T0305069

The Dynamics of Regions and Networks in Industrial Ecosystems

The Dynamics
of Regions and
Networks in Industrial
Ecosystems

Edited by

Matthias Ruth

University of Maryland, College Park, Maryland, USA

Brynhildur Davidsdottir

University of Iceland, Reykjavik, Iceland

Edward Elgar

Cheltenham, UK • Northampton, MA, USA

Published by
Edward Elgar Publishing Limited
The Lypiatts
15 Lansdown Road
Cheltenham
Glos GL50 2JA
UK

Edward Elgar Publishing, Inc.
William Pratt House
9 Dewey Court
Northampton
Massachusetts 01060
USA

A catalogue record for this book
is available from the British Library

Library of Congress Control Number: 2009922759

Mixed Sources
Product group from well-managed
forests and other controlled sources
www.fsc.org Cert no. SA-COC-1565
© 1996 Forest Stewardship Council

ISBN 978 1 84720 742 5

Printed and bound by MPG Books Group, UK

Contents

List of contributors   vii
Foreword by John R. Ehrenfeld   xvii
Acknowledgments   xxi
List of abbreviations   xxii

PART I   CONCEPTS AND METHODS

1   The dynamics of regions and networks in industrial
    ecosystems: background and concepts   3
    Matthias Ruth and Brynhildur Davidsdottir

2   Dynamics of geographically based industrial ecosystems   6
    Marian R. Chertow

PART II   REGIONAL DYNAMICS AND INDUSTRIAL
          ECOSYSTEMS

3   Regional dynamics and industrial ecosystems: an introduction   31
    David L. Rigby

4   Spatial and temporal life cycle assessment: ozone formation
    potential from natural gas use in a typical residential building
    in Pittsburgh, USA   38
    Shannon M. Lloyd and Robert Ries

5   Estimating generalized regional input–output systems: a case
    study of Australia   55
    Blanca Gallego and Manfred Lenzen

6   The economic and environmental consequences of reduced
    air transport services in Pennsylvania: a regional input–output
    life cycle assessment case study   83
    Gyorgyi Cicas, Chris T. Hendrickson and H. Scott Matthews

7   Design approach frameworks, regional metabolism and
    scenarios for sustainability   97
    Tim Baynes, Jim West and Graham M. Turner

PART III   EVOLUTION OF NETWORKS IN INDUSTRIAL
           ECOLOGY

 8 Learning and evolution in industrial ecosystems: an
    introduction   121
    Peter M. Allen

 9 A framework for analysis of industrial networks   128
    Ruud Kempener, Brett Cohen, Lauren Basson and Jim Petrie

10 Understanding and shaping the evolution of sustainable
    large-scale socio-technical systems   156
    Igor Nikolic, Gerard P.J. Dijkema and Koen H. van Dam

11 Futures scenarios of industrial ecosystems: a research design
    for transportation planning   179
    *Paul Beavis, John A. Black, James Lennox, Graham M. Turner
    and Stephen J. Moore*

12 PowerPlay: developing strategies to promote energy efficiency 201
    *Matthias Ruth, Clark Bernier, Alan Meier and
    John 'Skip' Laitner*

13 The dynamics of regions and networks in industrial
    ecosystems: retrospect and prospect   224
    Brynhildur Davidsdottir and Matthias Ruth

Index   233

Contributors

Peter M. Allen, BSc PhD is Head of the Complex Systems Research Centre in the School of Management at Cranfield University. He is part of the PhD and DBA programme at Cranfield and is an Invited Professor on the PhD Programme in the Economics Department of the University of Paris I, as well as contributing to Masters and Doctoral programs at Warwick and Aston Business Schools. He is an Editor in Chief of the journal *Emergence: Complexity and Organization*. He is currently running a large ESRC research project jointly with Sheffield University studying the use of complexity science to understand the evolution of the supply chain of aerospace companies. His research is directed towards the application of the new ideas concerning evolutionary complex systems to socio-economic sustainability, resilience and security. He has a PhD in Theoretical Physics and from 1970 to 1987 worked with Professor Ilya Prigogine at the Université Libre de Bruxelles. He has written and edited several books and published well over 200 articles in a range of fields including ecology, social science, urban and regional science, economics, systems theory and physics. He has been a consultant to the Defence Evaluation and Research Agency (DERA), the Civil Contingencies Secretariat, the Canadian Fishing Industry, Elf Aquitaine, the United Nations University, the European Commission and the Asian Development Bank. He has managed a number of large European and UK research contracts.

Lauren Basson is a lecturer at the Centre for Environmental Strategy (CES) within the School of Engineering at the University of Surrey, UK. Lauren holds BS and MS degrees in chemical engineering from the University of Cape Town, South Africa, and a PhD in chemical engineering from the University of Sydney, Australia. Her principal area of interest is decision support for complex decision situations. Prior to commencing with the PhD, Lauren worked as an environmental process engineer in an environmental consulting firm in Johannesburg, South Africa, where she consulted principally to the mining and minerals processing industries. She has also consulted extensively to the South African electrical utility (Eskom) on a range of projects including the selection of cleaner technologies for coal-based power generation, the screening of greenhouse gas reduction projects for the Clean Development Mechanism of the Kyoto Protocol and the incorporation of sustainability considerations into the performance evaluation of senior management.

Tim Baynes has led a diverse career in applied physics, publishing in international journals on magnetics and biophysics and completing a PhD in applied physics from the University of New South Wales in 2002. In recent years he has turned his attention to industrial ecology, complex systems science and sustainability analysis and currently works as a systems analyst within the Urban Systems Program of the Commonwealth Scientific and Industrial Research Organisation (CSIRO)'s Sustainable Ecosystems Division. The research activities Dr Baynes undertakes include the material and energy accounting of the physical economy and the application of complex system dynamics to problems of urban function and development.

Paul Beavis is currently a doctoral candidate with the School of Civil and Environmental Engineering at the University of New South Wales. He graduated with an Honors degree in environmental engineering (water) in 2001. While pursuing his degree he worked with Sydney Water Corporation in their wastewater planning section on reviews of plant augmentation. Since graduation he has worked for the Centre for Water and Waste Technology in the field of environmental life cycle assessment (LCA). Projects he has been involved with have entailed sustainability assessments of centralized and decentralized water and wastewater plants and solid waste treatment processes and logistics.

His PhD thesis topic deals with service in transportation infrastructure as a means to reduce material and energy throughput of the Australian economy. His case studies focus on developing smart infrastructure hubs (intermodal terminals and their production systems) in the Sydney basin as an attempt to reconcile logistics demands and infrastructure supply in the container freight and the waste management industries respectively.

Clark Bernier, at the time of writing, was an assistant faculty researcher at the University of Maryland's School of Public Policy. In addition to developing PowerPlay (an interactive energy efficiency role-playing game), he has worked with the University of Massey in New Zealand on the Climate's Long-Term Impacts on New Zealand Infrastructure (CLINZI) model and with the Joint Global Change Research Institute to develop a model of US power plant and transportation equipment retirement. He has a Masters of Public Policy from the University of Maryland and a BA in Political Economy from Knox College. He currently works as an efficiency program evaluation analyst in Sonoma, California.

John A. Black is a Professor in the Planning Research Centre at the University of Sydney and Director of the University of New South Wales

(UNSW), Botany Bay Studies Unit – a transdisciplinary research center that researches sustainability issues of the bay and its urbanized hinterland. He is a visiting professor in the Graduate School of Environmental Studies, the Laboratory for Sustainable Transport and Spatial Development at Nagoya University, Japan. He was Foundation Professor of Transport Engineering at the UNSW from 1984–99. He earned his PhD in transport engineering from Bradford University, a Masters in urban and regional planning from Sydney University, and a BA with Honors in urban geography from Manchester University.

Since 1968, he has undertaken research on land use, transport and the environment, and has an international reputation in transport planning and the economic, social and environmental impacts of transport infrastructure and services. He specializes in strategic planning and has advised government on numerous futures studies. Dr Black has acted for over 25 years as a high-level consultant to international agencies, such as the World Bank and the United Nations Development Programme, the Australian Commonwealth, state and local government agencies, and to the private sector and community groups.

Marian R. Chertow is Associate Professor and Director of the Industrial Environmental Management Program in the Center for Industrial Ecology at Yale University's School of Forestry and Environmental Studies. Broadly, her interests focus on industrial ecology and industrial symbiosis, environmental technology innovation, and business–environment issues. Her research focuses on evaluating public and private benefits of cooperative environmental business practices at the interfirm level and, ultimately, whether and how these practices might foster a shift to environmental sustainability. Professor Chertow came to Yale following ten years in state and local government and environmental business where she specialized in waste management.

Gyorgyi Cicas has a PhD in civil and environmental engineering from Carnegie Mellon and an MS in environmental engineering from the University of Pannonia, Hungary. She has worked as a trainer and consultant for TEQUA International (2000–02) and as a project manager of the Pollution Prevention and Environmental Management System Consultation project (1998–2000).

Brett Cohen holds both BS and PhD degrees in chemical engineering from the University of Cape Town, South Africa. He is currently employed as a part-time Senior Research Fellow at the University of Cape Town, and as Partner in the GreenHouse Consultancy in Cape Town. He has a wide range of experience in environmental management and sustainability strategy issues, having worked both in academia and in the private sector. His current work focus includes the development and implementation of tools for the support of complex decision-making and strategic planning towards sustainable outcomes in industrial and infrastructure networks.

Brynhildur Davidsdottir is Associate Professor of Environment and Natural Resources at the University of Iceland, and is the Director of the Graduate Program in Environment and Natural Resources. Before joining the University of Iceland in 2006, Dr Davidsdottir was an associate at Abt Associates Inc., Cambridge, Massachusetts, and a lecturer at Boston University. Much of her research has focused on complex systems modeling of resource and environmental policy issues, such as regional responses within the United States to various climate change policy options and the impact of those responses on the natural environment; adaptation of different cultures to changes in their external economic and natural environment as exhibited through natural resource use and management; and the development of sustainable energy development indexes.

Gerard P.J. Dijkema is Associate Professor of Energy and Industry, Delft University of Technology, Department of Technology, Policy and Management. In research and education he specializes in innovation for sustainability in industry and infrastructure networks, notably the understanding, development and transition of large-scale socio-technical systems. Drawing from technology, policy and management, his research involves model-based decision support, to help stakeholders to develop sustainable policies and strategies. By general election he is a member of the general council of the water authority Hoogheemraadschap van Delfland. An active advisor to regional and national authorities and companies, he has (co-)authored more than 100 papers and reports, among which are four patents and a dozen journal papers. Dr Dijkema graduated as a chemical engineer (Hons) and holds a PhD from Delft University of Technology.

John R. Ehrenfeld is Executive Director of the International Society for Industrial Ecology. He currently serves on the Council of the Society for Organizational Learning. His current research focus is on sustainability and culture change. A book on this subject is forthcoming in 2009 from the Yale Press. He retired in 2000 as the Director of the MIT Program on Technology, Business and Environment. In October 1999, the World Resources Institute honored him with a lifetime achievement award for his academic accomplishments. He holds a BS and ScD in Chemical Engineering from MIT, and is author or co-author of over two hundred papers, books, reports and other publications

Blanca Gallego completed her PhD in atmospheric and oceanic sciences at the University of California, Los Angeles, after which she joined the Centre for Integrated Sustainability Analysis at the University of Sydney, where she undertook research on environmental accounting systems, regional input–output economics and corporate sustainability reporting. Currently Dr Gallego is a Research Fellow at the Centre for Health Informatics at the University of New South Wales where she works on surveillance models of infectious diseases and decision support tools for clinicians and public health practitioners in the context of infectious disease management.

Chris T. Hendrickson is Duquesne Light Company Professor of Engineering and Co-Director of the Green Design Institute at Carnegie Mellon University. His research, teaching and consulting are in the general area of engineering planning and management, including design for the environment, project management, transportation systems, finance and computer applications. He has co-authored five books: *Environmental Life Cycle Assessment of Goods and Services: An Input–Output Approach* (Resources for the Future 2005), *Project Management for Construction* (Prentice-Hall 1989), *Transportation Investment and Pricing Principles* (John Wiley & Sons 1984), *Knowledge Based Process Planning for Construction and Manufacturing* (Academic Press 1989) and *Concurrent Computer Integrated Building Design* (Prentice-Hall 1994).

Ruud Kempener is a Research Fellow at the Energy and Environment Programme at SPRU – Science and Technology Policy Research, University of Sussex (UK). Ruud completed his PhD in the Complex Systems and Sustainability group of the School of Chemical and Biomolecular Engineering at the University of Sydney in 2008, and has an MS degree in technology and innovation policies from the Eindhoven University of Technology, the Netherlands. Ruud uses agent-based modeling to explore the consequences of individual behavior, business strategies and policy interventions on the sustainable development of supply chain and industrial network evolutions in the energy sector, chemical industries and agriculture.

John 'Skip' Laitner is a resource economist with more than thirty years of experience in science and economic impact studies, public policy analysis, and economic development planning. He currently serves as Senior Economist at the American Council for an Energy-Efficient Economy. He was awarded the EPA's 1998 Gold Medal for his work with a team of EPA economists that helped lay the foundation for the recent Kyoto Protocol on Greenhouse Gas Emissions. In 2003 he was acknowledged as a technology leader when given the 'CHP Champion' award by the US Combined Heat and Power Association.

James Lennox currently holds a research position at Landcare Research New Zealand Ltd. His research interests include environmental input–output analysis, the application of full cost accounting and other techniques to assess sustainability within organizations, and research into the impacts of tourism in New Zealand. Previously, Dr Lennox worked as a postdoctoral fellow at CSIRO Sustainable Ecosystems, Australia. In that position he helped to develop a stocks-and-flows model of the Australian economy, concentrating on industrial production processes. He also studied material and energy flows associated with Australian towns and cities, as well as the accumulation of cadmium in agricultural systems. Dr Lennox has a PhD (2002) and a Bachelors of engineering (chemical, with Honors, 1997) from the University of Queensland, Australia. His doctoral research concerned applications of multivariate statistical techniques to the detection of faults in biological wastewater treatment and verification of computer simulation models.

Manfred Lenzen is Professor of Sustainability Research at the Centre for Integrated Sustainability Analysis of the University of Sydney. After completing a PhD in nuclear physics at the University of Bonn in Germany, Professor Lenzen moved to Australia where he took up work on renewable energy technologies (solar-thermal electricity, passive solar architecture and wind turbines) at the University of Sydney. At present, Professor Lenzen works on the development of quantitative methods for integrated triple bottom line accounting, dynamic modeling of greenhouse gas emissions, land use and biodiversity, and multi-criteria decision analysis. Prof Lenzen has published nine book chapters and more than 60 articles in international peer-reviewed journals. He has worked as Visiting Professor at the University of Tokyo and the Federal University of Rio de Janeiro, and collaborates extensively with research groups in the UK, Japan, Brazil, the United States, Denmark, Norway and Germany. He is Chief Editor for the *Journal of Industrial Ecology and Economic Systems Research*.

Shannon M. Lloyd is a Principal Technical Advisor in Concurrent Technologies Corporation (CTC)'s Sustainability and Process Engineering Directorate. Dr Lloyd's research focuses on evaluating advanced or emerging technologies that can contribute to energy efficiency and security, environmental sustainability and pollution prevention. Of particular interest is using quantitative analysis and mathematical modeling to assess the economic and environmental implications of policy and investment decisions. Dr Lloyd has experience applying life cycle assessment, risk assessment, energy modeling and greenhouse gas accounting in a variety of industry and government settings. She is currently conducting research to incorporate quantitative uncertainty analysis, spatial differentiation and temporal differentiation in environmental life cycle assessment. Dr Lloyd received a PhD in engineering and public policy and an MS in civil and environmental engineering from Carnegie Mellon University and a BS in general engineering from the University of Illinois at Urbana-Champaign. Prior to joining CTC, she held positions at John Deere Harvester Works, Square D Company, and First Environment.

H. Scott Matthews is an Associate Professor of Civil and Environmental Engineering, and Engineering and Public Policy, at Carnegie Mellon University. He is also the Research Director of the Green Design Institute. His primary research interest is sustainable life cycle management of infrastructure, where infrastructure includes transportation and building facilities, as well as energy, utility and telecommunications networks. In assessing the efficiency of management methods, he considers private and social aspects such as externality costs of pollution.

Alan Meier is Senior Scientist at the Lawrence Berkeley National Laboratory. Dr Meier earned degrees in chemistry and economics, and a PhD in Energy and Resources from the University of California, Berkeley. Most of his research has dealt with understanding how energy is used and how it could be used more efficiently. His work relies heavily on field measurements of the energy use of buildings and equipment. About a decade ago he began to study the energy consumption of 'miscellaneous' equipment and, more recently, the energy use of appliances when they were switched off. This research sparked his interest in standby power and launched an unusually successful global effort to reduce standby power in all sorts of equipment. Dr Meier has published over one hundred papers and articles in journals, magazines and conference proceedings, mostly about energy efficiency. He founded the magazine *Home Energy*, and served as Editor-in-Chief of the journal *Energy and Buildings*. This chapter describes research undertaken while Dr Meier was a senior energy analyst at the International Energy Agency in Paris.

Stephen J. Moore has 12 years of experience in the public sector and private consulting in the fields of solid and hazardous waste management, and environmental management. He has a Bachelors degree in engineering (civil, with Honors) from the University of New South Wales (UNSW) and a Masters in engineering science from Adelaide University. He has been responsible for the preparation of environmental impact statements, reviews of large companies' environmental performance, creation of regional solid and hazardous waste management strategies, the design of transfer stations, recycling schemes, landfills and hazardous waste treatment plants.

In 1991 he joined the UNSW as Senior Lecturer in Waste and Environmental Management, where he is now Director of Studies, Environmental Engineering. He also coordinates and is principal lecturer for the coursework Masters degrees in waste management and environmental engineering. His research activities include the establishment of a national waste database for Australia and the development of analytical and design tools for improved environmental management at the corporate and regional level. This includes use of materials accounting tools such as life cycle assessment, material flow analysis, sustainable process index, ecological footprints, and total material requirements.

Igor Nikolic graduated as a chemical and bio-process engineer from Delft University of Technology. In his MSc thesis he presented an agent-based model of gene flow from genetically modified (GM) crops to surrounding plant populations. After his graduation, he spent several years as an environmental researcher and consultant at University of Leiden, Institute for Environmental Science (CML), where he worked on life cycle assessment/material flow analysis (LCA/MFA) and industrial ecology. In his research he specializes in applying complex adaptive system theory and agent based modeling of network evolution and industry–infrastructure networks. He is an active promoter of open source software and social software that enables group work and collaboration and has (co-)authored some 20 publications. Currently, he is completing his PhD at the Energy and Industry Group, Faculty of Technology, Policy and Management, Delft University of Technology.

Jim Petrie is Emeritus Professor of Chemical Engineering at the University of Sydney, and Honorary Professor at the University of Cape Town, South Africa. At Sydney, he leads a research group whose interests are centered on engineering for sustainability. Specific focus areas include environmental systems analysis based on life cycle thinking, decision support for complex decisions characterized by multiple objectives under risk and uncertainty, process modeling, and technology development. Much of this work has been in support of primary industries and infrastructure, including minerals and metals, power generation, water and waste industries. He consults widely to the resources sector in both South Africa and Australia. He is a Chartered Engineer in the UK and a Fellow of the Institution of Chemical Engineers.

Robert Ries is the Rinker Professor of Construction, Assistant Professor and Associate Director of the Powell Center for Construction and the Environment in the M.E. Rinker Sr School of Building Construction at the University of Florida. Dr Ries's primary research work is focused on improving the environmental performance of buildings and the built environment. His work includes environmental life cycle assessment (LCA) in the building domain, LCA studies of building systems, modeling construction processes, and building process modeling. His research also addresses developing LCA methodology, such as incorporating optimization, managing uncertainty, and assessing impact at variable temporal and spatial scales. Dr Ries has developed courses in green design and construction and sustainable development that are both required and elective courses in the undergraduate and graduate programs in the School.

David L. Rigby is a Professor in the Departments of Geography and Statistics at the University of California, Los Angeles. He received his MA and PhD in geography from McMaster University, Canada. His research interests include economic geography, technological change, evolutionary economics, regional growth and uneven development, political economy, and spatial statistics. Dr Rigby has published two books and more than 50 journal articles and book chapters.

Matthias Ruth is Roy F. Weston Chair in Natural Economics, Professor and Director of the Environmental Policy Program at the School of Public Policy, Director of the Center for Integrative Environmental Research at the Division of Research, and Co-Director of the Engineering and Public Policy Program at the University of Maryland. His research focuses on dynamic modeling of natural resource use, industrial and infrastructure systems analysis, and environmental economics and policy. His theoretical work draws heavily on concepts from engineering, economics and ecology, while his applied research utilizes methods of non-linear dynamic modeling as well as adaptive and anticipatory management. Dr Ruth has published 12 books and more than 100 papers and book chapters in the scientific literature. He collaborates extensively with scientists and policy makers in the USA, Canada, Europe, Oceania, Asia and Africa.

Graham M. Turner currently works on whole-of-system analysis involving whatIf coding of the Australian stocks-and-flows framework, capturing historical data and creating scenarios of Australia's future, and communicating these analyses to others. Topics have included Australian agriculture, fisheries, transport, and climate change impacts. He leads a small team developing an urban metabolism framework. At the global level, his research involves scrutinizing scenarios of the global socio-economic system, particularly those of the limits to growth. Dr Turner has earned his PhD in physics from the University of Sydney, Australia, modeling and measuring ionized gases used to create thin metallic films. He is now with CSIRO Sustainable Ecosystems searching for physically sustainable futures at the city, state, national and global levels.

Koen H. van Dam is a researcher and PhD candidate in the Energy and Industry Group, Faculty of Technology, Policy and Management, Delft University of Technology. Working on the topic of modeling infrastructures as multi-agent systems, his main research interests include intelligent infrastructures, multi-agent and complex systems, ontology design, knowledge acquisition, electricity infrastructure and industrial networks. A (co-) author of a dozen publications, Koen van Dam holds a Masters degree in knowledge engineering from the VU University, Amsterdam.

Jim West has a background in geology and computing, and now works as a systems modeler in the Urban Systems Program of CSIRO's Sustainable Ecosystems Division. He is interested in simulation and modeling tools generally, the applicability of such tools to enumerating and visualizing the physical outcomes of different development paths, and the question of how such physical outcomes might meaningfully be linked to estimating the subjective well-being of affected populaces.

Foreword

John R. Ehrenfeld

With this book, Matthias Ruth and Brynhildur Davidsdottir have made an important and substantial contribution to the still evolving field of industrial ecology. In the years that have transpired since the emergence of the idea that economic and industrial systems generally exhibit features analogous to natural ecosystems, the field has taken root. Industrial ecology now has associated with it activities in many universities, consultants with programmes based on industrial ecological principles, and applications of these principles showing up in corporate strategy, product design and public policy. The key principles spring from the above-mentioned ecological analogy and include such notions as loop closing and symbiosis, mimicking forms and processes found in *healthy* ecologies. The first chapter in the collection expands and comments on connections between the field and natural ecosystems.

The stressed term above, 'healthy', lends a normative dimension to the field, beyond the merely descriptive character of analogies. Environmental management and its successor concept, sustainability, have become firmly embedded in high-level societal activities in virtually every economic sector and industrialized nation. The relevance of these terms is tied to a still-growing consciousness of the fragility of the Earth's ecosystem and its criticality as the primary life support system of our species and indeed all life. International consensus about global warming and its impact on climate has now heightened interest in acting to preserve the environment for the present and for future generations.

Among many potential pathways toward sustainability, one stands out as the choice of most industrial and governmental strategies: eco-efficiency. Eco-efficiency, the idea of providing more value for less impact, is contained in many other prescriptive statements, such as dematerialization, decarbonization, detoxification, factor X reduction, cradle-to-cradle, and so on. Healthy ecosystems are naturally 'eco-efficient'. They recycle the nutrients found in their local environment by closing material loops. Detritivores turn the wastes produced in the food web into nutrients for species in other places in the web. The source of energy is renewable solar energy. It is only a very small jump to get from this observation to a normative possibility for industrial ecology: produce a more sustainable world by designing economic and industrial systems to look and behave more like ecosystems.

This possibility has taken hold in several important areas, for example, in the design of technological artifacts (design for environment) and in the design of industrial organization (eco-industrial development). In both of these cases, analytic and design tools, based on material and energy flows, have been developed and applied. Other analytic models and tools have been developed for larger systems, such as national or regional material economies (flows), but these have not achieved the level of design applications as the above two cases. It would seem, based on a patently unscientific assessment by this author, that the 'simpler' the system, as in product systems, the more the ideas of industrial ecology have found their way into practice. 'Simple' in this sense has several aspects, temporal and organizational. Products generally have shorter lifetimes than industrial systems, especially looking at common consumer products such as automobiles, mobile phones or computers.

The present generation of industrial ecological models and tools largely springs from relatively static analyses. The assumptions that are made in applying the tools generally assume that the context of the analysis approximates the conditions during the actual lifetime of the system under the analyst's lens. These tools also generally do not take into account sociological and organizational processes that are involved in putting the prescriptions into play. Again, for product systems, this limitation is not critical as to technical considerations although it is part of the reasons that the outcome that the designer or strategist had in mind may turn out differently.

Furthermore, these first generation models are almost exclusively based on assumptions of linearity with respect to the technical components and on normal rationality with respect to the human elements, in those cases where consideration of actor behavior enters the analytic framework. And finally, much of the work reflects the reductionist nature of the technical disciplines on which industrial ecology rests. This statement should not be read as a criticism of this sociological fact, but merely as an argument for expanding the intellectual basis for what has been the mainstream of research and analysis within industrial ecology.

If one stops for a moment and thinks about the more complex situations mentioned above, the next generation of analytic and design tools will have to incorporate models of processes that more realistically reflect the messy way that the world does, unfortunately for analysts, really work. As the editors of this volume point out, this requires that new ideas must be injected into industrial ecological thinking and research. For example, ways to account for changes in material stocks over long periods are now being incorporated into frameworks for analyzing material flows in large and long-lasting systems, as several chapters indicate.

Readers who have read my recent writings know that I believe that the limits of the present linear models, including those representing ecosystem processes, correspondingly limit the ability of the workers in the field to muster convincing arguments that industrial ecology can be a powerful new frame for thinking about and acting towards sustainability. Eco-efficiency thinking is extremely important in revealing ways to stop and even reverse the apparently inexorable trajectory towards breakdown and destruction of the natural world, with consequent immense potential social implications. But eco-efficiency, like efficiency in any setting, ignores possible absolute limits to growth. William Jevons, writing in 1865, noted that coal consumption in England eventually rose in volume even after the large increase in efficiency produced by Watt's steam engine. Jevons's notion lives today in the current notion of the rebound effect which implies that eco-efficiency (creating wealth in the process) will produce more investment and more consumption, eventually outstripping any gains from technological improvements.

Several of the chapters in this book delve into the area of complexity, invoking new models for the evolution of technical and associated human systems. This work helps make clear the important distinction between the complicated and the complex. The kinds of systems of interest to industrial ecologists have always been complicated, involving many interwoven processes, but processes that have been examined as separate pieces of the overall puzzle and with linear analytic bases. Typical product systems that have been examined often have hundreds of components and many tens of distinct materials involved, producing impacts on various environmental media in different places and times. Certainly not simple, but not complex. Complexity is reserved for systems that cannot be effectively analyzed by such reductionist methods. The key outcomes are the results of interconnected, often non-linear processes that cannot be reduced to analytic statements. Such systems may exhibit unpredictable and discontinuous behavior, possibly flipping from healthy regimes to unsustainable states. Human behavior and its role in establishing the dynamics of such systems cannot be modeled on standard concepts of rationality, even using Simon's notion of bounded rationality. The typical assumptions of stable preferences must be relaxed because the time frames involved are much longer than present models comfortably allow.

Models based on complexity foundations are much more likely to lead to more effective applications in dynamic circumstances, the primary setting for this book as the title denotes. This contextual feature is important when it comes to designing eco-industrial development, implementing national material and energy policies, and in governing product life cycles and supply chains.

This volume takes a large step into the world of complexity and other mostly uncharted domains in industrial ecology. The principle publications in the field, including the *Journal of Industrial Ecology*, have begun to include articles that fall outside or overlap the 'traditional' bounds of the field. (One should hesitate to use the term 'traditional' for a field as young as industrial ecology.) This collection of chapters is the most comprehensive assemblage of work that systematically probes the edges of the field from the perspective of many disciplines. The individual authors are leaders in their particular areas of expertise. For this reason alone, the book contains material that should support for many years the research of those working in the field and others who would like to enter it. Sustainability is a global problematique; the authors, appropriately, are drawn from around the globe.

Symbiosis is a core notion in industrial ecology. Drawn from ecology, it means simply the interaction of two or more organisms that produces mutual benefits. In a metaphorical sense, the whole is greater than the sum of the parts. So is the case for this book. Unlike many excellent edited volumes containing related, but independent parts, the overall contribution to the emerging field of industrial ecology is larger than the aggregate value of the chapters. Such an outcome is rare for volumes like this. The editors and authors deserve congratulation and kudos for their work.

REFERENCE

Jevons, William (1865), *The Coal Question: An Inquiry Concerning the Progress of the Nation and the Probable Exhaustion of our Coal-mines*, London and Cambridge: Macmillan and Co.

Acknowledgments

This volume is the product of many contributors working on several continents, engaged in theoretical advancement, data analysis, modeling, and support for investment and policy-making. Our appreciation for their efforts goes to them all, and to Mary Ellen Kustin at the University of Maryland's Center for Integrative Environmental Analysis, who helped shepherd the preparation of the manuscript. Tara Gorvine and her colleagues at Edward Elgar have provided much valued guidance along the way. Special recognition goes also to our colleagues, friends and families for their support throughout the years.

Abbreviations

ABM	agent-based model
ABS	Australian Bureau of Statistics
AI	artificial intelligence
AIPP	Allegheny Institute for Public Policy
AMAD	Arithmetic mean of absolute differences as a measure of matrix distance
AMRD	arithmetic mean of relative differences as a measure of matrix distance
AOIE	action-oriented industrial ecology
ASFF	Australian Stocks and Flows Framework
BAU	business as usual
BEA	US Department of Commerce Bureau of Economic Analysis
CA	cellular automata
CAS	complex adaptive systems
CES	Centre for Environmental Strategy
CHI	the χ^2 distribution of absolute differences as a measure of matrix distance
CIQ	cross-industry quotient assumption of intraregional trade
CORR	correlation coefficient as a measure of matrix distance
CRT	cathode ray tube
CSIRO	Commonwealth Scientific and Industrial Research Organisation
CTC	Concurrent Technologies Corporation
DCORR	de-correlation coefficient (1-CORR)
DERA	Defence Evaluation and Research Agency
DSE	Victorian Department of Sustainability and Environment
DSIM	dissimilarity index (1-SIM)
DSM	demand-side management
EIA	US Department of Energy – Energy Information Administration
EIO-LCA	economic input–output life cycle assessment
EPA	US Environmental Protection Agency
GHG	greenhouse gas
GM	genetically modified

GMAD	relative geometric mean of absolute differences as a measure of matrix distance
GMDf	gravity model assumption on interregional trade using data from freight movements
GMDs	gravity model assumption on interregional trade using distance between state capitals
GRIT	Generation of Regional Input–output Tables – technique for the generation of regional input–output tables
GSO	gross state output
GSP	gross state product
GWP	global warming potential
IAPs	interested and affected parties
IE	industrial ecology
IGCC	integrated gasification combined cycle
I–O	input–output
ISA	Integrated Sustainability Analysis group at the University of Sydney
kWh	kilowatt-hour
LCA	life cycle assessment
LCIA	life cycle impact assessment
LGA	local government area
LHS	Latin hypercube sampling
LQ	location quotient assumption on intraregional trade
MCDA	multi-criteria decision analysis
MCS	Monte Carlo sampling
MFA	material flow analysis
MIR	maximum incremental reactivity
MRIO	multiregional input–output model
mt	metric ton
MTCDE	metric tons of carbon dioxide equivalent
NAQETR	National Air Quality and Emission Trends Report
NGCC	natural gas combined cycle
NH	null hypothesis assumption (zero interregional trade)
NOx	nitrogen oxides
O&M	operation and maintenance
OFP	ozone formation potential
PCSO	President's Council for Sustainable Development
PEIP	planned eco-industrial park
pkm	passenger-kilometres
pre-RAS	preliminary estimate into RAS
PTR	passenger transportation revenue
R&D	research and development

RAS	bi-proportional matrix balancing technique
RCRA	Resource Conservation and Recovery Act
RDA	regional development agency
REIO-LCA	regional economic input–output analysis-based LCA
RIMS	regional input–output modeling system
RIOT	regional input–output model
RPC	regional purchase coefficient
RPM	revenue passenger miles
SDP	supply–demand pool assumption on intra-regional trade
SFA	substance flow analysis
SFF	stocks and flows frameworks
SIM	sequential inter-industry modeling
SIM	similarity index as a measure of matrix distance
SLQ	semi-logarithmic quotient assumption on intra-regional trade
SOHO	self-organizing hierarchical open
SOS	self-organizing symbiosis
SP	smog potential
tkm	metric ton-kilometers
TRACI	Tool for the Reduction and Assessment of Chemical and other Environmental Impacts
TRI	US Environmental Protection Agency Toxics Release Inventory
UNSW	University of New South Wales
US SEC	US Securities and Exchange Commission
VOCs	volatile organic compounds
VRSFF	Victorian Regional Stocks and Flows Framework
WDIF	weighted mean of absolute differences as a measure of matrix distance
λ-systems	large-scale socio-technical systems

PART I

Concepts and Methods

1. The dynamics of regions and networks in industrial ecosystems: background and concepts

Matthias Ruth and Brynhildur Davidsdottir

Industrial ecosystems consist of the interplay of producers, consumers and regulatory agencies that exchange materials, energy and information with each other and their environment. Many of the processes that character-ize such interplay are variable and changing over space and time – new technologies emerge and old ones are replaced, new materials and energy sources are developed, consumer needs and preferences evolve, and new resources and environmental repercussions are discovered. Regulatory interventions into materials and energy use by consumers and producers alter, and often are guided by, changes both at the process level and at the larger system level. For example, new understanding of the human health impacts of a material or recognition of global environmental harm from greenhouse gas emissions have prompted restrictions on the use of select substances, promotion of particular technologies, and implementation of incentives to reduce emissions.

Typically neither do the activities of producers, consumers and regula-tory agencies occur immediately in response to each other or to changes in the environment, nor are they typically in direct proportion to each other. Detection of environmental insult, for example, can take years or decades. Changing technologies, behaviors or institutions, likewise, is never instan-taneous. If and when changes occur, they do so with respect to a com-bination of past situations and expectations of the future. The resulting time-delayed, often non-linear cause–effect relationships between actions and reactions in the industrial ecosystem make the understanding of their dynamics and the management of their behaviors daunting tasks.

Since the complexity of industrial ecosystems is not simply a result of the connections of a myriad of system components – producers, consumers and the environment all interact with each other – but fundamentally and inherently related to our ability to comprehend and explain them, multiple disciplinary perspectives will be required to encompass the relevant system features. For example, an engineering perspective will provide valuable information on materials and energy conversions, gaps that may exist between existing practices and ideal conversion processes, and alternatives to close those gaps. Economic, legal and institutional analyses will be able to provide insights into opportunities and constraints for closing such gaps. Biological information will help quantify impacts of materials and energy use on the living environment. Public health insights can be used to assess implications for public and community health. Computer modeling may be required to relate the various pieces of information on the dynamics of industrial ecosystems to each other and make that information relevant to decision-makers in the public, private and non-profit sectors. How that information is perceived and acted upon, in turn, depends to a large degree on psychology, organizational structures of industry and government agencies, and the roles and responsibilities of civil society.

The complexity of dynamic industrial ecosystems results from the many possible interactions at the physical and technological levels; the many pathways through which their ramifications permeate environmental, economic and social systems; and the many, diverse perceptions and actions of the individuals making up those systems. A simple change anywhere in an industrial ecology may be buffered and never exert larger-scale system impact. Or it may ripple through the many interconnections among system components, ultimately to determine new behaviors, new materials and energy flows and new feedbacks among those components. The breakthrough associated with the steam engine stimulated the industrial revolution; a combination of institutional and technical changes triggered the agricultural revolution; the merger of information and telecommunication technology gave rise to an ever proliferating Internet. Simple physical descriptions of the associated materials and energy flows provide only one relevant piece of information to understand those changes.

An extension of physical descriptions of systems change to encompass a broader socio-economic and environmental context allows analysts better to comprehend bifurcations and developmental trajectories. Choosing multiple disciplines means embracing the complexity of industrial ecosystems. Most importantly, though, a diverse, multidimensional approach allows for the identification of added degrees of freedom for system intervention to promote self-organization and resilience outside the simply physical world.

In recent years, heightened interest in the dynamics of industrial ecosystems has been developing. Scholars and practitioners, from varied backgrounds and with different purposes in mind, attempt to gain a deeper understanding of the important features and dynamics of industrial ecosystems, some through analogies, others through application of first principles, yet others through case studies and modeling-based inquiries. Given the novelty of their perspective and the diversity of their approaches, the products of their work are widely dispersed in individual book chapters and journal articles. Yet, as interest in these perspectives is growing among researchers and decision-makers, the need to bring or hold the newly developing strands of interdisciplinary scholarship together, and to identify their relationships and differences, is growing. Without such an effort, continued fragmentation may result in lost opportunities to develop synergies among research programs and in reduced impact on thinking in industrial ecology, environmental research in general, and investment and policy-making.

This volume is one of two companion books that cover basic and advanced analytical concepts and tools to explore the dynamics of industrial ecosystems, and presents a wide range of applications. Here, we concentrate on the dynamics of regions and networks in industrial ecosystems. Elsewhere (Ruth and Davidsdottir 2008) we attend to the dynamics of materials and energy flows, and the associated behaviors of industrial ecosystems.

This volume contains three parts. Each of these parts contains its own introduction, provided by one of the leaders in the respective field, as well as chapters ranging from conceptual models to case study applications. The first part offers an introduction into the main themes and issues surrounding regional and networked industrial ecosystems. The subsequent two parts then broaden and deepen some of that discussion with emphasis, respectively, on the regional and network characters relevant for analysis and management. The scale of issues here ranges from buildings to regions to entire nations. Methods range from input–output analysis to computer-assisted simulation games. The volume concludes by drawing on the knowledge gained in previous chapters and the various areas of research to which they are related, and it offers directions for further scientific inquiry and applications.

REFERENCE

Ruth, M. and B. Davidsdottir (eds) (2008), *Changing Stocks, Flows, and Behaviors in Industrial Ecosystems*, Cheltenham, UK and Northampton, MA, USA: Edward Elgar.

2. Dynamics of geographically based industrial ecosystems

Marian R. Chertow

2.1 INTRODUCTION

Central to the field of industrial ecology is 'the biological analogy', which focuses on 'the flow and especially the cycling of materials, nutrients and energy in ecosystems as a potential model for relationships between facilities and firms' (Lifset and Graedel 2002). The seminal work by Frosch and Gallopoulos (1989) described an industrial ecosystem in which 'the consumption of energy and materials is optimized and the effluents of one process . . . serve as the raw material for another process'.[1] The industrial ecology subfield of industrial symbiosis, which arose to examine the dynamics of industrial ecosystems, pays resolute attention to the flow of materials and energy through networks of businesses in geographic proximity sharing resources including water, energy, by-products and wastes (Chertow 2000). The goal of this chapter is to explore these geographically based industrial ecosystems by comparing some of their dynamics with those of natural ecosystems, drawing on principles of industrial ecology, ecosystem science, and borrowings from thermodynamics and complex adaptive systems theory coupled with recent findings from the industrial symbiosis literature.

Several scholars, including Ehrenfeld (2004a, 2004b) and Levine (2003), have sought to analyze whether the relationship of ecology and industrial ecology is metaphoric (chosen to bring together dissimilar items for comparison), analogous (still comparing two unlike things but emphasizing key points of resemblance in some particulars) or even whether the two can be analyzed under the same framework (Spiegelman 2003), perhaps owing to similarities in structure (Baldwin et al. 2004) (see Table 2.1). This chapter focuses the comparison at the level of geographically-based industrial ecosystems and natural ecosystems.[2] In fact, ecologist James Kay (2002) has described 'an ecosystem approach for industrial ecology' and challenged industrial ecologists to examine arguments from the study of complexity and self-organization to understand industrial systems.

Table 2.1   Bases of comparison

Concept	Definition	Example
Homology	Similar in structure and evolutionary origin, but not in function	Seal flipper and human hand
Analogy	Similar in function, but not in structure or origin	A bird wing and an insect wing
Metaphor	One thing conceived as representing another; a symbol	My love is a rose

The first part of the chapter looks at the early ties made between industrial ecology and ecology, which, even at the level of metaphor, inspired the field. A review of some of the more recent findings in ecosystem ecology highlights the broad acceptance of ecosystems as complex adaptive systems. I offer a rationale for examining industrial ecosystems as complex adaptive systems, based on recent observations of which types of industrial ecosystems seem most viable. I bring in the need for multi-scale analysis, given the interconnections and embeddedness of industrial systems. I also suggest several emergent properties that may explain certain aspects of industrial ecosystem dynamics, as well as propose areas for further examination.

2.2   STAKING THE CLAIM: RELATING GEOGRAPHICALLY BASED INDUSTRIAL ECOSYSTEMS TO NATURAL ECOSYSTEMS

As with natural ecosystems, industrial ecosystems involve a web of connections based on the cycling and adaptive use of energy and materials. Beyond some common vocabulary such as 'flows', 'cycles' and 'closed loops', a first wave of industrial ecologists trying to put flesh on the bones of the biological analogy relevant to industrial symbiosis borrowed from the study of food chains and food webs, assigning trophic layers to a conceptual 'industrial food chain' and 'industrial food web' (Graedel 1996). Côté et al. (1994) in their project on 'industrial parks as ecosystems', highlighted four key actors in the food chains of mature ecosystems: producers, consumers, scavengers and decomposers, which enable elements and nutrients to be recycled for reuse. Through study of a large and diverse industrial park in Nova Scotia, the roles of scavengers and decomposers – the recyclers in the industrial park who return materials to producers and consumers – were identified and described in comparable terms to those in biological food chains.

An appealing analogy came with the term 'industrial symbiosis', based on the type of biological symbiosis labeled 'mutualism', in which at least two otherwise unrelated species exchange materials, energy, or information in a mutually beneficial manner. The term industrial symbiosis was first applied in the small municipality of Kalundborg, Denmark, where a well-developed network of firm interactions was described as functioning much like biological symbiotic relationships in nature. The primary partners in Kalundborg – including an oil refinery, power station, gypsum board facility, and a pharmaceutical company – share groundwater, surface water and wastewater, steam and fuel, and also exchange a variety of by-products that become feedstocks for other processes. These mutualistic relationships result in a high level of environmental and economic efficiency as well as additional spin-off benefits involving personnel, equipment and information sharing (Gertler 1995; Ehrenfeld and Chertow 2002; Jacobsen and Anderberg 2005; Lowe et al. 1995). Many other examples of industrial symbiosis have since been identified around the world, facilitating richer observations of dynamics. According to ecologist Thomas Burns (1993: 248):

> Mutualism is one of the most important relationships that may obtain between two living entities. This does not mean that mutualism occurs, as a local relationship, more frequently than other relationships. Rather, where and when mutualism does occur, there exists the potential for positive feedback leading to the growth and development of new ecological structures.

This insight from biology can be directly applied to industrial ecosystems that are adding exchanges to a core set of interactions. For example, a steam loop that efficiently provides energy to a growing number of actors can replace an older structure that required each entity to maintain its own boiler.

Miller (1994: 109) cites evidence that mutualism increases when resources become scarce, indicating that these types of benefits have survival value. This concept is applicable to industrial ecosystems in isolated areas where, in the absence of new energy or materials, cycling within the system becomes critical in determining total resource availability (Deschenes and Chertow 2004). Constrained water availability triggered resource sharing in Kalundborg, as well as in the successful siting of a power plant in the dry southeastern region of the island of Puerto Rico, which replaced the need for fresh water for a power plant with treated wastewater (Chertow et al. 2008).

In addition to mutualism, there are two other forms of biological symbiosis: commensalism, in which one party benefits and the other is unaffected;

and parasitism, in which one party benefits and the other is harmed (Miller 1994). Neither effectively meets the economic goals of industrial organisms, since seldom would an individual business do 'something for nothing' and never would a business choose to be harmed. At least at the level of analogy, however, one can imagine a joint venture that ends up being commensal or a hostile takeover that is parasitic. Since businesses, unlike natural organisms, consciously decide whether to participate in exchanges, they are seeking a collective benefit greater than the sum of individual benefits that could be achieved by acting alone (Lowe et al. 1995). This insight has generated the first collective action model proposed in the field (Boons and Janssen 2005). The boundaries of an industrial ecosystem, like that of its natural counterpart, are largely constructed by analysts defining units for study (Miller 1994).

2.3   RE-EXAMINING ECOSYSTEM ECOLOGY

Our understanding of ecology and ecosystems has changed greatly over the last several decades. The older, more static equilibrium view was encompassed in the notion of the 'steady state' or the 'balance of nature' (McCann 2000; Ruth 1996; Oliver and Larson 1996). The current understanding of ecosystem dynamics instead recognizes the role of fluctuation and disturbance not as an exception to, but as an integral part of determining ecosystem outcomes. Coverage in the *New York Times* of a 1990 meeting of the Ecological Society of America was headlined 'The Real Constant is Eternal Turmoil' (Stevens 2001).

Four key topics from the contemporary ecosystem ecology literature are of great relevance to understanding the dynamics of geographically based industrial ecosystems. Each reflects the turning from simpler, more linear observations of natural systems to more complex views, often highlighting the sometimes hidden role of forces external to the specific ecosystems under study. These are: (1) diversity and stability; (2) open/closed and immature/mature systems; (3) non-equilibrium thermodynamics and self-organizing systems; and (4) food web dynamics and the role of detritus.

2.3.1   Diversity and Stability

The simple formula that the greater the species diversity in an ecosystem, the greater its ability to withstand or recover from stress has encountered many exceptions, making it difficult to generalize about thresholds of stability beyond a minimal number (Miller 1994). Even if, on average, diversity (species richness) is positively correlated with ecosystem stability, it is not at all clear that diversity is the driver; rather, other mechanisms are likely to be at play (McCann 2000). Central to this new argument is the role of variability (the waxing and waning of the density of a population) that enables species to respond differentially to aspects of their environ-ments, and thereby weakening the potential of any one competitor to overwhelm the system. In a review article in *Nature*, McCann (2000: 231) summarizes that although much work remains to be done regarding the diversity–stability relationship, 'it seems that community-level stability is dependent on the differential responses of species or functional groups to variable conditions, as well as the functional redundancy of species that have important stabilizing roles'.

The argument above that both variability and redundancy influence ecosystem stability is also seen in different types of industrial ecosystems. We have previously identified two basic industrial ecosystem types: 'multi-pecies industrial ecosystems' have symbiotic partners from many differ-ent industrial sectors such as Kalundborg, and 'single-species dominated industrial ecosystems' are led by a particular industry such as petrochem-ical complexes or pulp and paper clusters (Chertow and Ashton 2004). In Kalundborg, there is little redundancy of species – there is one power plant, one pharmaceutical company and so forth – yet the system has been stable. More redundancy is seen in larger mixed industrial clusters such as Styria, Austria or Burnside Industrial Park in Canada (Schwartz and Steininger 1995, 1997; Côté 2001).

With respect to single-species dominated industrial ecosystems, the petrochemical complex in Jurong Island, Singapore benefits from some variability. In this case, the variability is created by the inclusion of facili-ties of numerous sizes and emphases along the value chain that can take advantage of different parts of the carbon molecule. In a contrasting example where there was much redundancy but little variability, a large industrial park in China that represented much of the value chain for cathode ray tube (CRT) computer monitors felt the stress of technological change when the industry began to switch to flat screen monitors and, as a result, a large percentage of the companies did not survive (Yuan 2005).

2.3.2   Open/Closed and Immature/Mature Systems

While some elements of natural ecosystems are open – that is, they rely on resources outside of the system such as the sun – other elements such as materials and nutrient cycling are more closed. Consequently, categorizing ecosystems simply as open or closed does not recognize that these elements co-exist and therefore there is no fully closed-loop system. More signifi-cant is the distinction between immature and mature stages of ecosystem development. Earlier-stage, or immature ecosystems have simpler food webs, fewer interconnecting linkages, and are less efficient with respect to nutrient and energy cycling than more mature ecosystems. Structurally, immature systems have few decomposers and are dominated by producers. Whereas immature ecosystems have generalized ecological niches, mature systems have more specialized ones (Miller 1994). The fact that decomposers play a much larger role in the food webs of mature communities led Allenby and Cooper (1994) to conclude that 'mature communities "care" about waste, developing ones far less so'.

Characteristics of a mature industrial ecosystem can be drawn from the list of attributes above, especially a greater number of interconnecting links, increased specialization of niches, and the presence of many decomposers. An immature system would be one with few trades; for example, two companies may exchange water or share steam and electricity. These are generalized niches, as most industrial companies need water and energy, rather than the specialized niches occupied by the input materials of specific manufacturing processes. More research is needed to understand the mechanism of transitioning from immature to mature in industrial ecosystems.

2.3.3 Non-Equilibrium Thermodynamics and Self-Organizing Systems

The notion of open and closed systems, mentioned above, is important in thermodynamics, which examines changes in the quantity and quality of energy. While closed systems exchange energy (heat and work), open systems exchange both energy and matter with their environments. Just what happens with energy during these exchanges has spurred many theories related to the second law of thermodynamics (Rosen 1999). In the view of non-equilibrium thermodynamics, high-quality energy (exergy) is processed by open systems, which then moves that system away from equilibrium, even as nature tries to resist this movement through energy dissipation. As summarized by Kay (2002): 'When the input of exergy and material pushes the systems beyond a critical distance from equilibrium, the open system responds with the spontaneous emergence of new, reconfigured organized behavior that uses the exergy to build, organize, and maintain its new structure.'

This is the basis for Kay's theory in non-equilibrium thermodynamics of SOHO (self-organizing hierarchical open) systems which emerge whenever sufficient exergy is available to support them, because they are dissipative and must confront external gradients. From these structures new structures then emerge which, in turn, beget new structures – hence the term 'hierarchical' since each new structure is nested within the last.[3]

Rather than take their form from the outside, these new structures are self-organizing – just as flocks of birds or crystals forming are self-organizing – using a mechanism described by chemist Ilya Prigogine as 'order through fluctuations'. In non-equilibrium thermodynamic systems, even small changes can lead to fundamentally different system states including new mechanisms and new species (Ruth 1996).

The question of spontaneous emergence of structures is not unique to physics and biology. Economists and geographers describe, for example, spontaneous development of industrial districts in old London where, based on firm co-location, various economies emerged among businesses with related labor pools and input requirements (Duranton and Puga 2003; Desrochers 2001). Kalundborg has frequently been described as emerging spontaneously (Jacobsen and Anderberg 2005), thus raising one of the central questions of industrial symbiosis (Chertow 2007): are sustainable industrial ecosystems predominantly self-organizing or are they centrally planned?

2.3.4   Food Web Dynamics and the Role of Detritus

The modern view of food webs is that they are highly interconnected structures rather than strictly linear chains of discrete trophic layers (Polis and Strong 1996). A higher degree of interconnectivity adds buffering capacity and reduces the chance of dramatic external impacts disrupting the whole web. Recent research emphasizes the important role detritivores play in determining the overall structure and productivity of developed ecosystems, since they increase nutrient availability, which is often the limiting factor for plant growth. They do this not at one homogeneous trophic level, but at all levels (Polis and Strong 1996). Recently, some researchers have suggested that 'through its influences on food web composition and dynamics, detritus often increases system stability and persistence' (Moore et al. 2004).

In parallel, we see by-product and waste reuse boost production in industrial ecosystems, for example, when calcium sulfate residue from power plant scrubber sludge is used to replace virgin gypsum in wallboard manufacture. Such cycling is the goal of by-product reuse and is especially attractive when locally available by-products that can be used as process inputs reduce transportation or inventory costs. Husar (1994) has noted, however, a lack of efficient material recyclers in human systems compared to natural ecosystems. He found that the physical separation of consumers, producers and recyclers is much greater in human than natural systems, where close physical proximity and functional matching assures little energy is used on transport.

The structure of food webs and their interlinkages is of considerable interest to industrial ecologists (Graedel 1996). Hardy and Graedel (2002) experimented with a central tool for evaluating biological food webs called connectance value. It is a quantitative measure defined as the number of direct interactions in a web divided by the number of possible interactions. The authors plotted connectance within 18 industrial ecosystems and found that the connectance values for biological and industrial food webs fall within similar ranges. If this finding can be shown more conclusively, it could bring industrial and natural ecosystems closer analytically.

The progression of ecosystem thinking described above, with non-linearities, discontinuities, the importance of variability, and the nature of disturbance has led ecologists to the generally accepted conclusion that ecosystems are, in the words of Simon Levin (1998), 'prototypical examples of complex adaptive systems'. Industrial ecosystems, too, are open systems (with many material and energy exchanges), and subject to rapid (market) changes in direction analogous to state changes of non-linear thermodynamic systems. Despite the differences in natural and industrial systems, overall, modern ecosystem theory seems a better fit with industrial ecosystems than older, simpler, rule-based ecology as described earlier. The following section argues that industrial ecosystems, too, should be considered to be complex adaptive systems.

2.4   INDUSTRIAL ECOSYSTEMS AS COMPLEX SYSTEMS

Allenby and Cooper (1994) speculatively argued, in the early days of industrial ecology, that industrial as well as biological systems are complex systems. Here, I take up this argument, more narrowly targeted toward industrial symbiosis. First, I argue that looking at industrial ecosystems as complex adaptive systems greatly helps to explain observed dynamics. Second, I focus more specifically on applications of contemporary ecosystem theory, including the work of Kay and Schneider (1994) described earlier as SOHO systems, to suggest some emergent properties.

An important question in the 1990s history of industrial ecology and industrial symbiosis was why dozens of plans to create eco-industrial parks inspired by Kalundborg never came to fruition (Gibbs 2003; Gibbs and Deutz 2004; Chertow 2007). There are many possible answers – lack of financing, inappropriate industrial mix, inability to work cooperatively – but considering industrial ecosystems as complex adaptive systems opens the door to another sort of explanation and consciousness about these developments. Based on examination of 51 real and potential industrial ecosystems through field work with Yale graduate students as well as attention to additional systems emerging from a review of the literature, I will contrast what I am calling the planned eco-industrial park (PEIP) model with the self-organizing symbiosis (SOS) model to see how these characteristics come into play. A brief description of each model with some observed examples follows.

2.4.1   Planned Eco-Industrial Park Model

This model includes a conscious effort to identify companies from different industries and locate them together so that they can share resources across and among them. Typical US planning for these systems has involved the formation of a stakeholder group of diverse actors to guide the process and the participation of at least one governmental or quasi-governmental agency with some powers to encourage development such as land use planning and/or zoning, grant-giving, or long-term financing. Of 15 projects identified by the US President's Council for Sustainable Development (PCSD) in 1996, only two were actualized along the lines of the PEIP model (Chertow 2007). The Port of Cape Charles Sustainable Technologies Industrial Park in rural Virginia featured solar energy, a water recycling loop and a constructed wetland for storm water run-off (Hayes 2003). The Londonderry Eco-Industrial Park in New Hampshire began with land acquired by the town adjacent to an active industrial area. Private developers bought the park and attracted the anchor tenant, a new 720 MW gas-fired combined cycle power plant that uses wastewater from a nearby treatment plant for its cooling water. Other tenants were attracted by the overall 'eco' theme of the project (Lowitt 2003).

2.4.2   Self-Organizing Symbiosis Model

In this model, an industrial ecosystem emerges from decisions by private actors motivated to exchange resources to meet goals such as cost reduction, revenue enhancement, resource availability or business expansion. The individual initiative to begin resource exchange faces a market test, and if the exchanges are successful and there is ongoing mutual self-interest, more may follow. In the early stages there is not consciousness by participants of an industrial symbiosis or inclusion in an industrial ecosystem, but this can develop over time as well. In Kwinana, Australia, an abundance of waste products from a diverse mineral processing region has led to a strong symbiosis with over 100 exchanges among the 37 members of the Kwinana Industry Council, with *post facto* encouragement from an organized group at Curtin University (Curtin University of Technology

2005). In the Styria region of Austria, the act of mapping flows across companies revealed an extensive network of self-organized exchanges consisting of hundreds of thousands of tons of materials including power plant gypsum, steel slag, saw dust, and recyclable paper and wood (Schwarz and Steininger 1995, 1997) which led to *post facto* coordination and encouragement (Milchrahm and Hasler 2002).

The PEIP model, conceptually, is an attempt to design and direct a closed-loop system in a circumscribed geographic unit. With ecology in mind, Côté and Cohen-Rosenthal (1998) initially identified some 'essential attributes' of an eco-industrial park, one of which was that it 'attracts companies that fill niches to encourage diversity, resiliency and stability'. Ironically, the PEIP model has not shown itself to be stable or resilient – indeed, many early projects documented in the eco-industrial park literature never moved beyond the early planning stages, and those that advanced to later planning stages often moved away from the eco-industrial theme (Gibbs et al. 2005; Chertow 2007).[4] Even the two projects cited earlier in Virginia and New Hampshire that reached implementation never became deeply embedded in their local habitats.

The park in Cape Charles, Virginia could not adjust to the fits and starts of attracting companies in the face of competing development goals, and was disbanded in 2005. The land was sold and rezoned, with the exception of the small office building (Slone 2005). The anchor tenant in the Londonderry, New Hampshire project faced challenges brought on by rising gas prices and disagreements over property taxes and declared bankruptcy, although the power station is still operating (Anonymous 2004). Looking more deeply, it seems that some problems with the power plant trace back to the California energy crisis. While green design elements continue to be incorporated in nearby buildings, the anticipated governance structure has not been realized. In the words of former Londonderry town planner Peter Lowitt (2005): 'achieving the steady state closed loop system originally envisioned has not come to pass, something more sporadic has occurred'.

Alternatively, the self-organizing symbiosis model more closely fits the pattern of a dynamic, non-linear, complex adaptive system on the basis that it is not planned, but has proven resilient to many perturbations. The Kalundborg symbiosis, for example, not only has a strong track record in achieving substantial environmental and economic savings (Symbiosis Institute 2005), but has withstood at least three types of disturbance:

1. change in footprint, including a doubling in the size of the oil refinery;
2. change in flows, including a switch in fuel at the power plant and a change in composition of sulfur residue after process improvements in the refinery; and

Table 2.2   Projects sharing characteristics of the self-organizing symbiosis model

Kwinana, Australia	Gladstone, Australia
Triangle J, North Carolina	Barceloneta, Puerto Rico
Guayama, Puerto Rico	Kalundborg, Denmark
Styria, Austria	Jyvaskyla, Finland
National Industrial Symbiosis Programme, UK	Guitang Group, China
	Alberta Heartland, Canada
Burnside Industrial Park, Canada	

3. change in organizations, including mergers and the division of the pharmaceutical plant into two separate companies (Ehrenfeld and Chertow 2002).

While the US PCSD set of projects provides a convenient, though non-random sample of PEIP model projects, we do not have a similar set of SOS model projects, in large part because, by definition, they come to light only after they have achieved some level of success when a conscious link to symbiosis is made in an act I have called 'uncovering' industrial symbiosis (Chertow 2007). Despite the problem of selection bias, I have identified 12 instances of the SOS model and statements about industrial ecosystem dynamics are drawn from observations of these (Table 2.2). All qualify as industrial symbiosis by meeting 'the 3–2 heuristic', in which at least three different entities, none of which are primarily engaged in recycling-oriented businesses, are involved in exchanging at least two different resources. The 3–2 heuristic enables my research team to distinguish a basic industrial eco-system, even if still immature, from other types of arrangements. All also satisfy, at least to some extent, what Kay (2002: 94) has identified as 'two broad themes to self-organization of ecosystems – coping with a changing environment, and making good use of available resources'. Two examples that illustrate these three standards follow.

2.4.2.1 Guayama, Puerto Rico

An industrial site in Guayama, Puerto Rico meets the 3–2 heuristic since there is a wastewater treatment plant providing cooling water for a power station and the power station, in turn, supplies steam to a refinery. With respect to good use of resources, analysis of the exchanges clearly shows significant emissions reductions at the refinery along with millions of dollars of savings on water at the power plant (Chertow and Lombardi 2005). With regard to coping with a changing environment, when the power station ash was rejected at an offshore location, the management was able to identify and implement several means for beneficial ash reuse in Puerto Rico.

2.4.2.2 Guangxi, China

The Guangxi Autonomous Region in China has a vast sugar refining industry. The Guitang Group, located there, has followed the flow of refining materials into two key by-product streams: molasses (sugar refining residue) and bagasse (fibrous waste product from sugar cane production). The company makes good use of resources by reusing ten by-products (Zhu and Côté 2004). One way the management has adapted to change was in response to market demand for more paper from bagasse. To increase the supply of bagasse, the private company that took over from the Guitang Group is purchasing it from outside sugar mills, expanding the purview of the symbiosis to external companies (Barnes 2004; Zhu et al. 2007).

Interestingly, the SOS model is not focused solely on loop-closing or by-product exchange, suggesting that the structural characteristics as described by Kay are more fundamental to the system than the loop-closing. Matthias Ruth (1996) has suggested that self-organization may be a more important characteristic for industrial symbiosis than by-product exchange. Actually, several candidates raised thus far could be more important organizing principles than sharing by-products, such as diversity, redundancy, variability, self-organization and network structure. Several issues taken up below suggest a relationship between the dissipative SOHO structures and self-organizing industrial ecosystems that could further illuminate their dynamics at broader scales and levels.

2.5   MULTI-SCALE ANALYSIS OF INDUSTRIAL ECOSYSTEMS

Borrowing again from ecology and biology, and recognizing, as Kay (2002) has written, that 'every system is a component of another system and is, itself, made up of systems' raises the opportunity to bring multi-scale analysis to industrial ecosystem dynamics. Positing that what we observe at one scale may not be what we observe at another scale, it is easy to see the relevance and importance of bringing systems thinking at multiple scales into the study of industrial ecosystems. The spatial scale in industrial symbiosis is one of its defining features, embodied in the requirement of geographic proximity. Yet, boundaries raise a key issue: while a production unit or facility may be unable to optimize inputs and outputs by itself, this challenge can be greatly assuaged by other facilities in the region and, in some cases, by importing materials from farther away. I argue that the temporal scale (how industrial ecosystems change over time) as well as the organizational scale (including issues of ownership, contractual relationships and organizational succession) are important for understanding industrial symbiosis characteristics.

2.5.1 Spatial Scale

Levels of the spatial scale range from a single operation or facility, to clusters of companies, to industrial areas, to cities, to regions, and to the export of products or by-products beyond the region. The importance of spatial scale comes into play when matching flows of materials, energy, water and information across entities to enable appropriate partnering or sufficient agglomeration underlying symbiosis. Ironically, the PEIP model overemphasizes the role of spatial proximity, expecting a core set of key resources to be exchanged in a narrow geographic range (for example the adjacent boundaries of an eco-industrial park) in spite of key obstacles such as the dynamic nature of business and the mobility of capital. In the SOS model, spatial boundaries are looser, which has allowed the 'uncovering' of industrial ecosystems such as Styria, Austria and the recycling network in the Oldenburger Münsterland region of Germany, both of which are spread over broad regions (Milchrahm and Hasler 2002). Five material exchange types at different spatial levels have been identified and used to categorize many industrial ecosystems (Chertow 2000; Graedel and Allenby 2003).

2.5.2 Temporal Scale

While natural ecosystems are often discussed in geologic time to find their origins, the businesses and industries associated with regions are dynamic and constantly evolving. Except where traditional industries are involved, businesses and industries usually do not require study periods greater than 50 to 100 years, and often much less. To be able to track the evolution of exchanges in Kwinana, Australia, for example, would require a researcher to go back to the 1950s (Bossilkov et al. 2005). Thus, it is difficult to compare the life cycles of natural and industrial ecosystems and perhaps more emphasis should go to the individuals and species within them that have shorter life cycles. A characteristic of projects along the lines of the SOS model is that they take decades to reach fruition. The PEIP model tries, in effect, to collapse time by recruiting key companies either to cleared or vacant real estate or to a site working in combination with companies that may already be located there. It is possible that the younger PEIP model needs more time and perhaps periods of disturbance and regrowth before coming to fruition.

2.5.3   Organizational Scale

Issues of ownership, contractual relationships and organizational succession indicate that the key levels of the organizational scale stretch from multinational corporations, to national companies, to regional companies, to small and medium-sized businesses, and from public to private ownership. Such issues do not pertain to natural ecosystems, but act as constant perturbations to industrial ones. In both the PEIP and the SOS models, resilience to change can be increased if companies rely on more than one supplier, plan ahead of corporate changeovers, and clearly specify how to handle outages and other interruptions in contract language. Kalundborg has withstood change in ownership of the gypsum board company from a smaller Danish enterprise to a British-owned company with similar operations across many countries (Ehrenfeld and Chertow 2002). In the Londonderry case, the investor group that purchased the Granite Ridge power station following its bankruptcy now runs it primarily as a peaking plant in response to high gas prices (Lowitt 2005). This turn of events is a far cry from the original conception and actually disrupts symbiotic flows owing to the part-time nature of the operation.

Because the three scales identified above coexist in time and space and the players interact, they should not be examined individually only. In fact, the interactions appear to be crucial to understanding industrial ecosystem dynamics cross-nationally. Ownership of key industrial operations such as telecommunications or energy is often a role of the government in many countries. In China, however, state ownership of a wide array of companies is quite common. One Chinese scholar, then, breaks the operations of a state-owned company into 'operational units', making it more comparable in scale to large industrial companies in the west (Yuan 2005). These ownership structures in China interact with specific temporal levels such as five-year plans, and spatial levels such as the vast industrial estates, much larger than in the West.

2.6   SOME EMERGENT PROPERTIES OF INDUSTRIAL ECOSYSTEMS

Thus far we have conceived of geographically based industrial ecosystems along the lines of complex adaptive systems theory from ecology and thermodynamics and applied a multi-scale view. Examination of Kalundborg and other examples of the SOS model suggests three emergent properties discussed below.

2.6.1   Linkages Beget Linkages, Trades Beget Trades

A characteristic of an open, non-equilibrium, thermodynamic view of ecosystems is that as more energy (exergy) is pumped into a system, more organization emerges to dissipate that energy. At this point, more complex structures can develop with more linkages, although the path is not predictable as new sets of interactions emerge (Kay and Schneider 1994). There are limits, however, which Ulanowicz has called a 'window of vitality' that bound a minimum and a maximum level when self-organization would occur. Without a continued source of exergy, the system would collapse (Spiegelman 2003).

With respect to scale, what is the spatial area over which this organization emerges? A catch phrase was developed in Kalundborg that spoke of 'a short mental distance between firms', emphasizing that not only were the firms in the same industrial district, but there was also a collegiality and commonality of views among them concerning the industrial ecosystem. Temporally, this short mental distance did not develop all at once, but took many years of intertwined work and community experiences. It is possible to see a momentum effect. In the first 20 years of the Kalundborg symbiosis (1959–79) there were seven symbiotic exchanges, whereas in the second 20 years (1979–99) a net of 11 new trades developed (Gertler 1995; Ehrenfeld and Chertow 2002). Trades did beget trades in the examples in Australia and China cited earlier, observable from the way they proceeded temporally. In Styria it may be possible to count trades begun and trades ended to see if the number is stable or variable. Organizationally, in industrial ecosystems, once cooperation has begun, it seems that a new psychology enters, which facilitates more (mutually beneficial) linkages and trades that might otherwise not have been acted upon.

2.6.2   Linkages Increase in Complexity as Industrial Ecosystems Mature

Kay (2002: 76) observed that as ecosystems mature they should 'develop more complex structures and processes with greater diversity, more cycling, and more hierarchical levels to aid exergy degradation'. We see in the example below that an industrial ecosystem might begin with simpler bulk exchanges and move, over time, toward more refined or complex ones. As nutrient and energy cycling increases within ecosystems, selective pressures become less concerned with the number of organisms (as in Emergent Property 1) and more concerned with their quality (Allenby and Cooper 1994).

Spatially, the size of the industrial ecosystem would be likely to expand as more actors fill niches in the system. Temporally, more complex structures follow simpler ones, although both types coexist and reversals are possible. Organizationally, more robust links may be needed across trading firms in the event that increasingly complex structures require investment or long-term commitments to provide sufficient returns. Indeed, Gertler (1995) observed that the first links in Kalundborg were simple ones, such as the sale of by-products like fly ash and steam, without significant pre-treatment or rerouting. Later exchanges were more complex, typically the outgrowth of pollution control technologies, which required altering processes and by-products for their intended use. To recover gypsum from the power station's scrubber sludge, for example, took investment in flue gas desulfurization and enhancement. The development of usable organic agricultural materials made from pharmaceutical production residues in Kalundborg took years of research and development as well as physical infrastructure.

2.6.3 Adaptability Sustains Industrial Ecosystems

An important tool for dealing with change in natural systems is adaptive management, embraced by ecosystem managers. A parallel regime would benefit industrial ecosystem management. How to translate adaptability for industrial ecosystems is elusive, but one key feature is organizational: the importance of a coordinative function working across companies. Indeed, the Styria project has recently hired a full-time manager to coordinate and advance exchanges.

Projects along the lines of the PEIP model in multi-industry systems often display success with shallow linkages, but not the deeper ones called for by real-time resource exchange. Gibbs et al. (2005) found that while eco-industrial parks focused initially on symbiotic interfirm exchange of energy and materials, a broader array of strategies is now considered part of such development. Some of these less ambitious (but more easily achievable) goals include implementation of environmental management systems, sustainable design, pollution prevention, green landscaping and job training. Indeed, many of the working eco-industrial developments these researchers examine are based on the less ambitious goals. One company implementing an environmental management system, for example, is not dependent on a nearby company doing so. Green landscaping is likely to require some cooperation, but not at the deeper level of sharing material inputs essential to core production. The researchers comment on the difficulty and frequent failure of trying to achieve deeper 'closed-loop' linkages.

What are the implications of the closed-loop model being difficult to achieve? In the near term, experimentation with adaptive management regimes will be needed to sustain symbiosis once it is found, which could require use of the scarce resources of money and time. Such cooperation has been seen as contrary, at least in the US, to the individualism of companies and entrepreneurs, suggesting that industrial ecology and sustainable development would represent a paradigm shift to a new, more collaborative model (Wallner 1999; Ehrenfeld 2000).

2.7   CONCLUSION

This chapter has focused not on the many differences between industrial and natural ecosystems, but rather on commonalities. Critically important is the reasoning from theory and experience to see both structures as complex adaptive systems, which also deepens the connections between them (Spiegelman 2003; Ehrenfeld 2004b). A key goal of the chapter has been to update thinking about industrial ecosystems based on more recent scientific findings from ecosystem studies. In this regard, industrial ecologists should continue to keep up on the ecology literature to sharpen intuition on the lessons for industrial ecology and industrial symbiosis.

Numerous topics have been introduced here, but many other ecological and scientific ones can be usefully added in the future, including the role of competition and predation, the role of information, the conditions surrounding flips to new attractors, and the mechanisms of the progression from immature to mature and simple to complex systems. More research is needed on many topics raised here emerging from other disciplines such as mutualism, SOHO systems, and the need to foster adaptive capabilities (Hollings 2001). There is almost no coverage here of social science applications of complexity theory including the role of path-dependence and the implications of rapid change, both of which would add depth to future discussions on management regimes for industrial ecosystems.

Some claims are made concerning the success of the self-organizing symbiosis (SOS) model in market systems over more centralized planning (the PEIP model). This should be seen as retrospective. Although there has been less success with the PEIP model to date, it is possible that highly industrialized countries where planning plays a critical role, such as China and Korea, will be able to learn the lessons of industrial ecosystems and apply them more fruitfully to future projects or retrofit industrial estates. Nor should we conclude that the role of the market erases the need for government policy. Rather, this role will need to be reinterpreted in light of a clearer view of the dynamics of sustainable industrial ecosystems.

I have written previously that 'the keys to industrial symbiosis are collaboration and the synergistic possibilities offered by geographic proximity' (Chertow 2000). I believe we will do well to continue the systematic exploration of the possibilities among proximate firms with an eye toward efficiency, effectiveness and ultimately ecosystem resilience.

ACKNOWLEDGMENT

Thanks to Dan Leistra for research assistance; to my colleagues in ecology, Chad Oliver and Os Schmitz for their insights; and to my colleagues who review and improve my work – Tom Graedel, Reid Lifset, John Ehrenfeld and Weslynne Ashton.

NOTES

1. The term 'industrial ecosystem' was examined in a book published by the National Academy of Engineering (Allenby and Richards 1994). The geographically based systems described in this chapter are considered as one type of industrial ecosystem. Other types in the study include the life cycle of a single product or material, an industry, or a group of interrelated subsystems at different temporal or spatial scales.
2. Many scholars have examined the biological analogy in industrial ecology broadly, beginning with another sort of biological analogy, that of industrial metabolism (for example Ayres 1989; Ayres and Simonis 1994). Other explorations include Patel (1992), Wallner (1999) and Korhonen (2001).
3. Kay (2002: 75) offers the example of the vortex formed in a bathtub as the water drains, as follows: 'The exergy is the potential energy for the water (due to the height of water in the bathtub), the raw material is the water, the dissipating process is water draining, and the dissipative structure is the vortex. A vortex does not form until the height of water in the bathtub reaches a certain level.'
4. Descriptions of many North American projects have appeared over the years on the former website of the Cornell Work and Environment Program (paper files now housed at Yale), the website of the National Center for Eco-Industrial Development housed at USC (http://www.usc.edu/schools/sppd/research/NCEID), and through a Canadian-based publication called the *Eco-Industrial Advantage*, which is the official publication of the Canadian Eco-Industrial Network (http://www.greenroofs.ca/cein/advantage.html). While Gibbs et al. (2005) document results of 35 US eco-industrial developments and find only six of the 35 to be operational, my own survey found the same generally low numbers but with some different interpretations of project status (Chertow 2007).

REFERENCES

Allenby, Braden and William Cooper (1994), 'Understanding Industrial Ecology from a Biological Systems Perspective', *Total Quality Environmental Management*, Spring: 343–54.

Allenby, Braden and Deanna Richards (1994), *The Greening of Industrial Ecosystems*, Washington, DC: National Academy Press.

Anonymous (2004), 'AES gives Granite Ridge plant back to bank', Platt's POWER, 1 July.

Ayres, Robert (1989), 'Industrial metabolism', in Jesse Ausubel and Hedy Sladovich (eds), *Technology and Environment*, Washington, DC: National Academy Press, pp. 23–49.

Ayres, Robert and Udo Simonis (eds) (1994), *Industrial Metabolism: Restructuring for Sustainable Development*, Tokyo: United Nations University Press.

Baldwin, James, R. Murray, B. Winder and K. Ridgway (2004), 'A Non-Equilibrium Thermodynamic Model of Industrial Development: Analogy or Homology?', *Journal of Cleaner Production*, **12**: 841–53.

Barnes, D. (2004), Personal Communication, 11 November.

Boons, F. and M. Janssen (2005), 'The Myth of Kalundborg: Social Dilemmas in Stimulating Eco-Industrial Parks', in J.C.J.M. van den Bergh and M. Janssen (eds), *Economics of Industrial Ecology: Materials, Structural Change, and Spatial Scales*, Cambridge, MA: MIT Press, pp. 313–36.

Bossilkov, A., D. van Beers, and R. van Berkel (2005), 'Industrial Symbiosis as an Integrative Business Practice in the Kwinana Industrial Area: Lessons Learnt and Way Forward', Presented at the 11th International Sustainable Development Research Conference, Helsinki, June.

Burns, Thomas P. (1993), 'Discussion: Mutualism as Pattern and Process in Ecosystems Organization', in H. Kawanabe, J.E. Cohen and K. Iwasaki (eds), *Mutualism and Community: Behavioural, Theoretical, and Food-Web Approaches*, Oxford: Oxford University Press, pp. 239–51.

Chertow, M. (2000), 'Industrial Symbiosis: Literature and Taxonomy', *Annual Review of Energy and Environment*, **25**: 313–37.

Chertow, M.R. (2007), 'Uncovering Industrial Symbiosis', *Journal of Industrial Ecology*, **11**(1): 11–30.

Chertow, M.R. and W.S. Ashton (2004), 'Differentiating Industrial Complexes and Industrial Symbiosis', Association of American Geographers Centennial Conference, Philadelphia, PA, 17 March.

Chertow, M.R. and D.L. Lombardi (2005), 'Quantifying Economic and Environmental Benefits of Co-located Firms', *Environmental Science and Technology*, **39**(17): 6535–41.

Chertow, M.R., W. Ashton and J. Espinosa (2008), 'Industrial symbiosis in Puerto Rico: Environmentally-Related Agglomeration Economies', *Regional Studies*, **42**(10): 1299–1312.

Côté, R.P. (2001), 'The Evolution of an Industrial Park: The Case of Burnside, Halifax, Canada', Paper presented at the International Conference and Workshop on Industrial Park Management, Manila, Philippines, April.

Côté, R.P. and E. Cohen-Rosenthal (1998), 'Designing Eco-industrial Parks: A Synthesis of Some Experiences', *Journal of Cleaner Production*, **6**(3–4): 181–8.

Côté, R.P., R. Ellison, J. Grant, J. Hall, P. Klynstra, M. Martin and P. Wade (1994), 'Designing and Operating Industrial Parks as Ecosystems', School for Resource and Environmental Studies, Faculty of Management, Dalhousie University, Halifax, NS.

Curtin University of Technology (2005), 'Cleaner Production', available at http://www.c4cs.curtin.edu.au/index.htm, accessed November 2005.

Deschenes, P.J. and M.R. Chertow (2004), 'An Island Approach to Industrial Ecology: Toward Sustainability in the Island Context', *Journal of Environmental Planning and Management*, **47**(2): 201–17.

Desrochers, P. (2001), 'Cities and Industrial Symbiosis: Some Historical Perspectives and Policy Implications', *Journal of Industrial Ecology*, **5**(4): 29–44.

Duranton, G. and D. Puga (2003), 'Micro-Foundations of Urban Agglomeration Economies', National Bureau of Economic Research Working Paper 9931, http://dsl.nber.org/papers/w9931.pdf, accessed November 2005.

Ehrenfeld, J.R. (2000), 'Industrial Ecology: Paradigm Shift or Normal Science?', *American Behavioral Scientist*, **44**(2): 229–44.

Ehrenfeld, J. (2004a), 'Can Industrial Ecology be the "Science of Sustainability"?', *Journal of Industrial Ecology*, **8**(1–2): 1–3.

Ehrenfeld, J. (2004b), 'Industrial Ecology: A New Field or only a Metaphor?', *Journal of Cleaner Production*, **12**: 825–31.

Ehrenfeld, J.R. and M.R. Chertow (2002), 'Industrial Symbiosis: The Legacy of Kalundborg', in R.U. Ayres and L.W. Ayres (eds), *A Handbook of Industrial Ecology*, Cheltenham, UK and Northampton, MA, USA: Edward Elgar, pp. 334–48.

Frosch, R.A. and N.E. Gallopoulos (1989), 'Strategies for Manufacturing', *Scientific American*, **266**: 144–52.

Gertler, N. (1995), 'Industrial Ecosystems: Developing Sustainable Industrial Structures', Dissertation for Master of Science, Massachusetts Institute of Technology, Cambridge, MA.

Gibbs, D. (2003), 'Trust and Networking in Inter-firm Relations: The Case of Eco-Industrial Development', *Local Economy*, **18**(3): 222–36.

Gibbs, D. and P. Deutz (2004), 'Implementing Industrial Ecology? Planning for Eco-Industrial Parks in the USA', *Geoforum*, **36**(4): 452–64.

Gibbs, D., P. Deutz and A. Proctor (2005), 'Industrial Ecology and Eco-Industrial Development: A Potential Paradigm for Local and Regional Development?', *Regional Studies*, **39**(2): 171–83.

Graedel, T.E. (1996), 'On the Concept of Industrial Ecology', *Annual Review of Energy and Environment*, **21**: 69–98.

Graedel, T.E. and B.R. Allenby (2003), *Industrial Ecology*, 2nd edition, Englewood Cliffs, NJ: Prentice Hall.

Hardy, C. and T.E. Graedel (2002), 'Industrial Ecosystems as Food Webs', *Journal of Industrial Ecology*, **6**(1): 29–38.

Hayes, Timothy (2003), 'Cape Charles Sustainable Technology Park: The Eco-Industrial Development Strategy of Northampton County, Virginia', in E. Cohen-Rosenthal and J. Musnikow (eds), *Eco-Industrial Strategies: Unleashing Synergy Between Economic Development and the Environment*, Sheffield: Greenleaf Publishing, pp. 288–99.

Hollings, C.S. (2001), 'Understanding the Complexity of Economic, Ecological, and Social Systems', *Ecosystems*, **4**: 390–405.

Husar, Rudolf B. (1994), 'Ecosystem and the Biosphere: Metaphors for Human-Induced Material Flows', in Robert U. Ayres and Udo E. Simonis (eds), *Industrial Metabolism: Restructuring for Sustainable Development*, United Nations University Press.

Jacobsen, N.B. and S. Anderberg (2005), 'Understanding the Evolution of Industrial Symbiotic Networks: The Case of Kalundborg', in J.C.J.M. van den Bergh and M. Janssen (eds), *Economics of Industrial Ecology: Materials, Structural Change, and Spatial Scales*, Cambridge, MA: MIT Press, pp. 313–36.

Kay, James J. (2002), "On Complexity Theory, Exergy, and Industrial Ecology', in C.J. Kilbert, J. Sendzimir and G. Bradley Guy (eds), *Construction Ecology: Nature as the Basis for Green Buildings*, New York: Spon Press, pp. 72–107.

Kay, J.J. and E. Schneider (1994), 'Embracing Complexity: The Challenge of the Ecosystem Approach', *Alternatives*, **20**(3): 32.

Korhonen, J. (2001), 'Four Ecosystem Principles for an Industrial Ecosystem', *Journal of Cleaner Production*, **9**(3): 253–59.

Levin, Simon A. (1998), 'Ecosystems and the Biosphere as Complex Adaptive Systems', *Ecosystems*, **1**: 431–6.

Levine, S. (2003), 'Comparing Products and Production in Ecological and Industrial Systems', *Journal of Industrial Ecology*, **7**(2): 33–42.

Lifset, R. and T.E. Graedel (2001), 'Industrial Ecology: Goals and Definitions', in R.U. Ayres and L.W. Ayres (eds), *A Handbook of Industrial Ecology*, Cheltenham, UK and Northampton, MA, USA: Edward Elgar, pp. 3–15.

Lowe, E.A., S.R. Moran and D.B. Holmes (1995), *A Fieldbook for the Development of Eco-Industrial Parks*, Report for the US Environmental Protection Agency, Oakland, CA: Indigo Development International.

Lowitt, Peter (2003), 'Sustainable Londonderry', in E. Cohen-Rosenthal and J. Musnikow (eds), *Eco-Industrial Strategies: Unleashing Synergy Between Economic Development and the Environment*, Sheffield: Greenleaf Publishing, pp. 300–306.

Lowitt, Peter (2005), Personal written communication, November.

McCann, K.S. (2000), 'The Diversity–Stability Debate', *Nature*, **405**: 228–33.

Milchrahm, E. and A. Hasler (2002), 'Knowledge Transfer in Recycling Networks: Fostering Sustainable Development', *Journal of Universal Computer Sciences*, **8**(5): 546–56.

Miller, G.T. (1994), *Living in the Environment*, Belmont, CA: Wadsworth Publishing Company.

Moore, J.C., E.L. Berlow, D.C. Coleman, P.C. de Ruiter, Q. Dong, A. Hastings, N.C. Johnson, K.S. McCann, K. Melville, P.J. Morin, K. Nadelhoffer, D.M. Post, A.D. Rosemond, J.L. Sabo, K.M. Scow, M.J. Vanni and D.H. Wall (2004), 'Review: Detritus, Trophic Dynamics and Biodiversity', *Ecology Letters*, **7**(7): 584.

Oliver, C. and B. Larson (1996), *Forest Stand Dynamics (Update Edition)*, New York: John Wiley & Sons.

Patel, C.K.N. (ed.) (1992), 'Industrial Ecology: Proceedings of a Colloquium held May 20 and 21, 1991, at the National Academy of Sciences of the USA, Washington, DC', in *Proceedings of the National Academy of Sciences of the USA*, **89**: 793–878.

Polis, G. and D. Strong (1996), 'Food Web Complexity and Community Dynamics', *American Naturalist*, **147**(5): 813–46.

Rosen, M.E. (1999), 'Second-Law Analysis: Approaches and Implications', *International Journal of Energy Research*, **23**(5): 415–29.

Ruth, Matthias (1996), 'Evolutionary Economics at the Crossroads of Biology and Physics', *Journal of Social and Evolutionary Systems*, **19**(2): 125–44.

Schwarz, E.J. and K.W. Steininger (1995), 'The Industrial Recycling Network Enhancing Regional Development', Research Memorandum No. 9501, April.

Schwarz, E.J. and K.W. Steininger (1997), 'Implementing Nature's Lesson: The Industrial Recycling Network Enhancing Regional Development', *Journal of Cleaner Production*, **5**(1&2): 47–56.

Slone, Dan (2005), Personal written communication, 18 April.

Spiegelman, J. (2003), 'Beyond the Food Web: Connections to a Deeper Industrial Ecology', *Journal of Industrial Ecology*, **7**(1): 17–23.

Stevens, W.K. (2001), 'The Eye on Nature: The Real Constant Is Eternal Turmoil', *New York Times*, pp. C1–C2.

Symbiosis Institute (2005), http://www.symbiosis.dk/, accessed June 2005.

Wallner, H.P. (1999), 'Towards Sustainable Development of Industry: Networking, Complexity and Eco-Clusters', *Journal of Cleaner Production*, **7**: 49–58.

Yuan, Z. (2005), Personal communication, May.

Zhu, Q. and R.P. Côté (2004), 'Integrating Green Supply Chain Management into an Embryonic Eco-Industrial Development: A Case Study of the Guitang Group', *Journal of Cleaner Production*, **12**: 1025–35.

Zhu, Q., E. Lowe, Y. Wei and D. Barnes (2007), 'Industrial Symbiosis in China: A Case Study of the Guitang Group', *Journal of Industrial Ecology*, **11**(1): 31–42.

PART II

Regional Dynamics and Industrial Ecosystems

3. Regional dynamics and industrial ecosystems: an introduction

David L. Rigby

3.1 INTRODUCTION

An industrial ecosystem might be broadly conceived as a network of producers and consumers that transform resources and that are more or less loosely connected by flows of materials and energy (Allenby and Richards 1994; Ayres and Ayres 1996; Graedel and Allenby 2003). If we do not specify too closely the nature of the interaction between economic agents, then the world economy as a whole might be considered a single, large industrial ecosystem. As we adjust the resolution of our analysis and examine subsets of flows, attention focuses on particular branches of industry, for example the automobile or pulp and paper sectors, on particular economies such as Canada, Los Angeles or Kalundborg, or on individual industries within specific regions, for example semiconductor production in Silicon Valley. There are significant trade-offs to consider as we shift scales of analysis. At larger scales the industrial ecosystem is generally more complex and it displays greater heterogeneity (more economic agents, more industries, more institutions, more technologies), though at smaller scales drawing meaningful boundaries around subsets of economic agents in sectoral or spatial terms is difficult, and flows of energy, materials, wastes and information across system boundaries will likely be large.

Cross-border flows imply that regions are not isolated or independent. For example, how much of the materials flows that sustain individual economies such as the United States are located within those same economies? From the standpoint of the ecologist, such flows might not represent a significant problem, for fluxes of energy, materials and waste can be measured or estimated. However, for the regional scientist or the economic geographer, these flows typically mean that processes of competition and economic development cannot be understood simply by examination of region-specific relationships. Simple trade flows between regions shift patterns of supply and demand and make analysis of regional industrial ecosystems more complex, but not impossible. However, as we begin to think of a mosaic of regions, each characterized by somewhat different mixes of resources, economic agents and institutions, and each more or less integrated with one another in an emerging global economy, understanding how the pieces of this economy function becomes considerably more difficult. And, when we add dynamics to the mix and begin to think about our capacity to regulate industrial activity at any spatial scale, the task appears daunting.

This chapter explores representations of regional economic dynamics within the emerging field of industrial ecology. In the sections that follow, attention is directed toward identification of the boundaries of industrial ecosystems, at regional differences in the characteristics and behaviors of heterogeneous economic agents, and on how the dynamics of regional industrial ecosystems rest on choices by those agents operating in environments with imperfect information.

3.2 IDENTIFICATION OF INDUSTRIAL ECOSYSTEMS

To date, most analyses of industrial ecosystems have tended to focus on individual sectors of an economy like pulp and paper production or steel, or on a more diverse set of industrial activities found within particular regions (Ehrenfeld and Gertler 1997; Ruth and Harrington 2004; Ruth et al. 2004; Kincaid and Overcash 2001). Bounding the system under study, using sectoral or spatial constraints, makes it more manageable. Boundaries also serve to focus attention on a limited set of energy and materials flows within particular jurisdictions and this may be crucial from the perspective of policy that is often limited in reach (Richards and Forsch 1997). It must also be recognized, however, that setting boundaries around an industrial ecosystem is a difficult exercise and it is one that significantly impacts evaluation of the potential for industrial symbiosis, or 'closing the loop'. If we fix narrow boundaries we run the risk of artificially isolating producers and industries and limiting waste reuse. Fixing broad boundaries adds complexity and perhaps identifies linkages between components of the industrial ecosystem that are not viable.

What information and criteria do we need to identify an industrial ecosystem? Ideally, we need a complete mapping of energy and material flows throughout an economy. In terms of comprehensive industrial data, the best we currently have at our disposal are national-level, input–output accounts of the flows of commodities between industrial sectors on an annual basis (Leontief 1966; Miller and Blair 1985). Those accounts also provide limited information on different kinds of energy inputs into the production system as well as inputs from households. Input–output accounts, based on survey data, are available for many industrialized nations on a reasonably regular temporal basis. Some regional accounts exist, but they should not be used for identifying potential industrial eco-systems as smaller economies tend to be more specialized and thus might fail to capture industrial linkages present in larger regions.

While input–output data are useful, they aggregate complex bundles of energy and different substances into commodity form. We need to unpack these bundles in order to assess inputs and outputs between industrial sectors at a more elemental level. This is important because even if two industries are closely linked through commodity trade, this does not mean that the material (and other) wastes of the supply sector may be used as inputs within the downstream industry. Identification of substance flows is much more challenging, largely because individual producers may have little knowledge of the physical and chemical composition of the com-modities they consume and/or produce, or of the waste streams generated (Kincaid and Overcash 2001). For the most part, these data will have to be produced by expert analysts such as industrial chemists, process engineers and materials flow specialists. For some industrial sectors, for particular regions, and for specific substances these data are becoming available, often through materials flow analyses (Brunner and Rechberger 2004; Ayres and Ayres 1996; Desrochers 2002; Ruth et al. 2004). In turn, this information is supporting the rapid development of industrial materials exchanges at local, national and even international scales (see www.epa. gov/jtr/comm /exchanges.htm).

If we knew the amounts of different substances embodied within $1-worth of each commodity, combining this information with input–output data would yield a detailed map of materials (in aggregated or commodity form as well as in disaggregated form) flow throughout an economy. The economic input–output life cycle assessment (EIO-LCA) developed by Lave and associates at Carnegie Mellon University is a step in this direction. These linked materials and commodity data would provide more robust accounts of the potential for commodity and substance recy-cling; they would facilitate identification of industrial ecosystems or criti-cal reuse gaps within existing industrial complexes. Chapter 6 by Cicas, Hendrickson and Matthews uses an EIO-LCA to examine economic and environmental changes in Pennsylvania that result from a decrease in air transportation services.

A variety of methods have been used to identify functional groupings of industries from input–output data (see Feser and Bergman 2000). These methods typically group industries on the basis of relatively high levels of commodity exchange. These techniques are easily extended to identify sectors that exchange materials and commodities of any sort, indicating potential reuse linkages that are broader in scope than those resulting from commodity flows alone. These methods could be used to identify the components of an industrial ecosystem. A logical next step is then to examine whether existing economies contain these components. At this point geographical questions must enter the discussion for the energy and materials savings from reuse may be rapidly eroded by the environmental costs of transporting by-products between producers and users (Ruth and Dell'Anno 1997). These questions are readily handled by geographical information systems and various spatial statistics that allow exploration of the geographical distribution of establishments in specific industrial sectors across economies of varying scale (see Feser et al. 2005). This same combination of tools might be employed to design a regional industrial ecosystem from the ground up. Whether such a cluster of businesses, integrated in terms of materials flows, would be viable from an economic standpoint is an open question. Gallego and Lenzen, in Chapter 5, push these arguments further, exploring different approaches to estimating trade flows in multiregion industrial systems.

3.3   DYNAMICS OF THE REGIONAL INDUSTRIAL ECOSYSTEM

Techniques of production and interindustry relationships vary markedly over space (Saxenian 1994; Rigby and Essletzbichler 2006). These differences are not eliminated by competition; rather they tend to persist over time as trajectories of economic development push technologies along region-specific pathways (Dosi 1982; Rigby and Essletzbichler 1997). These results suggest that the industrial ecologist has to pay particular attention to how the characteristics of industrial ecosystems vary over space and how local and regional institutions maintain geographical uniqueness. Different sets of natural endowments and variations in place-specific attributes such as organizational form and institutional relations, industry mix, labor skills, the age structure of capital and knowledge flows all have a significant impact on technology, materials flows and firm performance (Rosenthal and Strange 2004; Baldwin et al. 2008). To these geographical concerns with the regional industrial ecosystem, Lloyd and Ries add an explicit temporal dimension. Their chapter explores not only how the potential impacts of pollutants vary over space, but also how they vary over time.

Regional industrial ecosystems, like their natural counterparts, are continually in flux. In aggregate, while the characteristics of these systems might appear relatively stable, that stability belies tremendous uncertainty and constant change at the level of individual agents. Jackson and Clift (1998) have recently called attention to the question of agency within industrial ecology, of identifying key actors and their motivation. Andrews (2001) makes a similar pitch as he searches for microfoundations. In part these calls may be understood as expressions of dissatisfaction with mainstream, neoclassical models of omniscient actors responding smoothly to exogenous signals that shift the economy from one equilibrium to another. In Chapter 7, Baynes, West and Turner use the design approach to examine questions of sustainability and different growth scenarios for the city-region of Melbourne, Australia. This simulation model forces users to specify the characteristics of the decision-making process and to explore how system-wide constraints limit choice and the characteristics of alternative futures.

How should we characterize the agents that operate within the economy or within an industrial ecosystem? Mayr (1984) offers two visions. A first, typological perspective focuses on representative individuals, or ideal types with fixed and uniform characteristics. According to this perspective, variety in the characteristics of the entities under study is irrelevant to understanding the movements of the broader system in which those entities operate. A second, population perspective focuses on diversity in the characteristics and behaviors of the units under study and examines how heterogeneity among those units drives system-wide change. Choosing between these perspectives has important implications for understanding dynamics within the industrial ecosystem.

The population perspective provides the most compelling vision of a regional industrial ecosystem as an inherently dynamic set of characteristics and relationships. That perspective, increasingly associated with evolutionary economics, seeks to understand the processes that jointly influence the behavior of economic agents and the environment within which they operate (Hodgson 1993; Metcalfe 1998; Nelson and Winter 1982). Population-based approaches embody a dynamics that results from the process of competition among heterogeneous agents. However, that process of competition does not simply eliminate variety, as much standard economic theory suggests, but rather it also produces novelty and thus the heterogeneity on which continued change depends. Heterogeneity renders concepts like equilibrium, the representative agent and the aggregate production function of questionable value. Historically, these have been some of the key tools that have been used to assess change within industrial ecosystems. Population models suggest replacing these familiar deterministic arguments with a stochastic framework where key arguments are represented with random variables and where attention focuses on the varied micro-processes that drive change within the industrial ecosystem as a whole.

REFERENCES

Allenby, B. and D. Richards (eds) (1994), *The Greening of Industrial Ecosystems*, Washington, DC: National Academy Press.

Andrews, C. (2001), 'Building a Micro-Foundation for Industrial Ecology', *Journal of Industrial Ecology*, **4**: 35–51.

Ayres, R. and L. Ayres (1996), *Industrial Ecology: Towards Closing the Materials Cycle*, Cheltenham, UK and Brookfield USA: Edward Elgar.

Ayres, R., L. Ayres and B. Warr (2004), 'Is the US Economy Dematerializing? Main Indicators and Drivers', in J. van den Bergh and M. Janssen (eds), *Economics of Industrial Ecology: Materials, Structural Change, and Spatial Scales*, Cambridge, MA: MIT Press, pp. 57–93.

Baldwin, J., D. Beckstead, W. Brown and D. Rigby (2008), 'Agglomeration and the geography of localization economies in Canada', *Regional Studies*, **42**: 117–32.

Brunner, P. and H. Rechberger (2004), *Material Flow Analysis*, Boca Raton, FL: Lewis.

Desrochers, P. (2002), 'Cities and Industrial Symbiosis', *Journal of Industrial Ecology*, **5**: 29–44.

Dosi, G. (1982), 'Technological Paradigms and Technological Trajectories: The Determinants and Directions of Technical Change and the Transformation of the Economy', *Research Policy*, **11**: 147–62.

Ehrenfeld, J. and N. Gertler (1997), 'Industrial Ecology in Practice', *Journal of Industrial Ecology*, **1**: 67–79.

Feser, E. and E. Bergman (2000), 'National Industry Cluster Templates: A Framework for Applied Regional Cluster Analysis', *Regional Studies*, **34**: 1–19.

Feser, E., S. Sweeney and H. Renski (2005), 'A Descriptive Analysis of Discrete US Industrial Complexes', *Journal of Regional Science*, **45**: 395–415.

Graedel, T. and B. Allenby (2003), *Industrial Ecology*, 2nd edition, Upper Saddle River, NJ: Pearson, Prentice-Hall.

Hodgson, G. (1993), *Economics and Evolution: Bringing Life Back into Economics*, Cambridge: Polity.

Jackson, T. and R. Clift (1998), 'Where's the Profit in Industrial Ecology?', *Journal of Industrial Ecology*, **2**: 3–5.

Kincaid, J. and M. Overcash (2001), 'Industrial Ecosystem Development at the Metropolitan Level', *Journal of Industrial Ecology*, **5**: 117–26.

Leontief, W. (1966), *Input–Output Economics*, New York: Oxford University Press.

Mayr, E. (1984), 'Typological versus Population Thinking', in E. Sober (ed.), *Conceptual Issues in Evolutionary Biology: An Anthology*, Cambridge, MA: MIT Press, pp. 157–60.

Metcalfe, S. (1998), *Evolutionary Economics and Creative Destruction*, London and New York: Routledge.

Miller, R. and P. Blair (1985), *Input–Output Analysis: Foundations and Extensions*, Englewood Cliffs, NJ: Prentic-Hall.

Nelson, R. and S. Winter (1982), *An Evolutionary Theory of Economic Growth*, Cambridge, MA: Harvard University Press.

Richards D. and R. Forsch (1997), 'The Industrial Green Game: Overview and Perspectives', in D. Richards (ed.), *The Industrial Green Game: Implications for Environmental Design and Management*, Washington, DC: National Academy Press, pp. 1–34.

Rigby, D. and J. Essletzbichler (1997), 'Evolution, Process Variety, and Regional Trajectories of Technological Change in US Manufacturing', *Economic Geography*, **73**: 269–84.

Rigby, D. and J. Essletzbichler (2006), 'Technological Variety, Technological Change and a Geography of Production Techniques', *Journal of Economic Geography*, **6**: 45–70.

Rosenthal, S. and W. Strange (2004), 'Evidence on the Nature and Sources of Agglomeration Economies', in V. Henderson and J. Thisse (eds), *Handbook of Regional and Urban Economics*, Amsterdam: Elsevier, pp. 2119–71.

Ruth, M., B. Davidsdottir and A. Amato (2004), 'Dynamic Industrial Systems Analysis for Policy Assessment', in J. van den Bergh and M. Janssen (eds), *Economics of Industrial Ecology: Materials, Structural Change, and Spatial Scales*, Cambridge, MA: MIT Press, pp. 125–64.

Ruth, M. and P. Dell'Anno (1997), 'An Industrial Ecology of the US Glass Industry', *Resources Policy*, **23**: 109–24.

Ruth, M. and T. Harrington (2004), 'Dynamics of Material and Energy Use in US Pulp and Paper Manufacturing', *Journal of Industrial Ecology*, **1**: 147–68.

Saxenian, A. (1994), *Regional Advantage*, Cambridge, MA: Harvard University Press.

4. Spatial and temporal life cycle assessment: ozone formation potential from natural gas use in a typical residential building in Pittsburgh, USA

Shannon M. Lloyd and Robert Ries

4.1 INTRODUCTION

Life cycle assessment (LCA) is a systematic, analytical process for assessing the inputs and outputs associated with each life cycle stage of a product or system. For a residential building this includes materials use, energy use, environmental discharges, and waste associated with extracting raw materials that make up the building, manufacturing building components or products, transporting and installing building materials and products, and operating, maintaining and decommissioning the building. The spatial and temporal aspects of a building's life cycle are important because environmental inputs and outputs vary over the building's long life span; the materials, components and subsystems which form a building are produced in many different locations; and the environmental impact depends not only on the building system, but also on its interaction with the natural environment and its occupants (Ries and Mahdavi 2001; Ries 2002). An industrial ecology perspective requires an understanding of the interactions between industrial systems supporting the building life cycle and the affected natural ecosystems. An industrial ecology approach can be better optimized by understanding when, where and to what extent these interactions occur.

In LCA, inputs and outputs are typically aggregated across a product's entire life cycle. The potential impact for different environmental impact categories (for example climate change and photochemical smog) is estimated by multiplying aggregate emissions by established characterization factors. Characterization factors estimate the potential impact for individual pollutants based on physico-chemical mechanisms which influence how they affect human and environmental health. Local, regional, national or global characterization factors may be more appropriate for some impacts. For example, characterization factors have been developed for each greenhouse gas to convert greenhouse gas emissions to global warming potential based on the radiative forcing properties of the gases. Since global warming occurs on a global scale, global characterization factors make sense. In contrast, photochemical smog occurs on a local level and depends on pollutant concentrations and meteorological conditions. In this case local characterization factors may make more sense.

The importance of spatial and temporal aspects in life cycle impact assessment has been recognized (Heijungs et al. 1992; Fava et al. 1993). It is also important to recognize the differences in the spatial and temporal characteristics of life cycle impact categories and to consider these differences when interpreting results (Owens 1997). Local and regional characterization factors have been developed for impacts such as acidification (Potting et al. 1998) and human toxicity (Pennington et al. 2005), and regional factors are included in life cycle impact assessment methods such as TRACI (Tool for the Reduction and Assessment of Chemical and Other Environmental Impacts) (Bare et al. 2002). However, while characterization factors for local and regional impacts are commonly developed for the conditions of a specific area, they rarely, if ever, consider the conditions at the time of the release. In the case of ozone-forming pollutants, developing a dynamic model that links temporally and spatially disaggregated pollutant emissions and local meteorological conditions to generate characterization factors for photochemical smog may make more sense.

This chapter presents a proof-of-concept LCA framework with temporal and spatial resolution. To illustrate the proposed framework, we evaluate the ozone formation potential of discontinuous methane emissions that results from producing and using natural gas for residential hot water heating in Pittsburgh, Pennsylvania. We focus only on the use-phase since it tends to dominate the hot water heater life cycle, but recognize that construction and maintenance of the infrastructure and systems will also impact upon ozone formation. Life cycle methane emissions are translated into smog potential using a temporally and spatially informed characterization factor. The results are compared to an application of a prevailing life cycle impact assessment characterization factor for photochemical smog that does not consider the spatial and temporal aspect of the dynamic system to demonstrate the additional insights on the magnitude and distribution of environmental impact.

4.2 LIFE CYCLE MODEL

The scope of the hot water heating life cycle, illustrated in Figure 4.1, includes natural gas from the wellhead where it is extracted and processed, through transmission via pipelines and storage facilities to the consumer. While an end use in the Pittsburgh region is presented as an example, geographically the regions between the Gulf of Mexico and Pittsburgh, PA are affected (see Figure 4.2). The scale of the Pittsburgh region is the metropolitan area.

The hot water heating life cycle model was built with Analytica software. Analytica's interface improves model transparency by graphically displaying the model's structure and by using nested, hierarchical modules that enable comprehensible organization of model components. Analytica models can also use simulation to propagate parameter uncertainty. To capture uncertainty in input parameters, median Latin hypercube sampling with a sample size of 500 was used. The top-level Analytica model for the hot water heater life cycle is shown in Figure 4.3. As shown, the dynamic hourly hot water use and therefore energy consumption are influenced by local meteorological conditions. In addition, the characterization factors are also calculated on an hourly basis and are also influenced by the

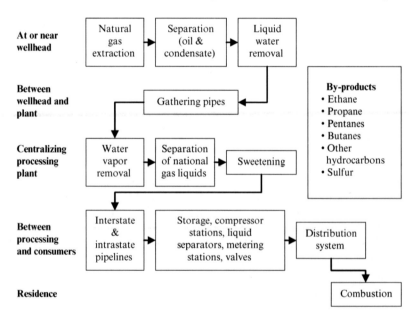

Figure 4.1   Overview of life cycle stages from wellhead to residence for producing and using natural gas in residential buildings

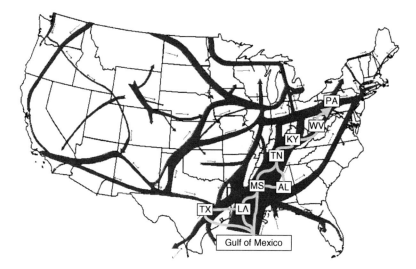

Source: Energy Information Administration (2005).

Figure 4.2 *Assumed flow of natural gas to Pittsburgh, overlaid on interstate natural gas flow map*

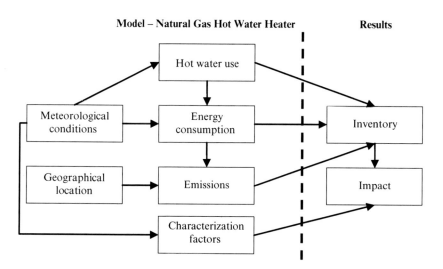

Figure 4.3 *Top-level Analytica model for hot water heater life cycle assessment*

local climate. The amount of emissions are influenced by the geographical location of natural gas production, distance to point of use and end use natural gas combustion.

4.2.1 Inventory of Hot Water Use

Hourly hot water use was estimated using the following residential hot water consumption model initially developed for the Electric Power Research Institute and later expanded by the Lawrence Berkeley National Laboratory and used on its Home Energy Saver website (Lutz et al. 1996; Pinckard et al. 2005):

$$
\begin{aligned}
\mathrm{Use}_{wh} = \Big[& a_0 + a_1 occupants + a_2 age1 + a_3 age2 \\
& + a_4 age3 + a_5 T_{tank} + a_6 tank\_size + a_7 T_{inlet} \\
& + a_8 T_{outdoor} + a_9 adult\_at\_home + a_{10} spring \\
& + a_{11} summer + a_{12} fall + a_{13} winter - dish \\
& - clothes + dwGals + (loads_{clothes} \times use_{clothes})/168 \\
& + (loads_{dish} \times use_{dish})/168 \Big] \\
& \times senior \times no\_pay \qquad (4.1)
\end{aligned}
$$

where a_0 through a_{13} are model coefficients, occupants is the total number of occupants in the household, *age1* is the number of people between 0 and 5 years, *age2* is the number of people between 6 and 13 years, *age3* is the number of people 14 years and older, T_{tank} is the water heater thermostat setting, *tank_size* is the rate volume of the water heater, T_{inlet} is the inlet water temperature, and $T_{outdoor}$ is the outdoor air temperature, *adult_at_ home* is a dummy variable to capture whether an adult is home during the day, *spring, summer, fall* and *winter* are dummy variables for each season, *dish* and *clothes* are adjustments for hot water used by a dishwasher and clothes washer embedded in the original Lutz equation, *loads_clothes* and *loads_dish* are the number of loads of clothes and dishes washed per week, *use_clothes* and *use_dish* are the amount of hot water used per each load, *senior* approximates the effect of senior-only households, and *no_pay* approximates the effect of occupants not paying for hot water.

Sampling methods and distribution parameters for model inputs were assigned using several different data sources. For example, variables describing the occupants of Pittsburgh residences were defined using information from the 2000 US Census (US Department of Commerce 2000).

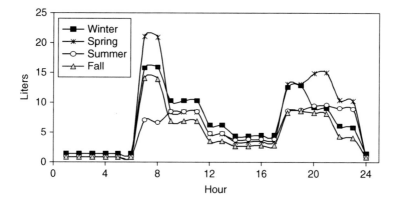

Figure 4.4   Average modeled hourly hot water use for a single residence in Pittsburgh for one weekday in each season

Temperature was defined using hourly temperature data from a weather station in Pittsburgh from 1961 to 2005 (Pennsylvania State Climatologist 2005).

The inlet temperature was assumed equal to ground temperature at pipe depth and was estimated using the following ground temperature profile model reported in the *Canadian Building Digest* (Williams and Gold 1976):

$$T(x, t) = \overline{T} + A\exp\left(-x\sqrt{\frac{\pi}{\alpha t_0}}\right)\cos\left(\frac{2\pi t}{t_0} - x\sqrt{\frac{T}{\alpha t_0}}\right) \qquad (4.2)$$

where T is the temperature at a given time, x is the depth below the surface, t is time, $T(bar)$ is the average temperature over one complete cycle, A is the amplitude of the surface temperature over one cycle, α is the thermal diffusivity of the ground, and t_0 is the time for one complete cycle.

Average modeled hourly hot water usage rates for a single residence in Pittsburgh for the weekday schedule are shown in Figure 4.4. Based on modeled results, the annual hot water usage for a single residence in Pittsburgh is 50 000 liters with a standard deviation of 27 000 liters.

4.3   ENERGY USE

The following equation, based on the Lawrence Berkeley National Laboratory Home Energy Saver model (Pinckard et al. 2005), was used to estimate hourly water heater energy use:

$$Q_{in} = \frac{use_{wh} \times dens \times Cp \times (T_{tank} - T_{in})}{RE}$$

$$\times \left[1 - \frac{UA \times (T_{tank} - T_{amb})}{Pon} \right] + UA \times (T_{tank} - T_{amb}) \qquad (4.3)$$

where Q_{in} is the amount of energy used, use_{wh} is hot water usage and was modeled using equation (4.1), *dens* is the density of water, C_p is the specific heat of water, T_{tank} is the temperature setting on the hot water heater, T_{in} is the heater inlet water temperature, *RE* is the recovery efficiency of the water heater, *UA* is the standby heat loss coefficient of the water heater, T_{amb} is the air temperature around the water heater, and *Pon* is the rated input power of the water heater.

The following equation, used by the Lawrence Berkeley National Laboratory model (Lutz et al. 1996; Pinckard et al. 2005), is used to calculate the standby heat loss coefficient:

$$UA = \frac{\dfrac{1}{EF} - \dfrac{1}{RE}}{67.5 \times \left(\dfrac{24}{Q_{out}} - \dfrac{1}{RE \times Pon} \right)} \qquad (4.4)$$

where *EF* is the energy factor of the water heater, *RE* is recovery efficiency of the water heater, and *Pon* is the rated input power of the water heater. Q_{out} is the energy content of water drawn from water heater during 24-hour test based on a DOE Energy Factor test procedure for water heaters (US Department of Energy 1993).

Based on modeled results, the annual energy usage for hot water heating for a single residence in Pittsburgh is 4000 kWh with a standard deviation of 1000 kWh.

4.3.1 Methane Emissions

Figure 4.1 illustrates the life cycle stages from wellhead to consumer for producing and using natural gas in residential buildings. Natural gas is extracted and processed throughout the United States and moved by pipelines from the centralized processing plants to consumers. Several types of emissions occur from the production, distribution and use of natural gas. This model quantifies the methane emissions that result from unintentional leaks in natural gas equipment, intentional venting, and exhaust emissions from combustion.

The US Environmental Protection Agency and the Gas Research Institute estimated methane emissions from the US natural gas industry

Table 4.1   Methane emissions for five stages of the natural gas life cycle

Life cycle stage	Emissions
Production[a]	0.38 ± 0.17 percent of natural gas produced
Processing[a]	0.16 ± 0.09 percent of natural gas processed
Transmission/Storage[a]	0.53 ± 0.26 percent of natural gas transmitted
Distribution[a]	0.35 ± 0.24 percent of natural gas distributed
Combustion[b]	0.037 ± 118% grams per m^3 natural gas combusted

Notes:
[a] Precision based on a 90% confidence interval (Kirchgessner et al. 1997).
[b] Precision expressed as the relative standard deviation (Eastern Research Group 1998).

from wellhead to the customer meter (Kirchgessner et al. 1997). The US Environmental Protection Agency's AP-42 series provides methane emissions factors for the combustion of natural gas (Eastern Research Group 1998). Table 4.1 summarizes the emission rates from these studies used in our model.

To incorporate spatial resolution in the life cycle, we needed to determine where the natural gas was produced. The amount of natural gas produced in Pennsylvania is approximately 24 percent of the amount that is consumed in Pennsylvania (US Department of Energy 2004). Therefore, we assumed that 24 percent of the natural gas used by residents in Pittsburgh is produced in Pennsylvania and 76 percent of the natural gas consumption in Pennsylvania flows in from other states. Roughly 33 percent of the natural gas entering Pennsylvania comes from Maine and New York, 23 percent comes from Ohio, and 43 percent comes from West Virginia (US Department of Energy 2004). Since the Pittsburgh region is near West Virginia and in the direction of natural gas flow, we assumed that the remaining 76 percent of the natural gas used by residents in Pittsburgh came from out-of-state transmission through West Virginia.

Figure 4.2 illustrates the flow of natural gas from the Gulf Coast region, through West Virginia, and to Pittsburgh. Of the states overlaid on the interstate natural gas flow map, only West Virginia (WV), Alabama (AL), Louisiana (LA) and Texas (TX) produce more natural gas than they use. We developed and used the following equation to estimate the percentage of natural gas used in Pittsburgh produced in each state and the Gulf of Mexico:

$$\% \text{ NG from state } i = \frac{\text{NG transported towards PA}_i}{\sum_i^n \text{NG transported towards PA}} \times (100 - 24) \qquad (4.5)$$

Table 4.2   Description of natural gas fields assumed to be serving
Pittsburgh for the purpose of this model

Location	Latitude	Longitude	%	Distance to POU (km)
Greene County, PA	39.86	80.16	24	68
Wyoming County, WV	37.62	−81.54	1	359
Vermillion Parish, LA	29.97	−92.13	2	1786
Panola County, TX	32.16	−94.32	12	1843
Gulf of Mexico	28.32	−88.82	61	1573

Natural gas is extracted from many fields in each of these states and in the Gulf of Mexico. For this model, we selected a large natural gas field from each of these and assumed that all natural gas used in Pittsburgh comes from one of these sites. Table 4.2 summarizes the geographical location of each of these fields, distance to Pittsburgh, and the percentage of Pittsburgh's natural gas requirements assumed to be met by each field.

We assume that natural gas production and processing occur within the same geographical region – near the wellhead, and that distribution occurs in the same geographical region as the natural gas customer. However, natural gas transmission occurs across large geographical areas. Based on the transmission emission rate provided by Kirchgessner et al. (1997), US Department of Energy (2004) information about annual natural gas production, interstate exchanges, and instate production and consumption, and distances between state centers and from state centers to state borders, we estimated emissions to be 0.0004 percent (standard deviation of 0.0001) of the natural gas transported per kilometer.

Figure 4.5 summarizes the methane emissions resulting from each stage of the natural gas life cycle. Based on modeled results, total annual methane emissions are 3.5 kg with a standard deviation of 1.2 kg. Transmission accounts for 34.5 percent, production for 27.8 percent, distribution for 25.6 percent, processing for 11.8 percent, and combustion for 0.4 percent. Geographically, these emissions occur throughout the natural gas supply chain and at the point of use, as illustrated in Figure 4.2. We assume that distribution and combustion emissions occur within the Pittsburgh metropolitan area. The smog potential of these emissions is evaluated in the next section based on when they occur and the meteorological conditions in Pittsburgh.

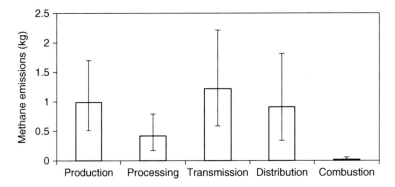

Figure 4.5   *Annual methane emissions from producing and using natural gas for a single household's hot water heating in Pittsburgh (mean with 5 percent and 95 percent confidence intervals)*

4.3.2   Smog Potential

Tropospheric ozone is formed by the photochemical oxidation of volatile organic compounds (VOCs), such as methane, and carbon monoxide in the presence of nitrogen oxides (NOx) and sunlight. High levels of tropospheric ozone and other photo-oxidants, in combination with certain meteorological conditions, can result in photochemical smog. Due to the variation in pollutant levels and meteorological conditions over time and space, photochemical smog tends to occur intermittently on a local scale. In this study we evaluate the ozone formation potential of methane emissions occurring from use-phase combustion and distribution in the Pittsburgh metropolitan area.

Most life cycle impact assessment (LCIA) models tend to quantify the average or maximum ozone formation potential of ozone-forming pollutants for some geographical area. We evaluate the ozone forma-tion potential of methane emissions using the characterization factor for methane employed by the Tool for the Reduction and Assessment of Chemical and Other Environmental Impacts (TRACI) developed by the US Environmental Protection Agency. The characterization factors in TRACI for local and regional impacts were developed specifically for the US.

TRACI uses the maximum incremental reactivity (MIR) scale provided by Carter (2000) to characterize the ozone formation potential of VOCs. These values are in moles of ozone produced per mole of VOC emitted and estimate the relative contribution of VOCs to photochemical smog when NOx availability is moderately high. As such, the MIR reflects the short-term contribution of VOCs to photochemical smog when they have

Table 4.3   Parameters of high, moderate and low oxidant formation ranges

Oxidant formation range	Relative humidity (%)	Temperature (°C)	Wind (m/s)	Ozone formation potential
High	20–55	30–41	1–6	1.0
Moderate	25–65	27–35	1–6	0.67
Low	30–90	25–30	0–5	0.33

their strongest influence on ozone formation (Bare et al. 2002). In TRACI, the MIR for each VOC is converted into a characterization factor that quantifies the grams of NOx with the same potential for smog formation as 1 gram of the VOC. This is referred to as the smog potential (SP) for that VOC and is expressed in NOx equivalents (Lippiatt 2002). The total smog index is calculated using the following equation:

$$\text{Smog Index} = \sum m_i \times SP_i \qquad (4.6)$$

where m_i is the mass of releases for pollutant i and SP_i is the smog potential in NOx equivalents for the pollutant. The smog potential for methane is 0.003675 grams NOx equivalent per gram methane.

Chock et al. (1982) determined oxidant trends within three ranges of meteorological parameters in the South Coast Basin of California. The three ranges favor high, moderate and low oxidant formation. To capture both the contribution of methane to ozone formation and the variability of meteorological conditions, we use three of the meteorological parameters identified by Chock et al.: temperature, relative humidity and wind speed. We use the parameter ranges summarized in Table 4.3 for high, moderate and low ozone formation potential. The wind speed ranges are the same as those found by Chock et al. The ranges for temperature and relative humidity were adjusted to be more in line with Pittsburgh conditions during ozone events.

The maximum ozone formation potential is set at 1 for the high oxidant formation range, 0.67 for the moderate range, and 0.34 for the low range. Since temperature is the most important meteorological determinant of ozone formation, we adjusted the ozone formation potential within each range using linear interpolation. For example, we developed and used the following equation to calculate an ozone formation potential between 0.67 and 1 for times when meteorological conditions fell within the high oxidant formation ranges:

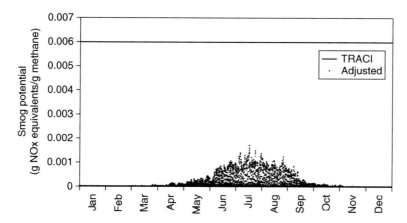

Figure 4.6   *Comparison of the TRACI smog potential and the mean adjusted smog potential based on metrological conditions in Pittsburgh for methane*

$$\text{OFP} = 0.67 + \frac{(T_{outdoor} - T_{lower})}{(T_{upper} - T_{lower})} \times (1 - 0.67) \qquad (4.7)$$

where $T_{outdoor}$ is the outdoor temperature, T_{upper} is the upper temperature of the high oxidant formation range, and T_{lower} is the lower temperature of the high oxidant formation range. Using equation (4.7), we calculated an OFP for methane emissions in Pittsburgh for every hour. We then developed and used the following equation to calculate an hourly adjusted smog potential using the smog potential value from TRACI and the hourly OFP described above:

$$SP_{adj} = SP_{TRACI} \times \text{OFP} \qquad (4.8)$$

The adjusted smog potential can only be equal to or less than the smog potential defined in TRACI. The adjusted and TRACI smog potentials will be equal if the OFP is in the high oxidant formation range and the temperature is equal to the maximum temperature for that range.

Figure 4.6 compares the TRACI SP with the mean adjusted smog potential over the course of a year for methane emissions in Pittsburgh. The TRACI smog potential is a constant and the adjusted smog potential varies with meteorological conditions, being the highest during the summer. Figure 4.7 compares the TRACI SP with the adjusted SP for methane on a day in the middle of July. Using the adjusted SP approach, the smog potential is highest during late afternoon and early evening. As shown in

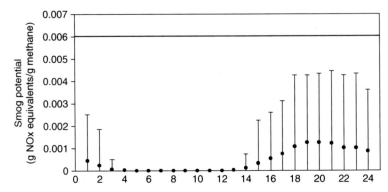

Figure 4.7   Comparison of adjusted and TRACI ozone formation potential
for a day in July in Pittsburgh for methane (mean with 5
percent and 95 percent confidence intervals shown for the
adjusted impact method)

Figures 4.6 and 4.7, the 95th percentile for the adjusted smog potential
never reaches the TRACI smog potential, which reflects a situation in
which methane has its strongest influence on ozone formation.

4.3.3   Smog Index

We developed and used the following equation to calculate the smog index
from methane emissions from distributing and combusting natural gas for
heating a single residence in the Pittsburgh area:

$$SI = \sum E_i \times SP_{adj,i} \qquad (4.9)$$

where E_i is methane emissions from distributing and combusting natural
gas at hour i and $SP_{adj,i}$ is the smog potential for Pittsburgh at hour i.
Figure 4.8 shows the cumulative distribution function for the resulting
smog index from methane emissions caused by distributing and combusting natural gas for heating water for a single residence in Pittsburgh for one
year. The results are presented from using both the TRACI smog potential
and the adjusted smog potential for methane emissions. The mean smog
index using the TRACI SP is two orders of magnitude higher than the
mean adjusted smog index – reflecting a situation where methane always
has a strong influence on ozone formation.

The smog index from methane emissions from natural gas production, processing and transmission requires calculation of SPs for areas
where natural gas fields and major pipelines are located. Emissions from

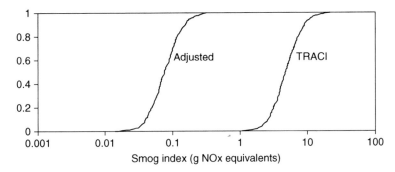

Figure 4.8   Comparison of the smog index CDF using the TRACI smog
potential and the adjust smog potential for methane emissions
from distributing and combusting natural gas for hot water
heating in a single residence in Pittsburgh

these processes may occur at a more stable rate than the distribution and
combustion emissions since natural gas is typically produced and stored
throughout the warmer seasons to meet indoor heating needs during colder
seasons. While less variability is expected in pollutant releases, regional
variability in meteorological conditions in these regions will result in
regionally variable impact. The SP from TRACI and meteorological conditions in these regions could be used to translate emissions into a smog
index for the production, processing and transmission life cycle stages.

4.4   DISCUSSION AND CONCLUSION

The model described uses a spatially and temporally disaggregated
approach to life cycle assessment. The approach combines a regional
hourly demand-side model for generating an inventory and hourly weather
data, and an impact assessment model to develop characterization factors
to evaluate the potential impact. Taking a regionally variable approach
has benefits as well as costs. While the model presents only the use-phase
emissions of a single pollutant and the potential impact for one impact cat-
egory, the results indicate that spatial and temporal resolution may reveal
significant differences between smog potentials if meteorological conditions at the time of the release are considered. This approach may have
improved the estimation for one impact indicator and can be extended to
the entire building life cycle. In order to investigate this more fully, current
work is evaluating smog potential in other geographic regions. However,
a relatively large model was used to simulate a small amount of life cycle

information for only one building system. Compared to current life cycle impact assessment, which aggregates life cycle inputs and outputs across time and space, this increases the amount of modeling and therefore the resources required for life cycle assessment.

Buildings typically have a long use-phase that is responsible for most building life cycle energy requirements. Most buildings are not mobile, and demand-side models with spatial and temporal impact assessment can be created for use-phase energy consumption. Often, spatial and temporal resolution cannot be determined for building and infrastructure construction materials from the demand side. For example, in manufacturing it may not be possible to determine the specific location or time when the steel for a component was produced. In this case, a materials flow analysis may be used in conjunction with spatial and temporal LCA to determine the likelihood of location and time and to develop characterization factors based on the typical production distribution for these locations.

A temporal and spatial understanding of a product's life cycle will more accurately identify the aspects of the product system with large environmental impact. Understanding where and when resources are consumed and effluents occur will help industrial ecologists identify opportunities for closed-loop cycles in industrial ecosystems and reduce the life cycle impact of products. Additional research is required to determine the appropriate level of temporal and spatial resolution in LCA and to determine where the greatest needs are, how to best apply it, and what the most appropriate modeling and analysis tools are.

ACKNOWLEDGMENTS

This work was supported by the Mascaro Sustainability Initiative at the University of Pittsburgh.

REFERENCES

Bare, J.C., G.A. Norris, D.W. Pennington and T. McKone (2002), 'TRACI: The Tool for the Reduction and Assessment of Chemical and Other Environmental Impacts', *Journal of Industrial Ecology*, 6 (3–4): 49–78.

Carter, W. (2000), 'Updated Maximum Incremental Reactivity Scale for Regulatory Applications', Sacramento, CA: California Air Resources Board, available at http://www.engr.ucr.edu/~carter/r98tab.htm.

Chock, D.P., S. Jumar and R.W. Herrmann (1982), 'An Analysis of Trends in Oxidant Air Quality in the South Coast Air Basin of California', *Atmospheric Environment*, 16: 2615–24.

Eastern Research Group (1998), 'Emission Factor Documentation For AP-42 Section 1.4 Natural Gas Combustion', prepared for the US Environmental Protection Agency.

Energy Information Administration (2005), *Natural Gas Annual 2004*, Washington, DC: US Department of Energy.

Fava, J., F. Consoli, R. Denison, K. Dickson, T. Mohin and B. Vigon (1993), *A Conceptual Framework for Life Cycle Impact Assessment*, Pensacola, FL: Society of Environmental Toxicology and Chemistry (SETAC).

Heijungs, R., J.B. Guinee, G. Huppes, R.M. Lankreijer, H.A. Udo de Haes and A. Wegener Sleeswijk (1992), 'Environmental Life Cycle Assessment of Products; Guide and Backgrounds', CML, Leiden, the Netherlands, available at https://openaccess.leidenuniv.nl/handle/1887/8061 and https://openaccess.leidenuniv.nl/handle/1887/8062.

Kirchgessner, D.A., R.A. Lott, R.M. Cowgill, M.R. Harrison and T.M. Shires (1997), 'Estimate of Methane Emissions from the US Natural Gas Industry', Chemosphere, **35**: 1365–90.

Lippiatt, B.C. (2002), *BEES 3.0 Building for Environmental and Economic Sustainability Technical Manual and User Guide*, National Institute of Standards and Technology NISTIR 6916.

Lutz, J.D., X. Liu, J.E. McMahon, C. Dunham, L.J. Shown and Q.T. McGrue (1996), 'Modeling Patterns of Hot Water Use in Households', Rep. No. LBL-37805 Rev. Ernest Orlando Lawrence Berkeley National Laboratory, Berkeley, CA.

Owens, J.W. (1997), 'Life Cycle Assessment: Constraints on Moving from Inventory to Impact Assessment', *Journal of Industrial Ecology*, **1**(1): 37–49.

Pennington, D.W., M. Margni, C. Ammann and O. Jolliet (2005), 'Multimedia Fate and Human Intake Modeling: Spatial versus Nonspatial Insights for Chemical Emissions in Western Europe', *Environmental Science and Technology*, **39**(4): 1119–28.

Pennsylvania State Climatologist (2005), 'Hourly Weather Data for Pittsburgh, PA, 1961–2005', http://climate.met.psu.edu/data/mesonet/datainv.php, accessed May 25, 2005.

Pinckard, M.J., R.E. Brown, E. Mills, J.D. Lutz, M.M. Moezzi, Celina Atkinson, C. Bolduc, G.K. Homan and K. Coughlin (2005), 'Documentation of Calculation Methodology, Input Data, and Infrastructure for the Home Energy Saver Web Site, Version 1.2, Rep. No. LBNL-51938', Ernest Orlando Lawrence Berkeley National Laboratory, Berkeley, CA.

Potting, J., W. Schöpp, K. Blok and M. Hauschild (1998), 'Site-Dependent Life-Cycle Impact Assessment of Acidification', *Journal of Industrial Ecology*, **2**(2): 63–87.

Ries, R.J. (2002), 'A Contextual Approach to Environmental Impact Assessment', *International Journal of Environmental Technology and Management*, **2**(1/2/3): 8–21.

Ries, R.J. and A. Mahdavi (2001), 'Integrated Computational Life Cycle Assessment of Buildings', *Journal of Computing in Civil Engineering*, **15**(1): 59–66.

US Department of Commerce (2000), *Census 2000*, US Census Bureau, available at http://www.census.gov/main/www/cen2000.html, accessed 7 November 2005.

US Department of Energy (1993), 'Technical Support Document: Energy Conservation Standards for Consumer Products: Room Air Conditioners,

Water Heaters, Direct Heating Equipment, Mobile Home Furnaces, Kitchen Ranges and Ovens, Pool Heaters, Fluorescent Lamp Ballasts, and Television Sets, Volume 3: Water Heaters, Pool Heaters, Direct Heating Equipment, Mobile Home Furnaces', Rep. No. DOE/EE-0009. US Department of Energy, Assistant Secretary, Energy Efficiency and Renewable Energy, Building Equipment Division.

US Department of Energy (2004), Energy Information Agency, *Natural Gas Annual 2003*, Washington, DC: US Department of Energy.

Williams, G. and L. Gold (1976), 'Ground Temperatures', *Canadian Building Digest*, **180**: 4.

5. Estimating generalized regional input–output systems: a case study of Australia

Blanca Gallego and Manfred Lenzen

5.1 INTRODUCTION

The past decades have seen a revival of input–output analysis, in particular that of generalized systems featuring physical factors such as energy, greenhouse gas emissions, or employment. The authors are part of a research initiative that uses the static input–output method for *ex post* reporting across a range of economic, social and environmental indicators (the 'triple bottom line'; see http://www.isa.org.usyd.edu.au) on individual, company, council, city, regional, state and national scales (Foran et al. 2005). One of the requirements of such an input–output-assisted reporting framework is that it should provide rich regional and commodity detail in order to be able to inform on a wide range of issues. This is especially true for a large country such as Australia, where regions differ substantially in their economic, social and environmental endowments.

Most statistical bureaus publish only national input–output tables, at least on a regular basis. Regionalizing national input–output systems has been a topic in the regional science literature for at least three decades. The main obstacle to estimating reliable regional input–output tables has been the lack of data, especially on interregional trade flows. The main encouragement has been the observation that reasonable holistic accuracy (that is, accuracy of impact measures such as multipliers) can be achieved if only a few but important trade flows are estimated with low enough uncertainty.

A viable way of building regional input–output tables in the absence of complete interregional trade data is making use of non-survey techniques based on theoretical considerations to estimate the missing data. The standard technique for updating or regionalizing input–output matrices is the so-called RAS balancing method.[1] Introduced by Stone and Brown (1962) and further extended by Junius and Oosterhaven (2003) and Lenzen et al. (2006), the RAS procedure consists of computing the data set closer to a preliminary estimate that satisfies a set of given constraints. It is well known that the choice of the preliminary (pre-RAS[2]) regional trade assumptions strongly influences the balance of regional tables and results of impact calculations (Round 1983).

At the University of Sydney, we have used an advanced RAS-type technique (see Lenzen et al. 2006) to assemble a detailed multi-regional input–output (MRIO) framework of Australia. This framework covers 344 industrial sectors over eight Australian regions, and makes use of a large and diverse amount of the latest survey data available. To our knowledge, this is the first such detailed framework estimated in Australia. In this article, we use our MRIO system with two aims: (1) to analyze the meaning and implications of a suite of pre-RAS regional trade assumptions; and (2) to provide a means of selecting one approach from this suite, based on the requirement that the balanced system matches real data as closely as possible. In doing so, we are able to identify the key players behind the regional dynamics of the Australian economy.

Furthermore, our MRIO system has been complemented with physical data on more than 1000 social and environmental parameters, such as employment, water use and greenhouse gas emissions (Centre for Integrated Sustainability Analysis n.d.). This generalization allows tracing social and environmental impacts along interregional supply chains, for example using structural path analysis (for example, Treloar 1997; Lenzen 2002; Wood and Lenzen 2003; Peters and Hertwich 2006). The trade specification in this model has a strong influence on evening out regional differences of environmental intensities of commodities bought by consumers. For example, due to Australia's variable climate, land and water use intensities in agriculture vary significantly across regions. These intensities become 'mixed' in a final consumer's commodity basket due to interregional trade. The extent of this dilution, and hence the magnitude of land and water intensities of regionally purchased commodities, depends critically on the specification of the trade model. This is important for characterizing the ecological footprint and other environmental impacts of regional populations, which have recently become widespread (for example, Lenzen et al. 2003; Lenzen and Murray 2003; Lenzen and Wood 2003; Global Footprint Network and ISA University of Sydney 2006). Because the dynamics of industrial ecosystems are embedded within larger-scale physical and economic transactions described in input–output frameworks, the insights gained from the use of generalized multiregional input–output models can be extended to the understanding of the long-term regional dynamics of industrial ecosystems.

This chapter is organized as follows: section 5.2 introduces the terminology and includes a literature review of regional trade in multiregional input–output systems. Section 5.3 describes our Australian case study. Section 5.4 presents the tests of the various estimates of regional trade described in section 5.3, and discusses the results. Section 5.5 concludes.

5.2 REGIONAL TRADE IN MULTIREGIONAL INPUT–OUTPUT SYSTEMS

5.2.1 A Brief Description

A multiregional input–output system is essentially a collation of input–output tables $\{T_{ij}^{rs}\}$ connecting not only – as in the single-region case – supplying industries i with using industries j, but also supplying regions r with receiving regions s. The system's basic architecture (see Table 5.1) consists of diagonal blocks ($\{T_{ij}^{rr}\}$, intraregional transactions) and off-diagonal blocks ($\{T_{ij}^{rs,r\neq s}\}$, interregional trade flows). The table is complemented with intra- and interregional final demand $\{y_i^{rs}\}$, primary inputs $\{v_j^{rs}\}$, and imports $\{m_j^s\}$. As Jensen et al. (1979) suggest, the model is formulated in basic prices, because these better complement physical factors in a generalized framework, and also show smaller fluctuations over time (see also Leontief and Strout 1963; Polenske 1970, 1980; Isard and Anselin 1982; Hewings and Jensen 1989).

The first MRIO system explicitly featuring all regions including their interregional trade flows was proposed by Isard (1951), but only a few operational MRIOs existed until the early 1960s. For a taxonomy of regional and multiregional approaches, see Batten and Martellato (1985: 41–9) and Hewings and Jensen (1989). For a history of developments, see Rose and Miernyk (1989). Mostly, input–output models of a single subnational region were estimated, with imports and exports as residual aggregates. Because of often prohibitive survey data requirements, a range of non-survey techniques based on theoretical considerations were needed to substitute missing data, particularly on interregional trade flows. With the introduction of the standard RAS matrix balancing method by Stone and Brown (1962), the role of these non-survey techniques became reduced to compiling the preliminary estimate for RAS before adding additional ('superior') data in a second step (Round 1978b), such as in the Generation of Regional Input–output Tables (GRIT) method (Jensen et al. 1979; Bayne and West 1989). The choice of regional trade assumptions in this preliminary estimate critically influences the structure of the regional input–output tables.

In what follows we discuss the methodologies that have been used in the literature for the definition of pre-RAS estimates in regional input–output models.

Table 5.1 Schematic of a regional input–output table

	domestic intermediate demand ($S \times J$)	+ domestic final demand ($S \times L$)	+ international exports (1)	= gross output
domestic intermediate supply ($R \times I$)	T_{ij}^{rs}: domestic interindustry transactions from sector i in region r to sector j in region s	$y_{il}^{d,rs}$: domestic final demand from sector i in region r for destinations l in region s	$y_i^{f,r}$: international exports of sector i in region r	X_i^r: gross state output (GSO) of sector i in region r
+ domestic primary inputs ($R \times K$)	v_{kj}^{rs}: domestic primary inputs of origin k in region r into sector j in region s	$v_{kl}^{d,rs}$: domestic primary inputs of origin k in region r into domestic final demand of destination l in region s	$v_k^{f,r}$: international exports of primary inputs of origin k in region r	V_k^r: gross state product (GSP) of origin k in region r
+ international imports (I)	m_{ij}^{s}: international imports from foreign sector i into domestic sector j in region s	$m_{il}^{d,s}$: international imports from foreign sector i into domestic final demand of destination l in region s	m_i^r: international re-exports of international imports from foreign sector i in region r	M_i^r: international state imports from foreign sector i in region r
= gross input	X_j^s: Gross state input (GSI) into sector j in region s	Y_l^s: Gross state expenditure (GSE) of destination l in region s	E: international state exports	

Note: Indices: i, j – industries; r, s – regions; k – domestic primary input origins (wages and salaries, gross operating surplus, net taxes on production, import duties); l – domestic final demand destinations (private and government final consumption, gross fixed capital expenditure, changes in inventories); d – domestic; f – foreign.

5.2.2 Literature Review

The simplest prediction for regional flows in the absence of any data except prescribed row and column sums is based on the assumption of import–export independence (compare Uribe et al. 1966: 209):

$$T_{ij}^{rs} = \frac{X_i^r X_j^s}{X^r X^s} \tag{5.1}$$

Here X_i^r represents gross output of sector i in region r. This estimate implies that flows from industry i in region r to industry j in region s are large if i in r exports much and j in s imports much. Since transport distances or other parameters do not play any role, this estimate is generally quite unrealistic (see Uribe et al. 1966: 215–18).

Therefore, most pre-RAS non-survey techniques attempt to estimate the technical coefficients $a_{ij}^{rs} = T_{ij}^{rs}/X_j^s$ by somehow scaling national coefficients down to the regional level.[3] It is important to note in this context that regional coefficients represent trade, and not technology: the more open a regional economy, the more regional production coefficients A^{rr} are likely to deviate from the national production recipe A^N, since inputs are increasingly sourced from outside the region.[4]

In his balanced model, Leontief (1953) distinguishes between 'regional commodities' that must be consumed not far from where they are produced, and 'national commodities' that can travel long distances.[5] First, the outputs of the latter are distributed between regions according to $X_i^r = \rho_i^r X_i^N$, where the superscript N refers to national values and the ρ_i^r are known locational constants describing the participation of region r in producing commodity i. The balance between inputs and outputs applies only to the nation. Second, applying the national production recipe A^N, and known regional final demand $y^{d,r}$, the regional balance $X_i^r - \sum_j a_{ij}^N X_j^r = y^{d,r}$ can be solved for the remaining outputs X_i^r (see Leontief 1953: 107–10). Finally, total input requirements $X_i^r - \sum_i a_{ij}^N X_j^r$ of each regional industry j are determined. Since the national production recipe is applied to regions, the model is blind with respect to spatial commodity origin: all inputs are taken from a common 'trade pool'.[6]

In their supply–demand pool technique Moore and Petersen (1955) take preliminary regional inputs $a_{ij}^N X_j^r$ based on the national production recipe and known regional outputs X_j^r, and replace these with superior survey data. In a final step, regional commodity demands and outputs are compared, positive or negative differences netted out so that either the commodity surplus or deficit is zero, with the remainders understood as regional imports and exports. Similarly, Shen (1960) takes into account survey data on industrial value added in order to capture regional differences in industry composition. These two models are therefore spatially sensitive.

A more recent approach uses trading coefficients τ_{ij}^{rs} in order to conclude from regional technical coefficients $a_{ij}^{s} = \sum_r a_{ij}^{rs}$ to regional flow coefficients via $a_{ij}^{rs} = a_{ij}^{s}\tau_{ij}^{rs}$ (see Round 1978a, 1978b; Oosterhaven 1984; Batten and Martellato 1985; Miller and Blair 1985). A common assumption is that regional and national production recipes are equal, so that $a_{ij}^{s} = a_{ij}^{N}$.[7] Interregional trading coefficients are bound by $\sum_r \tau_{ij}^{rs} = 1$.

One possibility for estimating trading coefficients is via location quotients:

$$LQ_i = \frac{X_i^r/X^r}{X_i^N/X^N} \tag{5.2}$$

The location quotient 'is a measure that is designed to reflect the relative importance of an industry in a region, as compared to its importance in the nation' (Morrison and Smith 1974: 7). Following their basic notion, location quotients 'may be ascertained by some function of the relative size of the supplying sector, the relative size of the purchasing sector, and the overall size of the region relative to the nation as a whole' (Round 1978a: 181). A location quotient $LQ_i = 1$ indicates self-sufficiency of the region for commodity i. Values smaller (larger) than 1 indicate regional production below (above) self-sufficiency, and import (export) orientation. When the location quotient exceeds 1 for a particular industry, it is assumed that all requirements of this industry's output are (and can be) met regionally, so that $a_{ij}^{rr} = a_{ij}^{N}$ for all j. If $LQ_i < 1$, then $a_{ij}^{rr} = LQ_i a_{ij}^{N}$ for all j. Regional imports (exports) are calculated residually for industries i with $LQ_i < 1 (>1)$.

A cross-industry quotient CIQ is a particular form of location quotient, which in addition to the relative size of the selling industry, also takes into account the size of the purchasing industry:

$$CIQ_{ij} = \frac{X_i^r/X_i^N}{X_j^r/X_j^N} = \frac{LQ_i}{LQ_j} \tag{5.3}$$

Equation (5.3) implies that intra-sectoral transactions ($i = j$) are always purely intra-regional, since $CIQ_{ii} = 1$ (Morrison and Smith 1974). As with the location quotient method, $CIQ_i < 1 \Rightarrow a_{ij}^{rr} = a_{ij}^{N}$ for all j, $CIQ_i < 1 \Rightarrow a_{ij}^{rr} = CIQ_i a_{ij}^{N}$ for all j, and regional imports (exports) are calculated residually for industries i with $CIQ_i < 1 (>1)$.

None of the approaches described so far allows simultaneous shipments of the same commodity in and out of the region, since exports and imports are netted out.[8] However, in reality, cross-hauling is often observed because products of aggregate industries are not homogeneous,[9] and because shipments in different directions occur at various times throughout one reporting year (Polenske 1970).[10] Results from these net-trade approaches tend to overstate intra-regional trade.[11] This shortcoming is overcome in the gravity model by Leontief and Strout (1963), where:

$$\sum_j T_{ij}^{rs} = \frac{X_i^r X_i^s}{X_i^N} q_i^{rs}, \tag{5.4}$$

and q_i^{rs} is a trade parameter which is a function of the cost of transferring commodity i from region r to region s (including factors such as transportation cost, distance, and so on). These q_i^{rs} reflect that especially interindustry transactions of bulky, low-value products are likely to involve spatially close industries (Czamanski 1971; Harrigan 1982).[12]

5.3 ANALYSIS OF REGIONAL TRADE IN A CASE STUDY OF AUSTRALIA

5.3.1 Methodology Overview

Various location quotient and commodity balance formulations have been analyzed by comparing the deviation of a generated table from a survey-based table for the same interregional system, and in most cases a clearly preferable candidate could not be established (see Hewings 1969; Round 1978a, 1978b; Morrison and Smith 1974; Harrigan et al. 1980b). Such a comparison is of course only possible if there exists a survey-based table. In most circumstances, regional analysts would want an indication for a preferred preliminary estimate without having to commission a complete survey-based table. In any case, if the latter were available, there would be no need for a preliminary estimate.

The idea put forward in this chapter is to base a quality measure for preliminary estimates on the superior data constraining the regional table. These superior data can be arranged in a vector c_{sup}, while its relations to the elements $\{T_{ij}^{rs}, y_{il}^{d,rs}, v_{kj}^{rs}$, and so on$\}$ of the regional transactions table $\mathbf{T}$ are collated in a matrix $\mathbf{K}$ so that under ideal balance, $\mathbf{KT} = c_{\text{sup}}$. In virtually all cases, a preliminary estimate $\mathbf{T}$ of a regional transactions table will not satisfy the constraints c_{sup} imposed by the superior data, but instead amount to actual values $c_{\text{act}} \neq c_{\text{sup}}$. The quality of the preliminary estimate can then be characterized by some measure of distance between c_{act} and c_{sup}.

The next section describes the different preliminary estimates analyzed in this chapter. Section 5.3.3 describes the compilation of the superior data used to constrain the multiregional input–output table c_{sup}, while section 5.3.4 describes the measures employed to determine the distance between c_{act} and c_{sup} and, therefore, the quality of the preliminary estimates of regional trade.

5.3.2   Preliminary Estimates

5.3.2.1   Intra-regional trading coefficients

In this work we follow the trading coefficients approach, and set $a_{ij}^{rs} = a_{ij}^{N}\tau_{ij}^{rs}$. For the intra-regional trading coefficients we appraise three location quotients: the simple location quotient (equation 5.5), the cross-industry location quotient (equation 5.6), and the semi-logarithmic location quotient (equation 5.7):

$$\tau_{ij}^{rr} = min(1, LQ_i^r), \quad LQ_i^r = \frac{X_i^r/X^r}{X_i^N/X^N}, \tag{5.5}$$

$$\tau_{ij}^{rr} = min(1, CIQ_{ij}^r), \quad CLQ_{ij}^r = \frac{LQ_i^r}{LQ_j^r}, \tag{5.6}$$

$$\tau_{ij}^{rr} = min(1, SLQ_{ij}^r), \quad SLQ_{ij}^r = \frac{LQ_i^r}{\log_2(1 + LQ_j^r)}. \tag{5.7}$$

For detailed discussions on these quotients see Schaffer and Chu (1969) and Round (1978b).

We further apply the supply–demand pool technique (see Leontief 1953; Round 1983) by assuming the trading coefficients as a first approximation equal to 1. If the regional outputs resulting from these estimates $\tilde{X}_i^r$ are larger than the known gross state outputs X_i^r then the corresponding trading coefficient is redefined as the ratio: $X_i^r/\tilde{X}_i^r$. This procedure may be rewritten in the form of a quotient as follows:

$$\tau_{ij}^{rr} = min(1, SDP_i^r), \quad SPD_i^r = \frac{X_i^r}{\sum_j a_{ij}^N X_j^r + \sum_l y_{il}^{d,r} + y_i^{f,r}} \tag{5.8}$$

5.3.2.2   Interregional trading coefficients

The interregional trading coefficients are estimated following a gravity law by which the trade from industry i in region r to industry j in region s is proportional to the size of i in r, and the size of j in s, and inversely proportional to the cost C_i^{rs} of transferring commodity i from r to s per dollar of commodity:

$$\tau_{ij}^{rs(r \neq s)} \propto \lambda_i^{rs}LQ_i^rLQ_j^s \text{ with } \lambda_i^{rs} = \frac{1/C_i^{rs}}{\sum_{r(r \neq s)} 1/C_i^{rs}}. \tag{5.9}$$

For commodities that require physical transport, C_i^{rs} can be estimated as a weighted product:

$$C_i^{rs(\text{transport})} = \sum_m C_{m,i}^{rs(\text{transport})} = \sum_m \left(D_m^{rs} c_m \frac{1}{p_i} \right), \qquad (5.10)$$

where D_m^{rs} is a measure of the distance between r and s, c_m is the cost of transporting one ton for one kilometer, and p_i is the specific value of one ton of commodity i. Four different modes of transportation – road, rail, sea and air – are distinguished and included in subscript m. For commodities that do not require physical transport (some services), we assume that the transfer cost is independent of the regions of origin and destination: $C_i^{rs(\text{no transport})} = C$. Whether a commodity is physically transported or not is reported in national data on transport margins $Z_{m,ij}^N$:

$$
\lambda_i^{rs} =
\begin{cases}
\dfrac{1/C_i^{rs(\text{transport})}}{\displaystyle\sum_{r(r \neq s)} 1/C_i^{rs(\text{transport})}}, & \text{if } \displaystyle\sum_{m,j} Z_{m,ij}^N \neq 0 \\[4ex]
\dfrac{1/C}{\displaystyle\sum_{r(r \neq s)} 1/C} = 1/(R-1), & \text{if } \displaystyle\sum_{m,j} Z_{m,ij}^N = 0.
\end{cases}
\qquad (5.11)
$$

The intra-regional and interregional trading coefficients cannot be determined independently since they are linked by the constraint $\sum \tau_{ij}^{rs} = 1$. This constraint can be exploited to calculate the proportionality constant in the interregional relationship $\tau_{ij}^{rs(r \neq s)} \propto \lambda_i^{rs} LQ_i^r LQ_j^s$:

$$\tau_{ij}^{rs(r \neq s)} = \frac{(1 - \tau_{ij}^{ss})}{\displaystyle\sum_{r(r \neq s)} \lambda_i^{rs} LQ_i^r LQ_j^s} \lambda_i^{rs} LQ_i^r LQ_j^s. \qquad (5.12)$$

5.3.2.3 Final demand and primary input coefficients

Domestic final demand $y_{il}^{d,rs}$ can be expressed in a similar way to inter-industry trade as $y_{il}^{d,rs} = y_{il}^{d,s} \tau_{il}^{y,rs}$, where $\tau_{il}^{y,rs}$ are the interstate trading coefficients dividing domestic production into final demand. These trading coefficients are estimated analogously to the trading coefficients into domestic production: $\tau_{il}^{y,rr} = min(1, LQ_i^r)$ for the simple location quotient; $\tau_{il}^{y,rr} = min(1, CIQ_{il}^{y,r})$ with $CLQ_{il}^{y,r} = (LQ_i^r)/(LQ_l^{y,r})$ and $LQ_l^{y,r} = (Y_l^r/Y^r)/(Y_l^N/Y^N)$ for the cross-industry quotient; $\tau_{il}^{y,rr} = min(1, SLQ_{il}^{y,r})$ with $SLQ_{il}^{y,r} = LQ_i^r/(log_2(1 + LQ_l^{y,r})$ for the semi logarithmic quotient; and $\tau_{il}^{y,rr} = min(1, SPD_i^r)$ for the supply–demand pool quotient. The interregional trading coefficient is defined as

$\tau_{il}^{y,rs(r \neq s)} \propto \lambda_i^{y,rs} LQ_i^r LQ_l^{y,s}$ with $\lambda_i^{y,rs}$ being like λ_i^{rs} but using its corresponding national transport margins.

Regarding primary inputs, we assume that income and profits are earned, and taxes paid only at the place of residence or production, so that interregional domestic primary inputs v_{kj}^{rs} and $v_{kl}^{d,rs}$ (where k denotes origin type) are assumed zero between states: $v_{kj}^{rr} = v_{kj}^r$, $v_{kj}^{rs(r \neq s)} = 0$, $v_{kl}^{d,rr} = v_{kl}^{d,r}$ and $v_{kl}^{d,rs(r \neq s)} = 0$.

5.3.2.4 Overview of models

Table 5.2 shows the 13 different scenarios analyzed in this chapter. The simplest one is what we call the 'null hypothesis' (NH), when all the intra-regional trading coefficients are set to 1 and all the interregional trading coefficients are set to 0. We explore combinations of the four estimations for intra-regional trading coefficients: location quotient, cross-industry quotient (CIQ), semi-logarithmic quotient (SLQ) (equations 5.5–5.7), and supply–demand pool (equation 5.8), together with the gravity model (equation 5.12) for the estimation of interregional coefficients. GMDs

Table 5.2   Scenarios for the 13 different preliminary estimates of the multiregional input–output table explored in this chapter

Scenario	τ_{ij}^{rr} (and similarly $\tau_{il}^{y,rr}$)	$\tau_{ij}^{rs(r \neq s)}$ (and similarly $\tau_{il}^{y,rs(r \neq s)}$)
NH	1	0
LQ + NH	$min(1, LQ_i^r)$	$\tau_{ij}^{rs(r \neq s)} = \dfrac{1 - \tau_{ij}^{ss}}{R - 1}$
CIQ + NH	$min(1, CIQ_{ij}^r)$	As above
SLQ + NH	$min(1, SLQ_{ij}^r)$	As above
SDP + NH	$min(1, SDP_i^r)$	As above
LQ + GMDs	$min(1, LQ_i^r)$	$\tau_{ij}^{rs(r \neq s)} = \dfrac{1 - \tau_{ij}^{ss}}{\sum_{r(r \neq s)} \lambda_i^{rs} LQ_i^r LQ_j^s} \lambda_i^{rs} LQ_i^r LQ_j^s$
		with D_m^{rs} = distance between state capitals
CIQ + GMDs	$min(1, CIQ_{ij}^r)$	As above
SLQ + GMDs	$min(1, SLQ_{ij}^r)$	As above
SDP + GMDs	$min(1, SDP_i^r)$	As above
LQ + GMDf	$min(1, LQ_i^r)$	$\tau_{ij}^{rs(r \neq s)} = \dfrac{(1 - \tau_{ij}^{ss})}{\sum_{r(r \neq s)} \lambda_i^{rs} LQ_i^r LQ_j^s} \lambda_i^{rs} LQ_i^r LQ_j^s$
		with D_m^{rs} = distance from freight movements
CIQ + GMDf	$min(1, CIQ_{ij}^r)$	As above
SLQ + GMDf	$min(1, SLQ_{ij}^r)$	As above
SDP + GMDf	$min(1, SDP_i^r)$	As above

refers to the application of the gravity model with the interregional transport distance estimated as the distance between state capitals. Meanwhile, GMDf estimates the transport distance as the ratio between interstate freight movements in tons $\times$ km and freight movements in tons.

5.3.2.5 Data sources for preliminary estimates

Most regional data sources are more aggregated than the national input–output tables. The integration of regional data into an input–output framework would be straightforward if all tables were aggregated to the largest overall common industry sector classification. This reduction in resolution, however, would severely limit the capabilities of the resulting model for impact analysis and decision-making. Especially, if additional indicators such as energy and land are to be integrated into a comprehensive Environmental and Economic Accounts System, it is desirable to compile the system of accounts at the maximum level of detail, and aggregate the results after impact analysis if necessary.

Recent work by the ISA[13] group at the University of Sydney has set the task of creating a standardized procedure to generate the most detailed generalized regional input–output framework possible. Choices of detail had to be made with respect to industry classification and spatial delineation. The Australian multiregional input–output model analyzed in this chapter distinguishes 344 industrial sectors, five primary input origins and six final demand destinations in the eight states and territories of Australia.

Regional transactions were leveraged off the national production recipe $\{a_{ij}^N\}$, which, together with final demand y^N and primary inputs v^N are documented in the input–output tables published by the Australian Bureau of Statistics (2004a, 2004b). Gross state output X^r can be derived from data on the number of business locations by turnover ranges (Australian Bureau of Statistics 2001a).

Regional primary inputs, v_{kj}^s and $v_{kl}^{d,s}$ are unknown, so that their preliminary estimates were derived from their corresponding national values and gross state values using the scaling $v_{kj}^s = v_{kj}^N V_k^s / \sum_s V_k^s$ and $v_{kl}^{d,s} = v_{kl}^N V_k^s / \sum_s V_k^s$. International imports and exports were similarly derived from national and state values by scaling $m_{ij}^s = m_{ij}^N M^s / \sum_s M^s$, $m_{il}^{d,s} = m_{il}^{d,N} M^s / \sum_s M^s$, $y_i^{f,s} = E_i^N E^s / \sum_s E^s$ and $v_k^{f,s} = v_k^{f,N} E^s / \sum_s E^s$.

Meanwhile, final private domestic $y_{iPr}^{d,s}$ and imported $m_{iPr}^{d,s}$ consumption are known from the Household Expenditure Survey, conducted every five years by the Australian Bureau of Statistics (ABS), with one being in this study's base year 1998–99 (Australian Bureau of Statistics 2000).

In the gravity model, distances D_m^{rs} between regions can be estimated either as the distance between state capitals (Lenzen 1999), or as the ratio between freight movements between regions (expressed in net-ton-kilometers) and freight movements between regions in tons (Australian Bureau of Statistics 2001b). Modal transport costs c_m were taken from Lenzen (1999), while mass-specific commodity prices p_i are documented by the Australian Bureau of Statistics (1997). National margins Z^N are documented along with the input–output tables published by the Australian Bureau of Statistics (2004a, 2004b). A shortcoming of our gravity model is the fact that our eight regions are rather large, resulting in the model favoring intra-state trade between two locations, even if they are farther away from each other than from other locations in different states (compare Moses 1960: 382). Such shortcomings can only be improved upon by increasing spatial detail.

5.3.3 Superior Data and Constraints

In order to constrain the preliminary estimate of the regional transactions table, it is important to incorporate as many sources of superior data as possible (Hewings and Jensen 1989: 347). We follow the idea of McMenamin and Haring (1974),[14] and subject the entire input–output system, including the value added and final demand blocks, to the estimation procedure. As in the GRIT method, we use 'good working knowledge of the region' (that is, engineering, geographic and economic information) in our constraints (West 1981: 857). Because of our focus on environmental impact of industrial ecosystems, we scrutinize those transactions that are likely to entail significant environmental burden (for example agriculture and energy transformation).

The constraints accounted for in this chapter can be classified into four main categories: constraints on national transactions, constraints on aggregated state expenditure and income components, constraints on the interstate trade of selected commodities, and internal accounting constraints. The superior data at a national level has been obtained from the Australia input–output tables and from unpublished data in form of 'commodity cards' both provided by the Australian Bureau of Statistics (2004a, 2004b). The constraints within each state have been built using the Australian State Accounts (Australian Bureau of Statistics 1999), which contain detail on state expenditure and income accounts, albeit at a relatively high degree of aggregation. Knowledge of selected interstate trade has been obtained from various industry surveys published by the ABS on single industry sectors (AusStats website http://www.abs.gov.au). Furthermore, for commodities that are unlikely to be transported far, mostly because of their weight, bulk, transportability, transport cost, low value and/or infrastructure requirements (compare Tiebout 1960: 398), a detailed manual survey was conducted, with information solicited via phone and email, resulting in a database of commodities that are produced and consumed only in the same state. These include minerals, livestock, energy carriers, water, agricultural by-products and construction materials. The final set of constraints is the result of imposing internal accounting consistency. For example, the sum of all the sales of industry i in region r to all domestic intermediate demand, domestic final demand and international exports should equal the gross state output of sector i in region r: $\sum_{j,s} T_{ij}^{rs} + \sum_{l,s} y_{il}^{d,rs} + y_i^{f,r} = X_i^r$. Or the sum of all domestic and international inputs into the final demand of type l of a given state should equal the gross state expenditure in that region: $\sum_{j,s} y_{jl}^{d,sr} + \sum_{k,s} v_{kl}^{d,sr} + \sum_l m_{jl}^{dr} = Y_l^r$.

5.3.4 Matrix Distance as a Quality Measure for Regional Flow Estimates

A number of authors (for example, Czamanski and Malizia 1969; McMenamin and Haring 1974; Morrison and Smith 1974; Lecomber 1975; Harrigan et al. 1980b; Jackson and Comer 1993) examine concepts of relative distance between two matrices in order to characterize the comparative performance of matrix balancing methods. According to Butterfield and Mules (1980: 293); 'there exists no single statistical test for assessing the accuracy with which one matrix corresponds to another. Analysts working in this area have tended to use a number of [complementary] tests.' For the purpose of measuring the distance between the constraints imposed by the superior data c_{sup}, and the actual values corresponding to a given preliminary estimate c_{act}, we have sourced six measures from the literature (Harrigan et al. 1980b; Günlük-Senesen and Bates 1988; Lahr 2001):

- the relative arithmetic mean of absolute differences:

$$AMAD = \frac{\sum_i |c_{act,i} - c_{sup,i}|}{\sum_i c_{sup,i}}; \qquad (5.13)$$

- the relative geometric mean of absolute differences:[15]

$$GMAD = \frac{\sqrt{\sum_i |c_{act,i} - c_{sup,i}|^2}}{\sqrt{\sum_i c_{sup,i}^2}}; \qquad (5.14)$$

- the Isard–Romanoff similarity index:[16]

$$DSIM = 1 - SIM = \frac{1}{N} \sum_i \frac{|c_{act,i} - c_{sup,i}|}{|c_{act,i}| + |c_{sup,i}|}; \qquad (5.15)$$

- the χ^2 distribution of absolute differences:

$$CHI = \sum_i \frac{(c_{act,i} - c_{sup,i})^2}{c_{sup,i}};$$

(5.16)

- the arithmetic mean of relative differences:

$$AMRD = \frac{1}{N} \sum_i \frac{|c_{act,i} - c_{sup,i}|}{c_{sup,i}};$$

(5.17)

- the correlation coefficient:

$$DCORR = 1 - CORR = 1 - \frac{\mathrm{Cov}\{c_{act,i}, c_{sup,i}\}}{\sqrt{\mathrm{Var}\{c_{act,i}\}}\sqrt{\mathrm{Var}\{c_{sup,i}\}}}.$$

(5.18)

We propose a further measure of the distance between c_{act} and c_{sup} incorporating the errors associated with the published 'measurement' of the superior data c_{sup}. It is generally the case that the values of c_{sup} are known within an interval $c_{sup,i} \pm \sigma_i$. Because the constraints are not independent of each other, even small deviations of $c_{sup,i}$ from their 'true' values cause serious incompatibilities. Therefore, attempting to satisfy $c_{act} = c_{sup}$ exactly is an impossible task. In order to reflect this reality we propose a measure of distance where the distance between each element of c_{act} and c_{sup} is weighted by the inverse of the corresponding standard error of the superior data:

$$WDIF = \frac{1}{N} \sum_i \frac{|c_{act,i} - c_{sup,i}|}{\sigma_i}.$$

(5.19)

Equation (5.19) reflects the fact that the better the knowledge of $c_{sup,i}$, the more important it is to have $c_{act,i}$ closer to it.

5.4   RESULTS AND DISCUSSION

5.4.1   Overview

The performance of the 13 different pre-RAS estimates described in Table 5.2 has been analyzed within the context of the Australian multiregional input–output system. For each preliminary estimate, a number on the order of 300,000 constraints has been computed using different linear combinations of the almost 9 million cells of our MRIO table (section 5.3.2.5).

The actual values c_{act} of these constraints are then compared to their known values c_{sup} using the seven distance measures described in section 5.3.4.

All our distance indices (equations 5.13–5.19) have been constructed to decrease as the relative distance between the vectors becomes smaller. The constraints have been defined such that $c_{sup,i} \geq 0$ for all i. A small number is added to both $c_{sup,i}$ and $c_{act,i}$ simultaneously whenever $c_{sup,i} = 0$ appears in the denominator. Note, however, that $c_{act,i}$ can take on negative values. For the computation of the weighted difference (WDIF), a small value of σ_i has been assumed for the accounting constraints that have otherwise $\sigma_i = 0$. Table 5.3 shows the results of these calculations normalized by the values resulting from the null hypothesis assumption.

Except for the dissimilarity index (DSIM), all of the distance indices change roughly in the same direction. More precisely, the correlation between each pair of indices is always positive and close to 0.99 with the exception of correlations with DSIM (see Table 5.4). The peculiar behavior of the dissimilarity index is possibly due to the presence of negative values of $c_{act,i}$.

All results are presented normalized by the values resulting from the null hypothesis assumption (NH), whose distance measures appear in parenthesis.

Except for the dissimilarity index (DSIM), all of the distance indices change roughly in the same direction. More precisely, the correlation between each pair of indices is always positive and close to 0.99 with the exception of correlations with DSIM (see Table 5.4). The peculiar behavior of the dissimilarity index is possibly due to the presence of negative values of $c_{act,i}$.

Our results show that the pre-RAS estimate generally improves as we move down in our intraregional assumption scenario from null hypothesis to the supply–demand pool model. This is particularly true in the absence of assumptions regarding interregional trade. The largest improvement occurs when comparing the null hypothesis and the rest of the scenarios. This reflects the importance of scaling regional transactions. Within the location quotient techniques, the models that include some measure of the size of the receiving industries (CIQ and SLQ) tend to perform better. However, this improvement is small.

The next most significant change occurs between the quotient techniques and the supply–demand pool model. This shows that considering the additional information (regional supply and demand balances as well as final demand) adds significantly to the quality of the estimate.

Regarding interregional trade, the gravity model always performs better than the null hypothesis. This means that when distributing interregional trade across states of origin it is better to do so considering some estimate of the cost of transportation, as a function of distance and/or weight.

Table 5.3   Performance in terms of seven distance measures (Equations 5.13–5.19) of the preliminary estimates described in Table 5.2

Assumptions on Intraregional trade	Assumptions on interregional trade		
	Null hypothesis	Gravity model with distances between state capitals	Gravity model with distances derived from freight movements
Null hypothesis	NH AMAD 1.0(2.8137E−01) GMAD 1.0(1.3440E−01) DSIM 1.0(2.3792E−02) CHI 1.0(1.4074E+25) AMRD 1.0(3.4291E+13) DCORR 1.0(8.9850E−03) WDIF 1.0(3.4492E+07)		
Location quotient	LQNH AMAD 0.7380 GMAD 0.7977 DSIM 1.0000 CHI 0.5674 AMRD 0.7226 DCORR 0.6391 WDIF 0.7242	LQGMDs AMAD 0.6751 GMAD 0.7445 DSIM 1.3121 CHI 0.4641 AMRD 0.6271 DCORR 0.5577 WDIF 0.6382	LQGMDf AMAD 0.6822 GMAD 0.7489 DSIM 1.3112 CHI 0.4686 AMRD 0.6313 DCORR 0.5642 WDIF 0.6433
Cross-industry quotient	CIQNH AMAD 0.7368 GMAD 0.7972 DSIM 1.0000 CHI 0.5665 AMRD 0.7214 DCORR 0.6383 WDIF 0.7230	CIQGMDs AMAD 0.6800 GMAD 0.7360 DSIM 1.5427 CHI 0.4472 AMRD 0.6186 DCORR 0.5450 WDIF 0.6311	CIQGMDf AMAD 0.6869 GMAD 0.7400 DSIM 1.5023 CHI 0.4512 AMRD 0.6236 DCORR 0.5509 WDIF 0.6369
Semi-logarithmic quotient	SLQNH AMAD 0.7349 GMAD 0.7968 DSIM 1.0000 CHI 0.5657 AMRD 0.7194 DCORR 0.6377 WDIF 0.7210	SLQGMDs AMAD 0.6779 GMAD 0.7378 DSIM 1.4732 CHI 0.4519 AMRD 0.6213 DCORR 0.5477 WDIF 0.6330	SLQGMDf AMAD 0.6848 GMAD 0.7422 DSIM 1.4433 CHI 0.4564 AMRD 0.6261 DCORR 0.5541 WDIF 0.6387

Table 5.3   (continued)

Assumptions on Intraregional trade	Assumptions on interregional trade		
	Null hypothesis	Gravity model with distances between state capitals	Gravity model with distances derived from freight movements
Supply–demand pool	SDPNH	SDPGMDs	SDPGMDf
	AMAD 0.7230	AMAD 0.6593	AMAD 0.6665
	GMAD 0.7932	GMAD 0.7364	GMAD 0.7407
	DSIM 1.0000	DSIM 1.3078	DSIM 1.3103
	CHI 0.5589	CHI 0.4489	CHI 0.4535
	AMRD 0.7068	AMRD 0.6080	AMRD 0.6122
	DCORR 0.6320	DCORR 0.5456	DCORR 0.5520
	WDIF 0.7085	WDIF 0.6202	WDIF 0.6254

Table 5.4   *Correlation coefficients between the seven distance measures (Equations 5.13–5.19) explored in this chapter*

	AMAD	GMAD	DSIM	CHI	AMRD	DCORR	WDIF
AMAD	1.0000	0.9944	−0.5678	0.9954	0.9897	0.9964	0.9939
GMAD		1.0000	−0.6431	0.9997	0.9967	0.9991	0.9985
DSIM			1.0000	−0.6272	−0.6772	−0.6124	−0.6540
CHI				1.0000	0.9949	0.9997	0.9973
AMRD					1.0000	0.9929	0.9994
DCORR						1.0000	0.9961
WDIF							1.0000

Furthermore, in the case of Australia, it is more accurate to use distances between state capitals rather than distances derived from statistics of freight movements.

5.4.2   Key Parameters of Interregional Dynamics

While interindustry trade on the whole is still governed by a technical production recipe, input can in principle be sourced from any region. Appropriately accounting for interregional trade in an input–output model is essential since the magnitude of the interregional linkages determines for example:

- how final demand shocks in one region ripple through the whole economy;
- how price hikes or taxation in one region affect consumers in other regions;
- the potential of closely located eco-industrial parks of substituting remote trade links;
- how production of capital commodities in one region influences growth in other regions; and
- how changes in particular intra-region interindustry links (for example technological innovation, or sudden disruptions) have repercussions across the entire economy (the 'field-of-influence' approach).

An interesting feature of the interregional structure of an input–output model is the magnitude of its interregional feedbacks. Interregional feedback effects refer to the changes in the output of a given region that are associated with changes in extra-regional demands and which themselves result from an initial change in the output of the region under consideration. One way of quantifying the interregional feedback effect in one region is by looking at the fraction of its gross output associated with intra-regional final demand in the presence of the other regions versus that in the absence of interregional trade (see Miller 1966).

In our model, the vector of gross output of a region r, X^r, can be expressed as the sum of requirements for production needed to satisfy final demand of intraregional products plus the requirements associated with final demand of extra-regional production:

$$X^r = [(I - A^{rr}) - A^{rS}(I - A^{SS})^{-1}A^{Sr}]^{-1}Y^r$$

$$+ [(I - A^{rr}) - A^{rS}(I - A^{SS})^{-1}A^{Sr}]^{-1}A^{rS}(I - A^{SS})^{-1}Y^S. \quad (5.20)$$

Here, the subscript S refers to all the regions other than r so that A^{ss} is a $N(R - 1) \times N(R - 1)$ matrix containing all the submatrices A^{pq} with $p, q \neq r$, Y^s is a $N(R - 1)$ vector that accounts for all final demand of production outside r, while Y^r refers to final demand for production in r and has dimensions of $N \times 1$. As a measure of interregional feedback effects, let us define the interregional feedback index in region r as the normalized difference between the first term of equation (5.20) and the gross output associated with Y^r that would exist in the absence of trade, that is:

interregional feedback index in r

$$= \sum_i \frac{|\{[(I - A^{rr}) - A^{rS}(I - A^{SS})^{-1}A^{Sr}]^{-1}Y^r\}_i - \{(I - A^{rr})^{-1}Y^r\}_i|}{\{(I - A^{rr})^{-1}Y^r\}_i} \quad (5.21)$$

The interregional feedback indices for each region in Australia, as defined above, have been computed for some of the regional trade assumptions analyzed in this chapter and are shown in Table 5.5. Overall they are small in magnitude. In the absence of gravity model assumptions, the interregional feedback indices for all pre-RAS estimates (other than for the null hypothesis which has zero interregional feedbacks) are roughly inversely proportional to the size of the economy of the state. The smaller indices appear in Victoria (gross state output $270 million) and New South Wales (gross state output ~ $400 million), and the larger indices in the Australian Capital Territory (gross state output ~ $22 million) and the Northern Territory (gross state output ~ $11 million). Furthermore, similar interregional feedback indices are obtained with the simple location quotient as with the supply–demand pool assumptions, and with the cross-industry quotient as with the semi-logarithmic quotient techniques, which directly consider the size of the receiving industries. The inclusion of an interregional trade that follows a gravity law, which improves the performance of the preliminary estimate, has the effect of evening-out interregional feedback effects across the states, increasing the interregional feedback index in the economically larger and spatially better connected states such as New South Wales, Victoria and Queensland and reducing it in others, particularly in the Australian Capital Territory and in distant Tasmania and the Northern Territory. This result points out the dependence of interregional feedback effects on the size of gross regional outputs and interregional transportation costs.

5.5 CONCLUSIONS

Modeling regional dynamics can produce results that are only as robust as the underlying database. Most data collecting and reporting to date is done on a national level, thus posing considerable challenges, for example for the estimation of regional interindustry tables suitable for dynamic analysis. The lack of key data requires the application of sophisticated balancing and reconciliation techniques. Two particular problems are that estimating a unique concordance matrix between two classification systems is often impossible (see Vardon et al. 2007), and that traditional RAS balancing techniques do not work when data are conflicting (see Lenzen et al. 2006). In the latter case, analysts often trace inconsistencies manually, and/or make subjective selections based on data quality. Optimization techniques can greatly assist and streamline previously manual adjustments to conflicting survey data (see *Economic Systems Research* 2004). Faced with these problems, an effort could be made to streamline data collection by

Table 5.5 *Interregional feedback index (Equation 5.21) for some of the different pre-RAS estimates explored in this chapter*

Interregional feedback Index	Regions							
	New South Wales	Victoria	Queensland	Western Australia	South Australia	Tasmania	Northern Territory	Australian Capital Territory
NH	0.00	0.00	0.00	0.00	0.00	0.00	0.00	0.00
LQNH	2.60	4.05	2.89	4.16	5.64	10.89	16.18	46.41
CIQNH	1.95	1.87	1.87	2.41	2.77	4.71	7.47	12.30
SLQNH	1.96	1.90	1.90	2.54	2.87	5.34	8.25	13.78
SDPNH	2.13	2.59	2.57	3.94	4.03	7.78	13.20	51.47
LQGMs	2.26	1.38	1.80	2.17	1.60	3.43	1.55	2.14
CIQGMs	3.27	2.51	2.66	2.51	2.67	4.19	2.34	2.22
SLQGMs	2.82	2.01	2.25	2.31	2.20	3.68	1.95	1.94
SDPGMs	2.12	1.55	1.92	2.54	1.76	3.65	1.84	2.16

using only one classification system. At present, the lack of such harmonization is ubiquitous, not only for Australian data, and has been deplored by analysts for a long time.

Ignoring the above data problems for the time being, it could be asked how the framework described in this work could aid dynamic modeling. In his essay on evolution, environment and economics, Gowdy (1999: 971) outlines the role that static, structural analysis plays for understanding and modeling temporal processes. He lists the examples of field-of-influence analysis (Hewings et al. 1988) and regional structural studies (Jensen et al. 1988), and stresses their potential to understand evolutionary processes in the environment–economy relationship. The work described in this chapter is in fact of the type mentioned by Gowdy.

Economic and technological change is strongly determined by the interdependent structure of the relationship between economic agents. This becomes obvious in dynamic input–output models (Leontief 1970), where the information of capital transactions is used to formulate the accelerator/feedback term in the dynamic differential equation (Gossling 1975). These dynamic models are often calibrated using historical time series data. A regional version of a historical structural decomposition analysis for Japan 1985–1990 is presented by Kagawa et al. (2002). If off-diagonal entries in regional transactions matrices are misestimated, the temporal feedback loops will necessarily be incorrect.

On three other counts, the iterative structure of the Taylor expansion of the Leontief inverse has been given a temporal interpretation. First, in ecological compartmental modeling, iterations of transactions are interpreted as resource cycling across trophic chains (Patten 1985; Higashi et al. 1993), with diagonal elements signifying storage periods. Second, Miyazawa's groundbreaking work on compartmentalizing semi-closed input–output systems applies to expenditure–income cycles, and the redistribution of income over regional or demographic segments of populations (Miyazawa and Masegi 1963; Miyazawa 1966; Lenzen and Schaeffer 2004). Finally, on a smaller scale, sequential inter-industry modeling (SIM) (Romanoff 1984; Romanoff and Levine 1986, 1993; Levine and Romanoff 1989) looks for examples at the temporal dynamics of project scheduling and allocation of human resources across project stages. All of the above disciplines utilize frameworks such as the one described in this work.

Finally, a number of authors have argued that long-term change is not governed by equilibrium processes such as modeled according to neoclassical economic theory, because the latter usually does not explicitly recognize uncertainty, irreversibility and the unpredictability of change (van den Bergh and Gowdy 2000). Structural economics may therefore be better geared to identify critical interindustry links or structures that can indicate the resilience or tolerance of economies for short-term instabilities and unexpected events (see Gowdy 1999: 974). In this respect, regional economics may learn from parallels in biology where evolutionary change is viewed as a sequence of 'punctuated' equilibria caused by external forces such as changes in climate (Gowdy 1999: 968). Bernstein (1981) for example states that 'natural systems are usually in transient rather than static equilibrium states', and that 'surviving ecosystems are those that have evolved means of absorbing the consequences of change'.

In summary, dynamic models often draw on static structural frameworks, extending these frameworks temporally. Regional dynamic models hence rely on comprehensive regional structural frameworks such as regional input–output tables in order to be able to produce meaningful outcomes. It is hence crucial that – as a first step – robust static regional frameworks are estimated. This work shows both challenges and solutions to this end.

ACKNOWLEDGMENTS

This study was financially supported by the Australian Research Council, Sydney Water Corporation and the University of Sydney through an ARC Linkage Grant. The authors are grateful for contributions by the Australian Conservation Foundation, and by their colleagues Richard Wood, Barney Foran, Christopher Dey, Graham Turner, James Lennox and Miles Foran.

NOTES

1. RAS is a bi-proportional matrix balancing technique. It consists of iteratively adjusting a given initial matrix to produce a second matrix bi-proportional to the first.
2. The term 'pre-RAS' can be understood in a temporal sense as 'non-survey techniques conceived before the invention of RAS', or in a procedural sense as 'preliminary estimate before applying RAS'. It happens to be that the 'non-survey techniques conceived before the invention of RAS' are in fact used as 'preliminary estimates before applying RAS'.
3. Approaches using $A^N = \{a_{ij}^N\}$ are based on the notion of a trade pool in which commodities are produced according to a uniform national production recipe, and interregional flows are balanced, consistent with regional total commodity inputs and outputs. This means there is no regionally characteristic production function, and that the regional origin and destination of commodities is irrelevant to producers. Shen (1960), Harrigan et al. (1980a) and other authors criticize the simple transfer of the national production structure on the grounds that compared to the nation, regional industries could: (1) employ different technology mixes; and (2) exhibit a different commodity output structure. While further survey data are needed to verify the first case (see Harrigan et al. 1980a), input–output studies at different levels of aggregation (for example Karaska 1968) have confirmed the difference between national and regional industry commodity

output structures. It has been argued that more sophisticated approaches would have to combine the non-survey technique with superior data that reflect regional features such as industry capacities, price competitiveness, production and transportation cost, or distance to purchasing regions. For a further discussion of these issues see Schaffer and Chu (1969: 88–92) and Jensen et al. (1979: 27–39).

4. See Round (1983) on the distinction between regional technical and trading coefficients. Oosterhaven et al. (1986) and Round (1983) suggest using an interregional model for the task of estimating a (subnational) single-region table, because it allows for easy incorporation of the national coefficients.

5. For a critique of the balanced model see Isard (1953a, 1953b) and Moore and Petersen (1955).

6. In their regional input–output (RIOT) model, Schaffer and Chu (1969) add another step to the regional balance: after estimating a sales matrix based on national coefficients, they compare for each industry regional sales with regional demands, establish pools of commodity surpluses and needs, and reallocate sales of surplus industries in order to increase supplies to industries in need. Their procedure yields the feasible maximum of regional trade, but the changes made to the regional interindustry trade are not checked against technological realities of production.

7. Note that these conditions are not applied to intra-regional trade a_{ij}^{ss}, but to the sum of intermediate inputs from within the region and all other regions. This is because technology can be assumed to be reasonably constant in the short term, but purely intra-regional trade is not necessarily stable since using industries can substitute spatially (compare Moses 1960: 375). A correction to this hypothesis was suggested by Round (1978b) to account for regional fabrication effects so that: $a_{ij}^s = \rho_j^s a_{ij}^N$. The fabrication effect of a given region and industry was defined as the proportion of total output of the industry due to intermediate inputs within the region divided by that within the nation, $\rho_j^s = (1 - (v_j^s/X_j^s))/(1 - v_j^N/X_j^N))$, with $v_j^s = \sum_{r,k} v_{kj}^{rs}$. For simplicity in this chapter we will always consider $a_{ij}^s = a_{il}^N$.

8. This is also true for linear programming approaches (for example Moses 1960), where economic agents are assumed to be in perfect competition and to possess perfect knowledge, and trade flows are optimized subject to capacity constraints in order to minimize total cost, so that one (domestic or foreign) region may have a complete advantage over another region in supplying a certain commodity. Moreover, since intra-regional transport costs are usually lower than interregional costs, within-region trade is maximized, and regions appear as unrealistically self-reliant.

9. On this point, Tiebout (1960: 405) illustrates: 'The failure to handle product mix adequately can lead to some ridiculous results in determining net exports and imports. In Wisconsin, for example, where the internal production of automobiles just about equals consumption, there would be no imports of automobiles. This implies, in turn, that Wisconsin residents drive only the local product, a Nash or Hudson. Clearly, this is one area where no further research is needed to see if Wisconsinites do actually drive only Nash or Hudson cars.'

10. In their interregional social accounting matrix, Madsen and Jensen-Butler (2002: 454) adopt an intermediate working hypothesis of a minimum of 10 percent imported demand.

11. For a quantitative treatment of the resulting bias see Jones et al. (1973).

12. In Australia, West et al. (1984) apply the Leontief–Strout gravity model in their interregional GRIT version. The regional purchase coefficient (RPC) by Stevens et al. (1983) provides another example for a gravity-type approach.

13. Centre for Integrated Sustainability Analysis (http://www.isa.org.usyd.edu.au)

14. For a critique see Giarratani (1975).

15. The square of this measure has also been referred to as 'Theil's inequality index' (Lahiri 1984).

16. $1 - SIM$ has been used as a 'dissimilarity index' by Thissen and Löfgren (1998).

REFERENCES

Australian Bureau of Statistics (1997), 'Manufacturing Production, Australia: Principal Commodities Produced, 1993–94', ABS Catalogue No. 8365.0, Australian Bureau of Statistics, Canberra, Australia.

Australian Bureau of Statistics (1999), 'Australian National Accounts: State Accounts 1998–99', ABS Catalogue No. 5220.0, Australian Bureau of Statistics, Canberra, Australia.

Australian Bureau of Statistics (2000), '1998–99 Household Expenditure Survey: Detailed Expenditure Items, Confidentialised Unit Record File', Electronic file (unpublished), Australian Bureau of Statistics, Canberra, Australia.

Australian Bureau of Statistics (2001a), 'Business Register Counts 2001', Customised Report No. 01/, Australian Bureau of Statistics, Canberra, Australia.

Australian Bureau of Statistics (2001b), 'Freight Movements, 2000', ABS Catalogue Number 9220.0, Australian Bureau of Statistics, Canberra, Australia.

Australian Bureau of Statistics (2004a), 'Australian National Accounts, Input–Output Tables, 1998–99', ABS Catalogue No. 5209.0, Australian Bureau of Statistics, Canberra, Australia.

Australian Bureau of Statistics (2004b), 'Australian National Accounts, Input–Output Tables, 1998–99, IOPC 8-digit Commodity Cards', Unpublished electronic data files, Australian Bureau of Statistics.

Batten, D. and D. Martellato (1985), 'Classical versus Modern Approaches to Interregional Input–Output Analysis', *The Annals of Regional Science*, **19**(3): 1–15.

Bayne, B.A. and G.R. West (1989), 'GRIT – Generation of Regional Input–Output Tables: User's Reference Manual', Australian Regional Developments Vol. 15, Australian Government Publishing Service, Canberra, Australia.

van den Bergh, J.C.J.M. and J.M. Gowdy (2000), 'Evolutionary Theories in Environmental and Resource Economics: Approaches and Applications', *Environmental and Resource Economics*, **17**: 37–57.

Bernstein, B.B. (1981), 'Ecology and Economics', *Annual Review of Ecological Systems*, **12**: 309–30.

Butterfield, M. and T. Mules (1980), 'A Testing Routine for Evaluating Cell by Cell Accuracy in Short-Cut Regional Input–Output Tables', *Journal of Regional Science*, **20**(3): 293–310.

Centre for Integrated Sustainability Analysis (n.d.), 'ISA Information Sheet 6: ISA Indicator Suite', http://www.isa.org.usyd.edu.au/research/ISA_TBL_Indicators.pdf.

Czamanski, S. (1971), 'Some Empirical Evidence of the Strengths of Linkages between Groups of Related Industries in Urban Regional Complexes', *Papers of the Regional Science Association*, **27**: 137–50.

Czamanski, S. and E.E. Malizia (1969), 'Applicability and Limitations in the Use of National Input–Output Tables for Regional Studies', *Papers of the Regional Science Association*, **23**: 65–77.

Economic Systems Research (2004), entire issue, **16**(2): 115–230.

Foran, B., M. Lenzen, C. Dey and M. Bilek (2005), 'Integrating Sustainable Chain Management with Triple Bottom Line Reporting', *Ecological Economics*, **52**(2): 143–57.

Giarratani, F. (1975), 'A Note on the McMenamin-Haring Input–Output Projection Technique', *Journal of Regional Science*, **15**(3): 371–3.

Global Footprint Network and ISA University of Sydney (2006), 'The Ecological Footprint of Victoria: Assessing Victoria's Demand on Nature', http://www.dse.vic.gov.au/CA256F310024B628/0/41F9DC419C7021A7CA256FE80024B3 2B/$File/Ecofootprint.pdf, EPA Victoria, Melbourne, Australia.

Gossling, W.F. (ed.) (1975), *Capital Coefficients and Dynamic Input–Output Models*, London: Input–Output Publishing Company.

Gowdy, J.M. (1999), 'Evolution, Environment and Economics', in J.C.J.M. van den Bergh (ed.), *Handbook of Environmental and Resource Economics*, Cheltenham, UK and Northampton, MA, USA: Edward Elgar, pp. 965–80.

Günlük-Senesen, G. and J.M. Bates (1988), 'Some Experiments with Methods of Adjusting Unbalanced Data Matrices', *Journal of the Royal Statistical Society A*, **151**(3): 473–90.

Harrigan, F.J. (1982), 'The Relationship between Industrial and Geographical Linkages: A Case Study of the United Kingdom', *Journal of Regional Science*, **22**(1): 19–31.

Harrigan, F.J., J.W. McGilvray and I.H. McNicoll (1980a), 'A Comparison of Regional and National Technical Structures', *Economic Journal*, **90**(360): 795–810.

Harrigan, F.J., J.W. McGilvray and I.H. McNicoll (1980b), 'Simulating the Structure of a Regional Economy', *Environment and Planning A*, **12**: 927–36.

Hewings, G.J.D. (1969), 'Regional Input–Output Models using National Data: The Structure of the West Midlands Economy', *Annals of Regional Science*, **3**: 179–91.

Hewings, G.J.D. and R.C. Jensen (1989), 'Regional, Interregional and Multiregional Input–Output Analysis', in H. Chenery and T.N. Srinivasan (eds), *Handbook of Development Economics*, Amsterdam: North-Holland, pp. 295–355.

Hewings, G.J.D., M. Sonis and R.C. Jensen (1988), 'Fields of Influence of Technological Change in Input–Output Models', *Papers of the Regional Science Association*, **64**: 25–36.

Higashi, M., T.P. Burns and B.C. Patten (1993), 'Network Trophic Dynamics: The Tempo of Energy Movement and Availability in Ecosystems', *Ecological Modelling*, **66**: 43–64.

Isard, W. (1951), 'Interregional and Regional Input–Output Analysis: A Model of a Space Economy', *Review of Economics and Statistics*, **33**: 318–28.

Isard, W. (1953a), 'Regional Commodity Balances and Interregional Commodity Flows', *American Economic Review*, **43**(2): 167–80.

Isard, W. (1953b), 'Some Empirical Results and Problems of Regional Input–Output Analysis', in W. Leontief, H.B. Chenery, P.G. Clark, J.S. Duesenberry, A.R. Ferguson, A.P. Grosse, R.N. Grosse, M. Holzman, W. Isard and H. Kistin (eds), *Studies in the Structure of the American Economy*, New York: Oxford University Press, pp. 116–81.

Isard, W. and L. Anselin (1982), 'Integration of Multiregional Models for Policy Analysis', *Environment and Planning A*, **14**: 359–76.

Jackson, R.W. and J.C. Comer (1993), 'An Alternative to Aggregated Base Tables in Input–Output Table Regionalization', *Growth and Change*, **24**: 191–205.

Jensen, R.C., T.D. Mandeville and N.D. Karunaratne (1979), *Regional Economic Planning*, London: Croom Helm.

Jensen, R.C., G. West and G.J.D. Hewings (1988), 'On the Study of Regional Economic Structure Using Input–Output Models', *Regional Studies*, **22**: 209–20.

Jones, L.L., T.L. Sporleder and G. Mustafa (1973), 'A Source of Bias in Regional Input–Output Models Estimated from National Coefficients', *Annals of Regional Science*, **7**(1): 67–74.

Junius, T. and J. Oosterhaven (2003), 'The Solution of Updating or Regionalizing a Matrix with both Positive and Negative Entries', *Economic Systems Research*, **15**: 87–96.

Kagawa, S., G. Gerilla, Y. Moriguchi and H. Inamura (2002), 'Spatial Structural Decomposition Analysis of the Chinese and Japanese Energy Demand: 1985–1990', presented at the 14th International Conference on Input–Output Techniques, Montreal, Canada, October, available at http://www.io2002conference.uqam.ca/english/the_conference/papers_k.html.

Karaska, G.J. (1968), 'Variation of Input–Output Coefficients for Different Levels of Aggregation', *Journal of Regional Science*, **8**: 217–27.

Lahiri, S. (1984), 'On Reconciling Purchases and Sales Estimates of a Regional Input–Output Table', *Socio-Economic Planning Series* **18**(5): 337–42.

Lahr, M.L. (2001), 'A Strategy for Producing Hybrid Regional Input–Output Tables', in M.L. Lahr and E. Dietzenbacher (eds), *Input–Output Analysis: Frontiers and Extensions*, London: Palgrave Macmillan, pp. 211–42.

Lecomber, J.R.C. (1975), 'A Critique of Methods of Adjusting, Updating and Projecting Matrices', in R.I.G. Allen and W.F. Gossling (eds), *Estimating and Projecting Input–Output Coefficients*, London: Input–Output Publishing Company, pp. 1–25.

Lenzen, M. (1999), 'Total Energy and Greenhouse Gas Requirements for Australian Transport', *Transportation Research Part D*, **4**: 265–90.

Lenzen, M. (2002), 'A Guide for Compiling Inventories in Hybrid LCA: Some Australian Results', *Journal of Cleaner Production*, **10**: 545–72.

Lenzen, M., S. Lundie, G. Bransgrove, L. Charet and F. Sack (2003), 'Assessing the Ecological Footprint of a Large Metropolitan Water Supplier: Lessons for Water Management and Planning Towards Sustainability', *Journal of Environmental Planning and Management*, **46**(1): 113–41.

Lenzen, M. and S.A. Murray (2003), 'The Ecological Footprint: Issues and Trends', ISA Research Paper 01-03, http://www.isa.org.usyd.edu.au/publications/documents/Ecological_Footprint_Issues_and_Trends.pdf, Centre for Integrated Sustainability Analysis, University of Sydney, Australia.

Lenzen, M. and R. Schaeffer (2004), 'Interrelational Income Distribution in Brazil', *Developing Economies*, **42**(3): 371–91.

Lenzen, M. and R. Wood (2003), 'An Ecological Footprint and a Triple Bottom Line Report of Wollongong Council for the 2001/02 Financial Year and the Wollongong population for the 1998/99 Financial Year', http://www.wollongong.nsw.gov.au/Downloads/Documents/WollongongTBL.pdf, Centre for Integrated Sustainability Analysis, University of Sydney, Sydney, Australia.

Lenzen, M., B.Gallego and R. Wood (2006), 'A Flexible Approach to Matrix Balancing under Partial Information', *Journal of Applied Input–Output Analysis*, **11&12**: 1–24.

Leontief, W. (1953), 'Interregional Theory', in W. Leontief, H.B. Chenery, P.G. Clark, J.S. Duesenberry, A.R. Ferguson, A.P. Grosse, R.N. Grosse, M. Holzman, W. Isard and H. Kistin (eds), *Studies in the Structure of the American Economy*, New York: Oxford University Press, pp. 93–115.

Leontief, W. (1970), 'The Dynamic Inverse', in A.P. Carter and A. Brody (eds), *Proceeding of the Fourth International Conference on Input–Output*

Techniques, Vol. 1: Contributions to Input–Output Analysis, Geneva, January 1968, Amsterdam: North-Holland Publishing Company, pp. 17–46.

Leontief, W.W. and A.A. Strout (1963), 'Multiregional Input–Output Analysis', in T. Barna (ed.), *Structural Interdependence and Economic Development*, London: Macmillan, pp. 119–49.

Levine, S.H. and E. Romanoff (1989), 'Economic Impact Dynamics of Complex Engineering Project Scheduling', *IEEE Transactions on Systems, Man, and Cybernetics*, **19**(2): 232–40.

Madsen, B. and C. Jensen-Butler (2002), 'Regional Economic Modeling in Denmark: Construction of an Interregional SAM with Data at High Levels of Disaggregation, Subject to National Constraints', in G.J.D. Hewings, M. Sonis and D.E. Boyce (eds), *Trade, Networks and Hierarchies: Modeling Regional and Interregional Economics*, Heidelberg: Springer-Verlag, pp. 445–56.

McMenamin, D.G. and J.E. Haring (1974), 'An Appraisal of Nonsurvey Techniques for Estimating Regional Input–Output Models', *Journal of Regional Science*, **14**(2): 191–205.

Miller, R.E. (1966), 'Interregional Feedback Effects in Input–Output Models: Some Preliminary Results', *Papers of the Regional Science Association*, **17**: 105–25.

Miller, R.E. and P.D. Blair (1985), *Input–Output Analysis: Foundations and Extensions*, Englewood Cliffs, NJ: Prentice Hall.

Miyazawa, K. (1966), 'Internal and External Matrix Multipliers in the Input–Output Model', *Hitotsubashi Journal of Economics*, **7**(1): 38–55.

Miyazawa, K. and S. Masegi (1963), 'Interindustry Analysis and the Structure of Income-Distribution', *Metroeconomica*, **15**(2): 89–103.

Moore, F.T. and J.W. Petersen (1955), 'Regional Analysis: An Interindustry Model of Utah', *Review of Economics and Statistics*, **37**(4): 368–83.

Morrison, W.I. and P. Smith (1974), 'Nonsurvey Input–Output Techniques at the Small Area Level: An Evaluation', *Journal of Regional Science*, **14**(1): 1–14.

Moses, L.N. (1960), 'A General Equilibrium Model of Production, Interregional Trade, and Location of Industry', *American Economic Review*, **42**(4): 373–97.

Oosterhaven, J. (1984), 'A Family of Square and Rectangular Interregional Input–Output Tables and Models', *Regional Science and Urban Economics*, **14**(4): 565–82.

Oosterhaven, J., G. Piek and D. Stelder (1986), 'Theory and Practice of Updating Regional versus Interregional Interindustry Tables', *Papers of the Regional Science Association*, **59**: 57–72.

Patten, B.C. (1985), 'Energy Cycling in the Ecosystem', *Ecological Modelling*, **28**: 1–71.

Peters, G.P. and E.G. Hertwich (2006), 'Structural studies of International Trade: Environmental Impacts of Norway', *Economic Systems Research*, **18**(2): 155–81.

Polenske, K.R. (1970), 'Empirical Implementation of a Multiregional Input–Output Gravity Trade Model', in A.P. Carter and A. Brody (eds), *Proceedings of the Fourth International Conference on Input–Output Techniques, Vol. 1: Contributions to Input–Output Analysis*, Geneva, January 1968, Amsterdam: North-Holland Publishing Company, pp. 143–63.

Polenske, K.R. (1980), *The US Multiregional Input–Output Accounts and Model*, Lexington, MA: DC Heath & Company.

Romanoff, E. (1984), 'Interindustry Analysis for Regional Growth and Development: The Dynamics of Manpower Issues', *Socio-Economic Planning Series*, **18**(5): 353–63.

Romanoff, E. and S.H. Levine (1986), 'Capacity Limitations, Inventory, and

Time-Phased Production in the Sequential Interindustry Model', *Papers of the Regional Science Association*, **59**: 73–91.

Romanoff, E. and S.H. Levine (1993), 'Information, Interindustry Dynamics, and the Service Industries', *Environment and Planning A*, **25**: 305–16.

Rose, A. and W. Miernyk (1989), 'Input–Output Analysis: The First Fifty Years', *Economic Systems Research*, **1**: 229–71.

Round, J.I. (1978a), 'An Interregional Input–Output Approach to the Evaluation of Non-Survey Methods', *Journal of Regional Science*, **18**: 179–94.

Round, J.I. (1978b), 'On Estimating Trade Flows in Interregional Input–Output Models', *Regional Science and Urban Economics*, **8**: 289–302.

Round, J.I. (1983), 'Nonsurvey Techniques: A Critical Review of the Theory and the Evidence', *International Regional Science Review*, **8**(3): 189–212.

Schaffer, W.A. and K. Chu (1969), 'Nonsurvey Techniques for Constructing Regional Interindustry Models', *Papers of the Regional Science Association*, **23**: 83–101.

Shen, T.Y. (1960), 'An Input–Output Table with Regional Weights', *Papers of the Regional Science Association*, **6**: 113–19.

Stevens, B.H., G.I. Treyz, D.H.J. Ehrlich and J.R. Power (1983), 'A New Technique for the Construction of Non-Survey Regional Input–Output Models and Comparisons with Two Survey-Based Models', *International Regional Science Review*, **8**: 271–86.

Stone, R. and A. Brown (1962), *A Computable Model of Economic Growth*, London: Chapman and Hall.

Thissen, M. and H. Löfgren (1998), 'A New Approach to SAM Updating with an Application to Egypt', *Environment and Planning A*, **30**(11): 1991–2003.

Tiebout, C.M. (1960), 'Regional and Interregional Input–Output Models: An Appraisal', in R.W. Pfouts (ed.), *The Techniques of Urban Economic Analysis*, West Trenton, NJ: Chandler-Davis Publishing Co., pp. 395–407.

Treloar, G. (1997), 'Extracting Embodied Energy Paths from Input–Output Tables: Towards an Input–Output-Based Hybrid Energy Analysis Method', *Economic Systems Research*, **9**(4): 375–91.

Uribe, P., C.G. de Leeuw and H. Theil (1966), 'The Information Approach to the Prediction of Interregional Trade Flows', *The Review of Economic Studies*, **33**(3): 209–20.

Vardon, M., M. Lenzen, S. Peevor and M. Creaser (2007), 'Water Accounting in Australia', *Ecological Economics*, **61**(4): 650–59.

West, G., J.B. Morrison and R.C. Jensen (1984), 'A Method for the Estimation of Hybrid Interregional Input–Output Tables', *Regional Studies*, **18**: 413–22.

West, G.R. (1981), 'An Efficient Approach to the Estimation of Regional Input–Output Multipliers', *Environment and Planning A*, **13**: 857–67.

Wood, R. and M. Lenzen (2003), 'An Application of an Improved Ecological Footprint Method and Structural Path Analysis in a Comparative Institutional Study', *Local Environment*, **8**(4): 365–84.

6. The economic and environmental consequences of reduced air transport services in Pennsylvania: a regional input–output life cycle assessment case study

Gyorgyi Cicas, Chris T. Hendrickson and H. Scott Matthews

6.1   INTRODUCTION

US Airways was the sixth-largest air carrier in the US in 2000 (US SEC 2000). With over 18,000 employees and two of its three major hubs located in Pennsylvania, the company had a major influence on both the region's economy and its environment. When US Airways reduced its service in Pittsburgh and entered Chapter 11 bankruptcy protection in 2004, the long-term effects became of considerable concern to employees, politicians, businesses and citizens in Pennsylvania. Beyond the direct effects on the air transport sector itself, the indirect effects of scaling down the supply chain are also of concern. The objective of this case study is to analyze the regional effects and policy implications of a 50 percent decrease in the economic activity of US Airways in Pennsylvania using our regional economic input–output life cycle assessment (REIO-LCA) model.

Our purpose is to illustrate the direct and indirect effects of such major economic impacts, as well as to introduce the use of the REIO-LCA model for such a purpose. Direct impacts herein are impacts on the air transport sector itself and its immediate suppliers. Indirect impacts are effects on the air transport sector supply chain, such as the supply of petroleum to refineries.

As important enterprises such as US Airways grow or contract, the dynamics of industrial ecosystems lead to multiple effects through the supply chain. This case study illustrates these effects within a region. The input–output (I–O) framework is useful since all the relevant supply chain interactions are included in the model (Hendrickson et al. 2006).

More extensive modeling might include that of dynamic time-lags of ripple effects through the economy or a dynamic, year-by-year simulation of the air transport sector's contraction. In this case study, we will only compare the overall effects of a single, significant contraction.

6.2   METHODOLOGY FOR REGIONAL ECONOMIC INPUT–OUTPUT LIFE CYCLE ASSESSMENT

The web-based national EIO-LCA model (Green Design Institute 2005) uses the 491-by-491 economic input–output matrix created for 1997 by the US Department of Commerce Bureau of Economic Analysis (BEA) and publicly available environmental data (for example, greenhouse gas emissions) provided by the US Environmental Protection Agency (EPA) to estimate the supply chain economic and environmental effects of production and services (Hendrickson et al. 2006). The national model was regionalized using gross state product (GSP) estimates provided by the BEA and state resource use and emission data (Cicas 2005). The regional model enables the estimation of economic and environmental effects occurring in the region where the analyzed service or production is located. In this section, we introduce the regional input–output model.

To develop a regional model, the national input–output table was modified using regional multipliers estimated as the ratio of regional sectoral GSP to the corresponding national GSP:

$$M_i^R = \frac{GSP_i^R}{GSP_i^{US}} \tag{6.1}$$

where: M_i^R = regional economic multiplier for industry i in region R. GSP_i^R = regional gross state product estimate for industry i in region R for 1997. GSP_i^{US} = national gross state product estimate for industry i for 1997.

For example, the GSP estimates for the air transport sector in the Mideast economic region (including Pennsylvania), and for the US are \$11,382 million and \$78,557 million, respectively (BEA 2005a). Consequently, the regional economic multiplier is:

$$M_i^R = \frac{GSP_i^R}{GSP_i^{US}} = \frac{11\,382}{78\,557} = 0.14. \tag{6.2}$$

Thus, we assume that 14 percent of the national output of the air transport sector occurs in the region.

The BEA defines GSP as the value added by property and labor located in a state (BEA 2005a). The entries of the regional input–output transaction matrices (representing purchases by one sector from another) were calculated based on the assumption that the fractions of the total national sectoral value added occurring in different regions might be used to distribute the annual industry outputs to those regions:

$$x_{i,j}^R = M_i^{R*}x_{i,j}^{US} \tag{6.3}$$

where: $x_{i,j}^R$ = regional dollar output of industry i used in production of industry j to its sectoral output in region R. $x_{i,j}^{US}$ = national dollar output of industry i used in production of industry j to its total annual output.

Using the multiplier for air transport in the Mideast region, and the benchmark input–output industry accounts provided by the BEA (2002), the regional output of the sector may be estimated:

$$x_i^R = M_i^R * x_i^{US} = 0.14 * \$119,445 \text{ million} = \$16,722 \text{ million} \tag{6.4}$$

where: x_i^{US} is the US output. The regional direct requirements matrices were estimated as defined in Leontief (1953):

$$a_{i,j}^R = \frac{x_{i,j}^R}{\sum\limits_{i=1}^{i=491} x_{i,j}^R + GSP_j^R} \tag{6.5}$$

where: $a_{i,j}^R$ = dollar output of industry i used by sector j to produce \$1 of its output.

Several state and regional input–output models exist, such as the regional input–output modeling system (RIMS) model provided by the BEA (2005b). See Hewings (1985) for a general review of regional input–output models. The model used here has two important characteristics for this work. First, we have based the model completely on publicly available data (equations 6.1, 6.3 and 6.5). Second, we have appended environmental effects for each sector in the model. The regional environmental effects can $(b_{y,k}^R)$ be calculated based on (Hendrickson et al. 2006):

$$b_{y,k}^R = e_k^{R*}[I - A^R]^{-1}*y \tag{6.6}$$

where: $b_{y,k}^R$ = environmental effect k resulted from output y in region R. e_k^R = environmental burden factor k estimated for region R as emission per million dollars of sector output. I = identity matrix. A^R = regional direct requirements matrix. y = final demand for the analysis case.

The effects calculation in equation 6.6 is widely used to assess direct and indirect economic impacts of the purchase of a good or service; in these applications, the environmental burden factor does not appear (or, identically, is set to 1 to obtain economic effects). With the addition of average environmental burdens, these economic effects are extended to estimate associated environmental burdens. Several environmental factors were created for the region using publicly available databases:

- electricity and fuel use (EIA 2005a);
- toxic releases (EPA 2004b);
- emissions of greenhouse gases (EPA 1997, 2005b);
- conventional pollutants (carbon monoxide, nitrous oxides, particulate matter, sulfur dioxide and volatile organic compounds) (EPA 2005a);
- hazardous waste generation and management (EPA 2004a).

We used the REIO-LCA model created for the Mideast to estimate the economic and environmental implications of the reduction of air transport services in Pennsylvania. The model incorporates data for the following states: Delaware, the District of Columbia, Maryland, New Jersey, New York and Pennsylvania. The purchases made outside of the region by the supply chain of US Airways operations in Pennsylvania are assumed to be negligible. This is a reasonable supposition since the major inputs are provided by the air transportation and supporting service sectors, and those facilities are most likely located in the region in order to ensure proper operation. However, the exclusion of even a small part of the total supply chain increases the uncertainty of the model results. In particular, we likely underestimate the total impact of the US Airways contraction. However, since the regional effects are included, the model results are pertinent for regional decision-makers. Of course, the national EIO-LCA model can be used to estimate the nationwide effects of the contraction.

6.3   SUPPLY CHAIN EFFECTS OF US AIRWAYS ON THE PENNSYLVANIA ECONOMY AND ENVIRONMENT

US Airways has significant impacts on the economy of Pennsylvania, having contributed approximately 6 percent of the total number of employees in the state transportation sector in 2000 (US Census Bureau 2000). Further, air transportation is a major contributor to greenhouse gas emissions, with nearly 12 percent of the annual national carbon dioxide emissions generated by the combustion of jet and aviation fuels by the industry (EPA 1997). In the decade 1993–2003, the number of total emplacements dropped by 43 percent at Pittsburgh International Airport (BTS 2004) due primarily to the US Airways contraction. Although the company emerged from bankruptcy in

2005, the case raised the question: What would happen to the state economy and consequently to the environment if US Airways had to decrease its service dramatically in Pennsylvania? We use a regional economic input–output life cycle assessment model (REIO-LCA) for our estimations in order to include both direct and indirect effects of the contraction. Direct effects result from the purchases made by US Airways from all industrial and service sectors of the economy of Mideast states needed to its operations in Pennsylvania. Indirect effects are the outcome of all purchases needed for the direct suppliers to produce the input they provided to US Airways.

6.3.1   Economic Effects

First, we estimated the direct and indirect economic and environmental effects of the six jet service airports located in the state for 2000. We used the operating and financial statistics that US Airways presented in its annual report to calculate the final demand for air transportation in Pennsylvania (US SEC 2000). It was assumed that the final demand might be approximated with the sum of annual passenger transportation revenue (PTR), calculated as the product of yield and revenue passenger miles (RPM), and the cargo and freight revenue (US SEC 2000). The total PTR and freight revenue in 2000 were $7662 million and $164 million, respectively. The ratio of the number of US Airways employees in Pennsylvania to the total number of US Airways employees (37.8 percent) was used to partition the final demand of air transportation between the state and the rest of the country.

Equation 6.7 shows the calculations described above. In contrast to the ratio of number of employees, the proportion of the total number of passengers emplaned in Pennsylvania to the total number of passengers emplaned in the US in 2000 was 29 percent (AIPP 2001; US SEC 2000), which we used to conduct sensitivity analysis on the model results.

$$y_{air-trans}^{PA} = (Yield * Revenue\ Passenger\ Miles + Freight)$$

$$* (EmployeesPA/EmployeesUS)$$

$$= (0.1628 * 47{,}065\ million + 164\ million) + (18{,}186/48{,}100)$$

$$= \$2{,}959\ million \tag{6.7}$$

The $2959 million final demand was used as input to our REIO-LCA model to estimate the purchases made by US Airways in the region. Table 6.1 presents the ten largest contributors in the supply chain. In recognition of the numerical uncertainty, all model results are rounded to two significant

Table 6.1   Ten largest contributors of the supply chain economic effects in Pennsylvania

Sector name	Sector output, M$	Share in supply chain total, %	Share in state total sectoral production, %
Air transportation	3000	49.00	62
Travel arrangement and reservation services	330	5.40	40
Scenic and sightseeing transportation and support activities for transportation	210	3.40	12
Petroleum refineries	200	3.30	4
Food services and drinking places	170	2.80	1
Real estate	160	2.60	1
Management of companies and enterprises	150	2.50	0.3
Telecommunications	140	2.30	1
Wholesale trade	130	2.10	0.5
Legal services	120	2.00	2
All other sectors	1490	24.00	
Total for all 489 sectors	6100	100	0.9

digits (Hendrickson et al. 2006). Approximately 1 percent of the total output of all industrial sectors occurred in Pennsylvania as the product of the supply chain of US Airways (including both direct and indirect effects). The air transportation and supporting service sectors provided 57 percent of the state's total economic activity. Although the major energy source used by the supply chain of the air transportation sector is jet fuel (Table 6.2), the contribution of petroleum refineries is only 3 percent of the total input. It is likely because of the relatively small regional share (9.4 percent) in the distillation capacity of the US petroleum refineries (EIA 2005b, 2005c).

We noted above that the regional model assumes purchases in the supply chain occur in the region. As an illustration of the difference between the regional and national model results, Table 6.3 shows the comparison of the regional and national models. As we expected, the results are similar for this case.

6.3.2   Environmental Effects

Regional electricity use, fuel use and greenhouse gas emissions were estimated using the environmental data described above. Table 6.2

Table 6.2   Comparison of supply chain electricity and fuel use to state energy consumption

Fuel	Total for all 489 sectors	Share in total (%)	Share in state total consumption (%)
Jet fuel, TJ	46 000	79	51
Natural gas, TJ	4 600	8	0.6
Coal, TJ	2 200	4	0.1
Motor gasoline, TJ	1 800	3	0.3
Distillate fuel, TJ	1 100	2	0.3
Residual fuel, TJ	770	1	1
Electricity, MkWh	470	1	0.5
LPG, TJ	400	1	1.9
Kerosene, TJ	4	0.01	0
Total energy, TJ	58 000	100	1.5

Table 6.3   Comparison of the largest supply chain economic effects estimated using REIO-LCA and the EIO-LCA models

Sector name	REIO-LCA result, million $	EIO-LCA result, million $
Transportation and warehousing	3300	3000
Manufacturing	640	840
Wholesale trade	130	120
Retail trade	11	12
Utilities	61	55
Mining	30	210
Construction	15	16
All other sectors	1913	1847
Total for all 489 sectors	6100	6100

summarizes the supply chain consumption of electricity and fuels, and it shows the comparison to Pennsylvania's annual energy use (EIA 2005a). These estimates include both direct and indirect environmental effects. The three most important fuels, accounting for 90 percent of the total energy use, were jet fuel, natural gas and coal. Seventy-nine percent resulted from the consumption of jet fuel by the air transportation sector. The majority of natural gas was used by petroleum refineries. Power plants were the second-largest consumer of natural gas (14 percent) and they used 94 percent of all coal.

Table 6.4   I–O sectors in the supply chain of US Airways with the largest energy consumption

Sector name	Total energy, TJ
Air transportation	47000
Power generation and supply	2900
Petroleum refineries	2700
Scenic and sightseeing transportation and support activities for transportation	840
Travel arrangement and reservation services	560
Water transportation	310
Paper and paperboard mills	300
Truck transportation	270
Natural gas distribution	170
Couriers and messengers	160

The 491 input–output sectors were rank-ordered based on their total energy use. Table 6.4 presents the ten largest consumers. Energy use is strongly correlated with many environmental effects, so these users represent targets for energy efficiency and pollution prevention strategies.

As can be seen in Table 6.5, the air transportation sector releases approximately 60 percent of the total nitrogen oxides (NOx) and 30 percent of all carbon monoxide (CO) associated with the operation of US Airways.

Although trucking is not one of the largest contributors to the supply chain, it has the greatest CO emissions, and releases significant amounts of volatile organic compounds (VOCs) and NOx due to high fuel intensity. The majority (more than 80 percent) of sulfur dioxide (SO_2) and VOC emissions are indirect (released by the supply chain). Both the petroleum refineries and power generation sectors consume 5 percent of the total energy; consequently, they are substantial contributors to all estimated criteria air pollution. The emission estimates were compared to the state total releases for 1999, obtained from the criteria air pollutant report of Scorecard (1999). Each emissions source accounts for less than 1 percent of the state annual release of a given pollutant.

Approximately 1 percent of Pennsylvania's total greenhouse gas (GHG) emissions is associated with the operation of US Airways (EPA 2005b). Table 6.6 presents the largest sectoral emissions and the estimated total emissions for the supply chain and the state. Similarly to the energy consumption, the air transportation, power generation, and petroleum refineries sectors release the majority of GHGs.

Table 6.5   I–O sectors in the supply chain of US Airways with the largest estimated air emissions

Sector name	CO, mt	NOx, mt	SO_2, mt	PM10, mt	VOC, mt	Total emissions
Truck transportation	2600	180	8	5	180	2973
Air transportation	2100	2500	62	280	13	4955
Waste management and Remediation services	500	47	7	77	100	731
Wholesale trade	320	90	2	0	18	430
Couriers and messengers	310	14	68	0	12	404
Petroleum refineries	310	270	820	39	110	1549
Iron and steel mills	68	15	9	6	2	100
Power generation and supply	54	400	1400	96	5	1955
Rail transportation	47	220	40	0	6	313
State and local government electric utilities	44	3	3	0	11	61
All other sectors	247	461	281	47	323	1359
Total for all 489 sectors	6600	4200	2700	550	780	14830
State total (Scorecard 1999)	3300000	940000	1200000	440000	620000	6500000

Table 6.6   I–O sectors in the supply chain of US Airways with the largest estimated greenhouse gas emissions

Sector name	CO_2, thousand TCDE	Share in supply chain total (%)
Air transportation	950	50
Power generation and supply	310	16
Petroleum refineries	280	15
Waste management and remediation services	43	2
Scenic and sightseeing transportation and support activities for transportation	42	2
Wholesale trade	36	2
Travel arrangement and reservation services	33	2
Oil and gas extraction	31	2
Paper and paperboard mills	20	1
Natural gas distribution	19	1
All other sectors	136	7
Total for all 489 sectors	1 900	100
State total (EPA 2005b)	243 000	

6.3.3   Potential Changes Due to Contraction

Our objective is to assess changes to the regional economy and environment resulting from a 50 percent decrease of passenger and freight transportation service provided by US Airways. In effect, 50 percent of the environmental effects shown in Tables 6.3–6.6 would be avoided. For the purpose of this analysis, we assume that only 40 percent of the passengers and goods transported by the company originated in Pennsylvania (Stifflemire 2001). Further, we presume that no other air carrier takes over the share of US Airways in the air transportation system of the state. The cargo and freight revenue altogether was 2 percent of the company's total revenue in 2000. The reduction of air transportation services provided by US Airways would result most likely in the termination of transit of products since the goods manufactured in the state still have to be shipped. However, since the per-ton-mile cost of air transportation is the largest compared to other modes (BTS 2005), we shall assume that the local manufacturers transporting their products by air cannot simply shift to trucking or rail transport. Thus, it may occur that these enterprises move their production out of the state. The diminished passenger transportation capacity affects approximately 8 million passengers in Pennsylvania. It can be assumed that the decrease of service would have major impacts on connecting passengers as well. At the same time, those passengers originating in or whose destination is Pennsylvania would have to travel to the next airport where the required service is provided. Since the public transportation by bus or train is less convenient, we shall assume that the passengers would drive, thereby increasing highway traffic and congestion, and creating demand for the expansion of the road system.

The 50 percent reduction of final demand would result in an approximately $3 billion loss over one year. As a matter of comparison, the budget of Pennsylvania was $40 billion in 2000 (Commonwealth of Pennsylvania 2000). The state energy consumption would decrease by 29,000 TJ, primarily resulting from a 610 000 cubic meter reduction in the use of jet fuel (EPA 2003). Although the contribution of the supply chain to criteria air pollution in the state is below 1 percent, the 1300 metric tons reduction of CO emission of trucks would be beneficial, since 77 percent of the emissions are related to transportation in highly populated urban areas (EPA 2005a).

6.4 CONCLUSIONS

Air transportation has a significant impact on the economy of Pennsylvania. As noted above, financial difficulties and changing strategy by US Airways resulted in a significant contraction of service within the state in the period 1993–2004. To analyze the effect of contractions, we hypothesized a 50 percent decrease in services for 1997 and assessed the impact on both the air transport sector itself and the sector supply chain (often referred to as direct and indirect effects). This 50 percent contraction by US Airways would result in an annual $3 billion loss, and it would affect approximately 8 million passengers. The most important environmental effect of the supply chain of air transportation is the emission of greenhouse gases, mostly caused (both directly and indirectly) by the use of jet fuel. At the same time, the majority of carbon monoxide comes from indirect emissions, released by the truck transportation industry. Other major contributors to the supply chain are the power generation and petroleum refineries sectors, accounting for significant GHG emissions. The direct environmental effects of reduced air transport service are below 1 percent of the state total emissions. These results illustrate the importance of including life cycle and supply chain approaches in assessing the losses due to dynamic changes in the industrial ecosystem. Important environmental effects may be due to indirect changes in the sector supply chain.

From a policy standpoint, we would like to obtain the reduction of environmental effects discussed above without suffering the economic dislocations associated with the service contraction. To pursue this goal, energy efficiency, green design and pollution prevention strategies can be pursued both in the air transport sector and in its supply chain.

The use of a regional model yields similar results to a national model in this case, but this may not be a general conclusion. Some sectors may have a more widespread supply chain for which regional indirect effects may be minor.

Finally, analyses of growth and contraction of this sort could be performed for any one or combination of the 491 sectors in the model. Air transport was selected as a case study because of the changes initiated by the region's dominant air carrier, US Airways.

Results from the modeling effort reflect some significant assumptions and limitations of the approach. First, as with other input–output applications, the regional economy is modeled linearly, even though non-linearities will likely exist. The analysis is comparative and static in nature, while dynamic effects may also be of interest. Finally, we neglected the substitution effects of other airlines entering the region or shifts in traffic to other modes. Additional work is needed to incorporate these other effects.

ACKNOWLEDGMENTS

This chapter is based upon work supported by the National Science Foundation under Grant Number: DMII – 0328071. Any opinions, findings, conclusions or recommendations expressed in this material are those of the authors and do not necessarily reflect the views of the National Science Foundation. We thank several reviewers for helpful comments.

REFERENCES

Allegheny Institute for Public Policy (AIPP) (2001), 'The Importance of US Airways to the Pennsylvania Economy', http://www.alleghenyinstitute.org/reports/01_03.pdf, accessed 28 November 2005.
Bureau of Economic Analysis of the United States Department of Commerce (BEA) (2002), 'Benchmark Input–Output Accounts of the United States, 1997', http://www.bea.gov/bea/ARTICLES/2002/12December/1202I–OAccounts2.pdf, accessed 18 April 2005.
Bureau of Economic Analysis of the United States Department of Commerce

(BEA) (2005a), 'Gross State Product', http://www.bea.gov/bea/regional/gsp. htm; accessed 13 April 2005.

Bureau of Economic Analysis of the United States Department of Commerce (BEA) (2005b), 'Regional Input–Output Modeling System (RIMS II) for Pennsylvania', CD-ROM.

Bureau of Transportation Statistics (BTS) (2005), 'National Transportation Statistics', http://www.bts.gov/publications/national_transportation_statistics/, accessed 20 July 2005.

Cicas, G. (2005), 'Regional Economic Input–Output Analysis-Based Life cycle Assessment', Unpublished PhD thesis, Department of Civil and Environmental Engineering, Carnegie Mellon University, Pittsburgh, PA.

Commonwealth of Pennsylvania (2000), '2000–2001 Budget in Brief', http://www.oit.state.pa.us/budget/lib/budget/2000-2001/BIB/index.html, accessed 28 November 2005.

Energy Information Administration (EIA) (2005a), 'State Data', http://www.eia. doe.gov/emeu/states/_states.html, accessed 28 November 2005.

Energy Information Administration (EIA) (2005b), 'Petroleum State Profiles', http://tonto.eia.doe.gov/oog/info/state/al.html, accessed 9 February 2005.

Energy Information Administration (EIA) (2005c) 'US Refineries and Refining Capacities, 1987–2004', http://www.eia.doe.gov/emeu/finance/usi&to/downstre am/update/index.html#tab4, accessed 9 February 2005.

Green Design Institute (2005), 'EIO-LCA web model', Carnegie Mellon University, Pittsburgh, http://www.eiolca.net/, accessed 28 November 2005.

Hendrickson, C.T., L.B. Lave, H.S. Matthews, A. Horvath, S. Joshi, F.C. McMichael, H. MacLean, G. Cicas, D. Matthews and J. Bergerson (2006), *Environmental Life Cycle Assessment of Goods and Services: An Input–Output Approach*, Washington, DC: Resources for the Future.

Hewings, G. (1985), *Regional Input Output Analysis*, Thousand Oaks, CA: Sage Publications.

Leontief, W. (1953), *Studies in the Structure of the American Economy*, Oxford: Oxford University Press.

Scorecard (1999), 'Criteria Air Pollutant Report: Pennsylvania', http://www.score-card.org/env-releases/cap/state.tcl?fips_state_code=42#emissions_summary, accessed 28 November 2005.

Stifflemire, Jr., P.F. (2001), 'Identifying and Dealing with Pittsburgh International Airport Problems', Allegheny Institute for Public Policy (AIPP), http://www.alleghenyinstitute.org/reports/00_05.pdf, accessed 3 November 2005.

United States Environmental Protection Agency (EPA) (1997), 'Inventory of US Greenhouse Gas Emissions and Sinks: 1990–2001', http://yosemite.epa. gov/oar/globalwarming.nsf/content/ResourceCenterPublicationsGHGEmissions USEmissionsInventory2003.html, accessed 23 February 2005.

United States Environmental Protection Agency (EPA) (2003), 'Inventory of US Greenhouse Gas Emissions and Sinks: 1990–2001, Annex Y – Constants, Units, and Conversions', http://yosemite.epa.gov/oar/globalwarming.nsf/Unique KeyLookup/LHOD5MJTCL/$File/2003-final-inventory_annex_y.pdf, accessed 30 August 2004.

United States Environmental Protection Agency (EPA) (2004a), 'Solid Waste and Emergency Response, 1999 National Biennial RCRA Hazardous Waste Report Data Files', http://www.epa.gov/epaoswer/hazwaste/data/brs99.htm, accessed 31 March 2004.

United States Environmental Protection Agency (EPA) (2004b), '2000 TRI Data Release', Toxics Release Inventory (TRI), http://www.epa.gov/tri/tridata/tri00/index.htm, accessed 1 April 2004.

United States Environmental Protection Agency (EPA) (2005a), 'Green Book, Criteria Pollutants', http://www.epa.gov/oar/oaqps/greenbk/o3co.html#Carbon%20Monoxide, accessed 28 November 2005.

United States Environmental Protection Agency (EPA) (2005b), 'State GHG Inventories', http://yosemite.epa.gov/OAR/globalwarming.nsf/content/EmissionsStateGHGInventories.html, accessed 21 February 2005.

United States Securities and Exchange Commission (US SEC) (2000), 'US Airways Group, Inc.: Annual Report', http://www.usairways.com/about/investor_relations/reports/report_2000.pdf, accessed 28 November 2005.

US Census Bureau (2000), 'Profile of Selected Economic Characteristics: 2000, Geographic Area: Pennsylvania', 10 October 2002, available at http://factfinder.census.gov/servlet/QTTable.

7. Design approach frameworks, regional metabolism and scenarios for sustainability

Tim Baynes, Jim West and Graham M. Turner

7.1 INTRODUCTION

As a physical entity, the whole of an urban economy may be considered as an industrial ecosystem; one that exists at several spatial and temporal scales and whose dynamics are affected by population growth and strategic planning among other factors.

The long-term (100 years) influence of policy and strategic planning is generally under-represented in such city region industrial ecosystems. The long-term, often indirect, impacts of policy choices have been demonstrated to be of critical importance to the vulnerability or sustainability of a region (Proust 2003). In the following we demonstrate an approach to simulating regional metabolism that addresses the broader implications for sustainability by explicitly incorporating strategic choices in its representation of the physical dynamics of a city region.

This is achieved through a computer model framework that incorporates the dynamics of the physical economy of a region and, simultaneously, functions as an integrated historical account of regional metabolism. Importantly, the framework is also a facility whereby decision-makers can use these attributes in combination with expert knowledge or other computer models to simulate and explore the physical implications of long-term strategies.

This framework has been constructed using the design approach (Gault et al. 1987). In contrast with some approaches to urban simulation and decision support such as those found in Brail and Klosterman (2001), the decision-maker is employed as an integral part of the mechanism by which simulations of the future are calculated.

The example here is the study area of the Victorian Regional Stocks and Flows Framework (VRSFF) which includes the city of Melbourne and regional urban centers, agricultural, forestry, and native vegetation areas

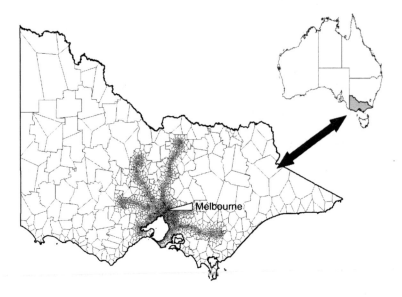

Note: Finer divisions shown are cells indicating the level of land use resolution in VRSFF used around urban and regional centers, and along major existing transport corridors.

Figure 7.1   Geographical disaggregation of the state of Victoria in VRSFF

for the state of Victoria in Australia (see Figure 7.1). Another example of the application of the design approach in regional planning is the Georgia Basin Futures Project (VanWynsberghe et al. 2003).

Firstly we describe the essential features of the design approach and stocks and flows frameworks (SFFs) constructed with this approach. We discuss how this type of dynamical analysis is important for address-ing issues of sustainability for a city region. Subsequently, we provide an example of how the design approach and SFF are used to explore population change and strategic planning as dynamical influences on the industrial ecosystem of Melbourne.

7.2   THE DESIGN APPROACH

The design approach has been applied to systems analysis on scales ranging from individual industries (Chan et al. 2004) to the globe (Hoffman 2001). From the design approach perspective the simulation of a complex system is separated into two parts: the user occupies 'control space' wherein choices are made in response to actions in the 'machine space' which is the locus

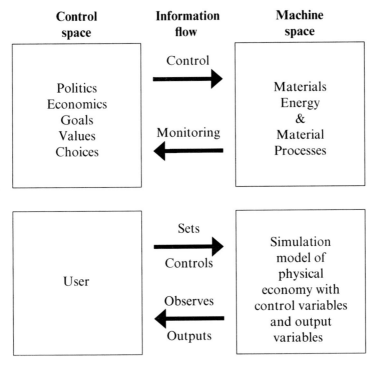

Figure 7.2   The design approach involves iterations of simulations by computer frameworks in the 'machine space', observation and response from the user and repeated simulations

of the computer code and calculations that describe the physical processes of the system. The corresponding description of the physical economy of a region separates the socio-economic actors from the industrial ecosystem (see Figure 7.2).

In common with systems dynamics approaches such as UrbanSim (Waddell 2002), design information, like engineering studies, is used to construct submodels which form part of a simulation framework to support the design of different scenarios. However, as Rotmans and van Asselt (2001) observed, 'modeling rationality and the policy rationality only converge if the two are brought together in one process' and the distinction between the design approach and systems dynamics is the direct involvement of the user as fundamental to the calculation of future scenarios.

The user might also have input to the construction of the framework, identifying inter- and intra-sectoral dynamics that must be represented, and identifying potential tensions (differences between requirements and provision in the physical economy) and designing relevant variables to expose tensions. End users and experts are consulted on where particular issues of sustainability might require sectoral models to be more detailed, and where and how inputs and outputs might be usefully disaggregated.

Most importantly, in the functioning framework the user provides the feedback bridge between simulated future physical circumstances and our (society's planned) response to them. Design of acceptable futures is achieved through iterations of computer simulation, learning and innovation from the user, and repeated simulation.

While agent-based models such as those presented in Perez and Batten (2006) and other simulators of human decision-making may be used, this would automate the resolution of tensions and forgo the potential convergence of modeling and policy rationality. The philosophy of the design approach is that having a human being form part of the modeling process is an efficient way to develop systems understanding in strategic decision-makers and simultaneously to incorporate human behavior in the long-term simulation of regional futures.

In the context of regional metabolism analysis, the submodels represent the dynamics and transactions of physical stocks (such as cars, houses and people) and flows (such as fuel consumption, waste from demolition, effluent and emissions) that describe sectors of the physical economy. The Victorian Regional Stocks and Flows Framework (VRSFF) is an example of a design approach framework for simulating a regional industrial ecosystem and the VRSFF is to be considered as synonymous with the design approach in the descriptions that follow.

7.3   THE DESIGN APPROACH AS APPLIED IN STOCKS AND FLOWS FRAMEWORKS

Frameworks such as the VRSFF are designed to house and manipulate a large amount of integrated data and it is, of course, sensible to have coding and data structures compatible with systems of national accounts. Consequently the code of the framework is a hybrid of systems dynamics and accounting and uses the whatIf? software platform (whatIf? Technologies Inc. 2006).

There are two main components to any SFF. The 'simulator' is the framework used to create scenarios and consequently learn about the trade-offs or interplay between sectors by interactively solving tensions. The 'calibrator' is an associated framework that incorporates historical data so that the simulator reproduces historical data as context for

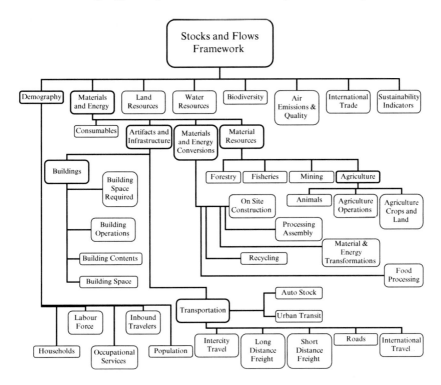

Note: The hierarchy shown is a conceptual map. There are many more connections between sectors encoded in the simulator framework.

Figure 7.3   Overview of a stocks and flows framework and the numerous sectoral submodels that are integrated for simulation

scenarios – context that both informs and constrains scenarios. Figure 7.3 shows the broad capture of the different components of the regional industrial ecosystem that is typical of an SFF simulator.

To represent multiple intersecting issues simultaneously, the VRSFF employs a combination of many disaggregate inputs, a wide coverage of intersectoral interactions and a linear format to calculations. The tractable nature of these linear calculations and their outputs allows the user to contemplate chains of cause and effect and information flows concerning single issues as they impact across multiple sectors and, conversely, the effect of multiple compound issues on one (or more) sector(s).

A more detailed explanation of the structure, mechanics and operation of the VRSFF can be found in West et al. (2005) and Baynes et al. (2005). A technical description of the input–output mathematics involved in the modeling of basic industries in SFFs can be found in Lennox et al. (2005). Here we simply want to convey the advantages and disadvantages of SFFs for representing the interaction of strategic policy and the industrial ecosystem. In particular, two fundamental features of SFFs, stock dynamics and disaggregation, are discussed with reference to sustainability assessment.

7.3.1   Advantages

The intellectual challenge of modeling the mechanics and behavior of the industrial ecosystem of a region is to be matched with an important social purpose: getting that knowledge into the heads of decision-makers. The advantage of involving the policy-maker in the simulation process is demonstrated in the following example.

Consider the chain of calculations suggested in Figure 7.4. An increasing population might have increasing demands for personal transport and this would have consequences for emissions. Thus far, these are all things that an SFF could process in linear calculations (in the 'machine space').

There might be direct health impacts from automobile exhaust fumes but the way the whole system (including government) responds could occur in different ways. There could be an adaptive response where special technology is developed to reduce emissions at the exhaust – this implies that governments would also legislate for its use and people would take up that technology. Alternatively there could be a preventative strategy where

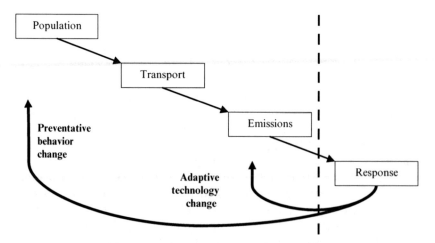

Figure 7.4   The user forms part of the intersectoral feedback loops in design approach frameworks allowing the exploration of multiple different responses to a given output

people are encouraged to live in places where mobility does not require automobiles as much. Or there could be a mixture of these two strategies or other strategies for example, involving the redesign of the urban plan.

This sort of 'control space' decision or calculation is exactly the sort of thing that policy-makers and other framework users are good at and it is often exactly the place where they have an intervention point. Consequently this sort of intersectoral feedback is not part of the computer code in the SFF. The feedback loops are closed overall in the iterative scenario-making exercise where we, in discussion with strategic decision-makers and stakeholders, are part of the loop (note that the user might very well come equipped with research or the results of other computer models). Response information is presented to the SFF 'machine space' for a revised iteration of the simulation and analysis by the user.

Within the sectoral calculators there is a deliberate simplicity to the mathematics. For example:

$$(number\ of\ automobiles) = (persons) \times (automobiles\ per\ person).$$

The sophistication is in the multitude of these simple calculations and bringing them all together for a very large number of variables, confronting each with the variables to which it is related, and making those variables readily available in context for policy consideration.

One of the more difficult aspects of sustainability is that it involves a confluence of issues that have to be addressed simultaneously: changes to the aggregate population, its age structure and its spatial distribution; the quantity and location of physical resources such as water and energy supply and transport infrastructure, and so on (Cocks 1996). Unfortunately, the innate capacity of humans to test and challenge alternative plans of action by 'what if?' storytelling appears to break down quite rapidly as the complexity of the causal linkages involved increases (Lempert et al. 2003).

To fully appreciate the interdependence and interactions between sectors and across scales of the physical economy, it is imperative to have a wide coverage of the whole system. Moreover, it is important to represent the physical economy with sufficient disaggregation and resolution to be able to depict the subtleties of these interactions. The VRSFF is an integrating tool capable of representing detailed compound scenarios across the whole regional system and, through compatibility with a national SFF, beyond the regional boundaries.

The characteristics of existing capital stocks and infrastructure constrain the vista of possible future sustainable pathways. The VRSFF analysis includes a deep history of capital stocks and infrastructure and considers several generations (of the capital and of humans) into the future. The VRSFF simulation time is 100 years.

7.3.2   Stock Dynamics

An important attribute of any industrial ecosystem is the age structure of the capital stocks and the consequent materials and energy flows that arise from the retirement, replacement and renewal of these stocks (Foran and Poldy 2002). Capital vintages are characterized by features such as their age, lifetime, input efficiency, rates of depreciation and so on. These aspects of extant capital and infrastructure influence the nature and timing of future capital additions. As Davidsdottir and Ruth (2005) have pointed out, it is important to represent explicitly the vintage structure of capital stocks and the dynamics of retirement, replacement and renewal to gain a more accurate picture of inertia in the industrial system and consequential constraints and opportunities for change.

A pervading feature of capital stock variables in the SFF is their characterization by age, efficiency, associated material and energy requirements, the discarded rate in a given time step and also the same considerations for co-dependent and replacement capital stock. Generations of historical capital stock data, input of expert knowledge and linear difference equations are combined to calculate the evolution of capital stocks throughout the physical economy.

It is also important to note that that the quantity and connectivity of variables in the VRSFF permit great flexibility in creating sophisticated compound scenarios. While the robust treatment of stock dynamics endows the framework with a long-term memory of capital and infrastructure, there is still the capability to explore simulations of shocks and sudden change.

7.3.3   Disaggregation

The typical quantity of different variables endows SFFs with a great deal of flexibility but one practical aspect of being comprehensive is answering the question: what level of detail is required to assess sustainability in a simulated physical economy? Choosing the smallest set of variables and the lowest level of disaggregation would benefit the usability of the framework but compromise its capacity to represent subtle interactions in the industrial system. The answer is for the framework developer, experts and/or the end user to assess the requirements for each sector and design variables with enough detail to learn about long-term physical sustainability. The guiding principle is to be as simple as possible but no simpler.

*Figure 7.5   Different variables of the VRSFF use appropriate
disaggregation: for example, 'surface water flow' requires the
regional geography to be disaggregated by catchment areas
shown*

For example the geographical disaggregation used to analyze urban
form (refer to Figure 7.1) was based on a desire to capture the materials, energy and labor signature associated with activity local to a given
area (and, implicitly, non-local materials, energy and labor transactions
between areas). Given the density and diversity of activities near the urban
centers and transport corridors, there is clearly a need to deal with these
areas in higher resolution than, for example, large areas devoted mostly to
national parks or agriculture. Thus the calculations are not encumbered
with the far more precise but more computationally intensive alternatives
such as a 1 km × 1 km square grid array applied over the entire 200,000 km²
region. For another, concurrent analysis, such as the distribution of water
resources, the VRSFF divides the regional map by different boundaries –
catchment areas and river basins (see Figure 7.5). Similarly, non-spatial
variables are disaggregated according to purpose.

Intersectoral calculations also influence the level of disaggregation.
Continuing the example above, 20 different land use categories were dis-
tilled from raw land zoning data that recognized more than 80 types of land

use. This level of resolution considered what land information the various other sectoral calculators might need and how sensitive their outputs might be to more or less detail. All this, while remembering that subtle, indirect interactions can have significant cumulative effects over many decades.

7.3.4   Disadvantages

SFFs are not intended to be information tools for short-term issues. Some of the fast-moving variables and behavioral feedbacks operating in markets, for example, are invisible to SFFs. The counterargument is that for decision support regarding sustainability in the long term, the slow-moving variables and dynamics of a regional industrial ecosystem will always conform to the physical laws of mass and energy balance, whereas the behavior of markets can only be forecast a few years hence at best.

SFFs are comprehensive and consequently they take some time to develop, although they can be constructed in modular form. There are also frequent issues with data availability. Here, however, the scope of SFFs is actually an advantage. It is rare that we know nothing. The connectedness of variables throughout the framework means that variables we do know about put bounds on possible values for those variables without any data. If we have no other information, we choose values in a reasonable range. Common sense or expert advice often helps us to do better and, in any case, this systematic treatment identifies a variable for which better data should be collected in the future.

7.4   POPULATION AND RESIDENTIAL LAND USE SCENARIOS

The following is a simple but practical example of the numerate way SFFs can be used to construct compound scenarios defined by settings of parameters throughout the framework. We present outputs of population and land use scenarios in the VRSFF and demonstrate a tension between the provision of residential land and the population-driven requirement.

7.4.1   Population

The 'regional population' submodel deals with basic demography, deriving the population in the region from variables such as fertility and immigration rates. All of the requirements that are driven by outputs from the regional population submodel can be monitored as they cascade through the various sector-specific calculators of the VRSFF (see Figure 7.6).

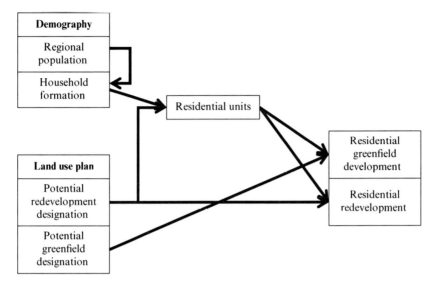

Note: The calculations about provision of land, directed by policy ('land use plan') are kept independent of those concerning the requirements of the population (starting from 'Demography') until they are accounted for together in the residential development calculators on the right.

Figure 7.6   The subset of VRSFF submodels used to represent the population and residential land use scenarios and information flows between them

Two population growth scenarios are considered which produce different age structures for the stock of people in simulations. One scenario sees the population of the region increase by 1 million people by 2030 through a higher fertility rate (2.1 children per female lifetime) and a net immigration rate of 7000 people per year. The other scenario also sees 1 million more people by 2030 but it has a lower fertility rate (of 1.8) and double the net immigration rate. This produces distinctly different age structures that are shown to impact on the future demands for labor (in this case, teachers) and infrastructure (households).

7.4.2   Implications of Population Scenarios

A feature of the VRSFF and SFFs in general is the long simulation times, well beyond the time frame generally considered in most planning frameworks. Figure 7.7a illustrates the sort of insight continuing a simulation beyond the time frame of immediate interest can bring.

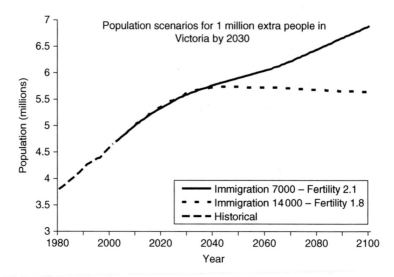

*Figure 7.7a   Two different population futures produce similar total
population until 2030 but thereafter they diverge because of
different age structures*

While delivering roughly the same population by 2030, the population
futures for the two scenarios are on radically different trajectories. By 2040,
the higher migration path has led to a slowly declining population, while
the higher fertility path has led to a rapidly expanding population.

The vintaging of stocks (in this case, stocks of people) combined with the
cross-sectoral linkages in the VRSFF yields other information of value in
assessing these two different population scenarios in the long term. The simulated total population in the region is of roughly the same size to 2030 under
both scenarios, but the age composition is quite different. This has implications for a number of components of the industrial ecosystem, including
both the availability of labor, and the requirement for different categories
of services and employees. Figure 7.7b shows one manifestation of this,
the strong and almost immediate divergence between the requirements for
teachers. This drives different requirements for classrooms, which in turn
has implications for how much material and energy needs to be dedicated to
more schools, in addition to the residential land and housing needs.

7.4.3   Land Use

To accommodate the growth in households, three scenarios of different
land release patterns were also simulated in concordance with those found

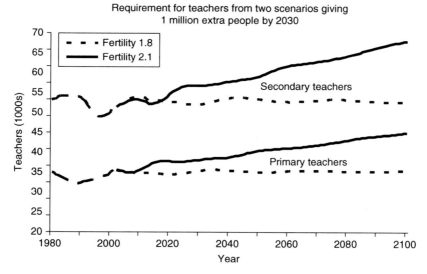

Note: The longer dashed lines show the common history of primary and secondary teachers for both scenarios.

Figure 7.7b   *The demand for primary and secondary teachers generated by the different age structures corresponding to the two different population scenarios*

in the regional government's long-term urban plan, 'Melbourne 2030' (Victorian Department of Infrastructure 2002). One land release option allows the city of Melbourne simply to expand outwards at the perimeter: 'perimeter growth'. Another scenario involves a greater density of housing within prescribed 'urban growth centers'. A third scenario encourages the development of 'regional centers'. While these are generic descriptions of residential development options, each of these scenarios was defined in the VRSFF through detailed numerate settings for development type, placement and priority.

The information flow between some of the submodels related to residential land use in the VRSFF has been shown in Figure 7.6. Similar chains of information flow also apply to other aspects of urban development, including employment activity, health care, education facilities and common land (parks and so on).

The number of households required by the population is calculated using a key exogenously defined variable: 'household formation rate'. Subsequently, the requirement for dwelling space is calculated in the 'residential units' submodel. This dwelling space requirement (including that required due to demolition) is split exogenously between greenfield and redeveloped units. The requirements are compared with land made available (and prioritized) through greenfield (and infill development) in the 'residential development' submodels.

In contrast with other modeling approaches, the strategy for redevelopment or greenfield release is not automatically calculated as a consequence of the requirements. Instead, land is provided (made available) in separate submodels: 'potential greenfield/redevelopment designation'. Consequently, there can be a mismatch – a tension – between the requirement and provision of land for dwellings. This is an example of the open feedback loop of the design approach in the operation of these submodels. If there is a tension it is up to the framework user to choose how to solve it.

Note that a higher net immigration scenario of population growth would have a higher impact on the total number of households in the near term because a greater proportion of immigrants are adults requiring immediate new accommodation. The scenario of a higher fertility rate would see this impact delayed until the children born of that higher fertility reached adulthood. The potential for a tension between housing requirement and provision in these scenarios is compounded by the features of different land use plans.

To retain some clarity in the following outputs, we only consider the combination of the three residential land use scenarios with the higher immigration, lower fertility population scenario.

7.4.4   Implications of Residential Land Use Scenarios

Where available residential land, designated by the land-use planning assumptions, is insufficient to accommodate the required number of dwellings, a tension will result. This is represented by a 'dwellings shortfall' which is explicitly calculated in the 'greenfield development' and 'redevelopment residential' submodels.

The four maps of Figure 7.8 display simulated residential land development. Figure 7.8a shows the distribution of residential dwellings in the base year of simulation, 2001. Maps b, c and d have been chosen to display the occurrence of any shortage in dwellings corresponding to the 'urban growth centers', 'regional centers' and 'perimeter growth' scenarios, respectively. It is understood that an actual deficit in available residential land, and the social impacts of homelessness, are unlikely to be allowable policies, but these outputs are designed to engage and inform the decision-maker about the timing and magnitude of such consequences.

The total shortfall in dwellings over the whole region is shown in the graph of Figure 7.8. The sudden onset of the shortfall arises because land

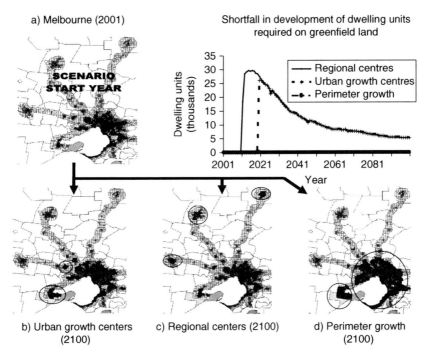

Note: The graph shows the onset and magnitude of dwellings shortfall, for the entire region, for each development scenario. For more information refer to text.

Figure 7.8   Residential dwellings distribution around Melbourne (a) in the base year, 2001 and simulated for 2100 according to the (b) urban growth centers, (c) regional centers and (d) perimeter growth scenarios

available for residential development abruptly runs out according to the limitations of the residential development plan. It is important to note that the graph is not a cumulative measure so the dwelling shortfall for each year reflects the decreasing rate of population increase, hence the diminishing tail of the graph.

The 'perimeter growth' scenario accommodates all new required residential development up to 2100. The land released in the 'urban growth centers' option is consumed by 2011 and the land available in the 'regional centers' scenario is used up by 2019. Undoubtedly each of these development scenarios has concomitant issues and trade-offs regarding, for example, transport, access to amenities and energy consumption, but for this demonstration we restrict ourselves to solving the tension of housing the population.

7.4.5   Solving the Tension

The way in which this tension may be resolved is very open, and goes to the core of why the design approach employs user initiated feedback loops rather than, for example, a 'hardwired' equilibrating allocation algorithm. A few of the relevant control variables in the VRSFF that could be used to resolve this tension include:

- Greenfield Development Density
- Greenfield Land designated for Potential Development
- Dwelling Units per Household
- Share Allocated to Redevelopment

For example, Figure 7.9 demonstrates the effect on the three different scenarios of increasing the 'greenfield development density' control variable from the value of 11.2 to 20 dwellings per hectare. The graphs indicate that this has resolved the tension at least to 2030 for the 'urban growth centers' option. With the same settings the tension under the 'regional centers' option has also been delayed. This, of course, is not merely an alternative setting for a physical parameter. It is an exploration of a socio-economic policy, specifically that of nearly doubling new housing

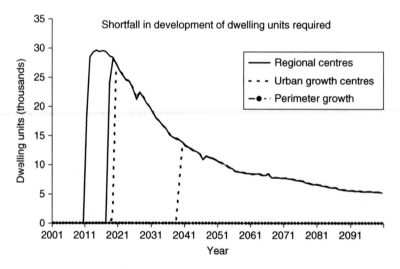

Figure 7.9   Changing the density at which dwelling units are developed on greenfield land from 11.2 dwellings/ha to 20 dwellings/ha delays the onset of the dwelling shortage in the 'regional centers' scenario from 2011 to 2019, and in the 'urban growth centers' scenario from 2019 to 2039

density. The sensible choice of the value for the density is provided by the user who has knowledge of market preferences, building costs and other socio-economic factors or other research such as in Troy (1996).

Scenarios where more basic drivers of the tension are altered can also be examined. For example, the policy assumptions about net immigration or fertility rates which underlie the output of total household numbers could be explored simultaneously with alternative settings of residential development parameters.

7.5   LEARNING WITH THE DESIGN APPROACH

To resolve the sort of tensions in the preceding section, an analyst must explicitly address them, effectively completing the feedback loops through numerical exogenous changes to suitable control variables. This has several strengths:

- It ensures that the analyst remains fully mindful of the assumptions being made to keep any individual scenario physically feasible. This would not be the case were the framework instead to resolve tensions in automated 'black box' feedback loops.
- The decision-maker learns about the system and its dynamics, dis-covering sensitivities and constraints.
- It is very flexible in terms of exploring different ways that the tension can be alleviated, avoiding any particular ideology or belief in how people and the economic system might respond.

Additionally the involvement of the user imbues the calculations of physi-cal entities with social and economic information. In the example of resi-dential development above, the desire to avoid homelessness and economic decay is represented in the settings of the submodels' control variables that house people over a given time, in a given location and at a particular density. The iteration of simulation, user learning and repeated simulation endows the VRSFF with a dynamical representation of strategic policy and planning in a rigorously defined physical framework.

7.6   REGIONAL SUSTAINABILITY IN THE NATIONAL CONTEXT

Australian cities are facing physical constraints on land use, housing, and energy, food and water security (Government of Western Australia 2003; Environmental Protection Authority of New South Wales 2003; Engineers

Australia 2005). However, the pressures faced by city regions should also be considered in the context of national sustainability. Australia is facing a confluence of difficult issues: climate change, an expanding and ageing population, water security that is, at best, highly variable, and land salinization are a selection of the national level sustainability challenges that intersect with regional issues (Australian Department of the Environment and Heritage 2001).

At the national level, a computer framework has already been developed: the Australian Stocks and Flows Framework (ASFF) is a modeling framework and database for simulating the physical economy of Australia over the long term (Foran and Poldy 2004). In a wide-ranging study, the ASFF was used to determine the physical implications of different population scenarios, for all sectors of the Australian economy over the next 100 years (Foran and Poldy 2002). The ASFF is an extremely powerful information tool and it continues to contribute to national-level analyses (Foran et al. 2005).

The scope of the VRSFF accommodates the potential expansion of the region's population and its material and energy catchment. Acknowledging that regions are rarely autonomous and often rely on physical transactions across their borders, the region itself should not be considered in isolation.

An example of a connection between the VRSFF and ASFF is the 'Victorian population' variable in the 'regional population' submodel of the VRSFF. This has a counterpart in the ASFF and data passed between the frameworks so that VRSFF and ASFF values can be compared and harmonized. Similar comparisons can be made for other appropriate variables such as land use allocation, water use and energy production and consumption. Movement or trade of physical quantities – goods, commodities, energy, people – are also be made explicit and compared with such flows in the national framework. These comparisons are intended to draw attention to issues that fall across geographic scales and to ensure that these are adequately represented from the level of the suburb to the nation.

7.7   CONCLUSIONS

Through frameworks like the VRSFF, the design approach presents a way to represent the current regional industrial ecosystem and narratives of potential physical futures that is rigorous and rich in detail but also accessible to decision-makers. This accessibility engages and includes strategic policy in the calculations concerning possible sustainable futures. The range of possible options is narrowed by the limitations of what are socially or economically acceptable physical futures. If, for example, we wish future society to retain a health care system, public transport system or a banking system, these institutions ultimately represent a physical cost and that cost confines the array of possible physical sustainable futures. The modeling and analysis we have presented here (and in other models using the design approach) are based on physical parameters, but far from precluding social or economic considerations, they rely on them.

If an analysis is isolated to any fraction of the regional industrial ecosystem then, no matter how thorough the research, it will have limited utility in answering questions of long-term sustainability. The starting point must be as comprehensive and integrated as possible. The wide scope of the VRSFF is augmented further by a deep capture of historical data so as to acquire the age profile and associated characteristics of capital stocks and infrastructure.

One consequence of this approach is the detail and disaggregation required for a given sectoral model within the framework. This depends on the strength and sensitivity of the connections between it and other sectors of the physical economy, but there is also a balance to be struck with regards to usability. This balance is achieved in the VRSFF through a design process strongly coupled with input from stakeholders, experts and other models.

It should also be acknowledged that regions are parts of larger physical economies and that there are important physical transactions between a region and the world outside of it. We have deliberately used a software platform and an approach in common with an existing national-level framework to provide a mechanism for realizing the impact a region or city has on areas beyond its geographic boundary. The VRSFF is part of an integrated effort to aid the design of a sustainable future for Australia's urban, regional and rural populations across the continent.

ACKNOWLEDGMENTS

This work inherits much from the data, methods, and results of the Australian Stocks and Flows Framework (ASFF) and we are grateful to the creators of the ASFF for their continuing support. In particular we would like to recognise the technical guidance of whatIf? Technologies who are the originators of the design approach and the software we used. This research was mostly supported through the Commonwealth Scientific and Industrial Research Organisation (CSIRO)'s Water for a Healthy Country Flagship and the State of Victoria Department of Sustainability and Environment.

REFERENCES

Australian Department of the Environment and Heritage (2001), *Australia State of the Environment 2001, Independent Report to the Commonwealth Minister for the Environment and Heritage*, Canberra, Australia: CSIRO Publishing.

Baynes, T.M., J. West and G.M. Turner (2005), *User Manual – Melbourne Region Stocks and Flows Framework*, Canberra, Australia: CSIRO Publishing.

Brail, R.K. and Richard E. Klosterman (2001), *Planning Support Systems*, Redlands, CA: ESRI.

Chan, A.W., R. Hoffman and B. McInnis (2004), 'The Role of Systems Modeling for Sustainable Development Policy Analysis: The Case of Bio-ethanol', *Ecology and Society*, **9**(2): 6; http://www.ecologyandsociety.org/vol9/iss2/art6.

Cocks, D. (1996), *People Policy: Australia's Population Choices*, Sydney, Australia: UNSW Press.

Davidsdottir, B. and M. Ruth (2005), 'Dynamic Industrial Systems Modeling: Issues in Integrating Economic and Physical Modeling', in *The 3rd International Conference of the International Society for Industrial Ecology Abstracts*, p. 218, www.isie-2005.org/home.

Engineers Australia (2005), *Victorian Infrastructure Report Card*, Melbourne, Australia: Engineers Australia.

Environmental Protection Authority of New South Wales (2003), *New South Wales State of the Environment 2003*, Sydney, Australia: Department of Environment and Conservation.

Foran, B. and F. Poldy (2002), *Future Dilemmas: Options to 2050 for Australia's Population, Technology, Resources, and Environment*, Report for the Australian Commonwealth Department of Immigration and Multicultural and Indigenous Affairs, Canberra, Australia: CSIRO Sustainable Ecosystems.

Foran, B. and F. Poldy (2004), 'Modeling Physical Realities at the Whole Economy Scale', in J.C.J.M. van den Bergh and Marco A. Jansen (eds) *Economics of Industrial Ecology: Materials, Structural Change, and Spatial Scales*, Cambridge, MA: MIT Press, pp. 165–94.

Foran, B., M. Lenzen and C. Dey (2005), *Balancing Act: A Triple Bottom Line Analysis of the Australian Economy*, Canberra, Australia: CSIRO Publishing and the University of Sydney.

Gault, F.D., K.E. Hamilton, R.B. Hoffman and B.C. McInnis (1987), 'The Design Approach to Socio-Economic Modeling', *Futures*, **19**(1): 3–25.

Government of Western Australia (2003), *Hope for the Future: The Western Australian State Sustainability Strategy*, Perth, Australia: Department of the Premier and Cabinet.

Hoffman, R. (2001), 'Interacting with the Global Systems Simulator', *CACOR Proceedings*, **3**(2), 7–12.

Lempert, R.J., S.W. Popper and S.C. Bankes (2003), *Shaping the Next One Hundred Years: New Methods for Quantitative Long-Term Policy Analysis*, Santa Monica, CA: RAND Corporation.

Lennox, J.A., G. Turner, R. Hoffman and B.C. McInnis (2005), 'Modeling Basic Industries in the Australian Stocks and Flows Framework', *Journal of Industrial Ecology*, **8**(4): 101–20.

Perez, P. and D.F. Batten (2006), *Complex Science for a Complex World: Exploring Human Ecosystems with Agents*, Canberra, Australia: ANU E Press.

Proust, K. (2003), 'Ignoring the Signals: Irrigation Salinity in New South Wales, Australia', *Irrigation and Drainage*, **52**(1): 39–49.

Rotmans, J. and M.B.A. van Asselt (2001), 'Uncertainty in Integrated Assessment Modelling: A Labyrinthic Path', *Integrated Assessment*, **2**(2): 43–55.

Troy, P.N. (1996), *The Perils of Urban Consolidation: A Discussion of Australian Housing and Urban Development Policies*, Sydney, Australia: Federation Press.

VanWynsberghe, R., J. Moore, J. Tansey and J. Carmichael (2003), 'Towards Community Engagement: Six Steps to Expert Learning for Future Scenario Development', *Futures*, **35**(1): 203–19.

Victorian Department of Infrastructure (2002), *Melbourne 2030: Planning for Sustainable Growth*, Melbourne, Australia: Victorian State Government.

Victorian Department of Premier and Cabinet (2005), *Growing Victoria Together: A Vision for Victoria to 2010 and Beyond*, Melbourne, Australia: Victorian State Government.

Victorian Department of Sustainability and the Environment (2004), *Victorian State Government Population and Household Projections 2001–2031*, Melbourne, Australia: Victorian State Government.

Waddell, P. (2002), 'UrbanSim: Modeling Urban Development for Land Use, Transportation and Environmental Planning', *Journal of the American Planning Association*, **68**(3): 297–314.

West, J., T.M. Baynes and G.M. Turner (2005), *Technical Manual: Melbourne Region Stocks and Flows Framework*, Canberra, Australia: CSIRO.

whatIf? Technologies Inc. (2006), http://www.whatiftechnologies.com.

PART III

Evolution of Networks in Industrial
Ecosystems

8. Learning and evolution in industrial ecosystems: an introduction

Peter M. Allen

The problem of learning, innovation and the evolution of industrial eco-systems goes beyond the 'dynamic'. Instead of thinking about a particular dynamical system – with corresponding equations capturing the flows of materials and value between different nodes – the issue of learning and of evolution considers the structural evolution of any such system from one 'dynamical system' (set of equations) to another. It asks not only how the stocks and flows of a traditional system dynamics change over time, but how new flows, new variables and emergent properties may appear over time. As Schumpeter correctly stated in 1938: 'the problem that is usually being visualized is how capitalism administers existing structures, whereas the relevant problem is how it creates them and destroys them.'

This correctly captures the idea that what really matters over time is the flow of creative, innovative initiatives and responses into and out of the system. In other words it is the dialogue of the apparent variables which typify system structure at any particular time with the non-average deviations and novelties around these. When deviance is suppressed by the system, the structure is stable; when deviance is amplified, instability, structural change and transformation occur. In considering the longer-term evolution of an industrial ecosystem, therefore, instead of just calibrating what is present at a given time, we must also attempt to explore what could possibly happen, and the possible frameworks within which such explorations could be considered.

In a series of papers (Allen and McGlade 1987; Allen 1994; Allen et al. 2006) the essential driving force of evolution and of complex systems was shown to be the micro-diversity (heterogeneous and idiosyncratic individuals) that exists below any chosen level of description of real systems. It was shown that micro-diversity provides an internal pool of adaptive and creative behaviors that drives the evolution of the system as a whole, through successive structures and organizations, changing both the macro-structure and also the internal beliefs, criteria and aims that underlie individual behavioral responses. In this way, the internal beliefs and views held by agents of a given kind are shaped by their experiences that in turn result from the organization and structures that they inhabit. These are, in their turn, also formed by the behavior and interactions of the individual agents. This is a circular system that either is self-reinforcing, marking a period of stability, or is not, marking the occurrence of an instability. The complex system that represents organizational evolution is therefore about periods of structural stability, when rational analysis and knowledge can exist, separated by instabilities, when new variables and aspects invade the system, and rational-decision making is impossible.

This can be understood by studying the assumptions and approximations made in arriving at a mechanical description or model of any evolved, and hence complex, part of reality. This is illustrated in Figure 8.1 where the different kinds of 'models' that correspond to successive, additional simplifying assumptions are shown.

This is illustrated in Figure 8.1 in which we see the different types of model and epistemology that arise as successively more constraining, simplifying assumptions are made.

With no assumptions, reality is simply subjective experience, and survival would rely on intuitive, spontaneous responses.

With the definition of a boundary, and with the ability to classify the elements and content of a situation, we would arrive at an evolutionary and learning view. Over time systems such as industrial ecosystems are characterized by a qualitatively changing structure, with new entities, technologies and knowledge emerging and earlier ones disappearing.

By considering only the present and taking the current structure (variables) as being given, we have a description in terms of 'noisy' differential or difference equations, expressing the coupled behavior of the system. Such systems would normally possess multiple possible dynamic attractors, and the noisy processes would make the system jump between different possible attractor basins. This kind of model constitutes the basis for contingency planning, risk analysis and for testing the resilience of an industrial ecosystem.

Making a further assumption that processes run smoothly at their average rate leads to a system dynamical description of the system. The behavior of the system is apparently predictable, but it entirely fails to capture the effects of evolution or learning, and the structural and behavioral transformations that could occur as a result.

One further assumption that is often made is that of equilibrium. In particular, such methods as cost–benefit analysis of a possible decision rely on comparing the initial (equilibrium) situation with the final one. This is appealingly simple, but does ignore the probable fact that the system and its environment are never at equilibrium, and hence the calculation is false.

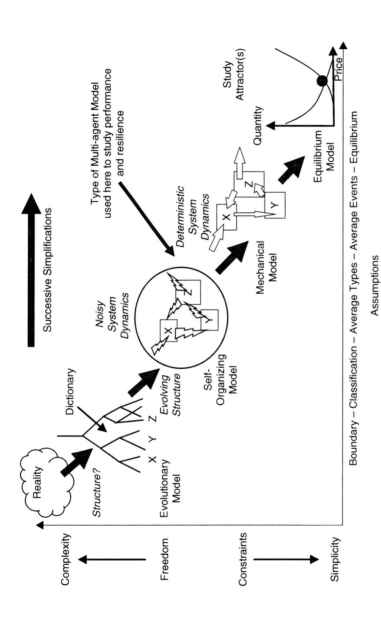

Figure 8.1 Successive assumptions are used to reduce reality to a simple, causal mechanical description, with models that can 'run' but not evolve

123

This series of assumptions concerns the degree of understanding that we have of a situation. Our understanding of reality is in terms of a set of inter-acting components that cannot evolve of themselves, and the changes and innovations that occur in reality are merely taken account of by making a new, revised model of that reality. The mechanical, system dynamic, view of the 'functioning' of the system at a given time is necessarily incomplete in that it does not include the micro-diversity within the agents that leads to new ideas and to learning, and will in fact change and modify things. Figure 8.1 tells us therefore that the key assumption in which we assume a description of the current situation in terms of the average types, or homo-geneous elements, currently present is the critical one in which the 'evolu-tionary potential' is lost. In the real, complex system there exits internal heterogeneity, multiple different perspectives and constructs, and differing aims and goals, and it is the interaction of these things over time that will lead to evolutionary, structural qualitative change.

This understanding of complexity underlines the importance of develop-ing frameworks within which to consider the problem of an evolutionary industrial ecosystem. We need to set up a broad and open system so that multiple examples and structures can be considered and explored. Indeed the whole point of this book has to be to allow the exploration of different possibilities of how industrial ecosystems may evolve in the future, and how our policies, actions and choices will affect these possibilities.

Clearly, an important way to gain understanding is to develop sophis-ticated 'gaming' within which players can both invent possible scenarios and responses and also begin to take in the multiple possible pathways into the future – and the different qualities of life associated with some of them. The modeling of such complex systems is not about the simulation of the present running deterministically into the future. It is about imagining and exploring possible futures so that we can modify our beliefs and intentions, and act in order to push the future in one direction rather than another. The paradoxical nature of seeing mathematical models as being predictive can be seen by considering, for example, climate change. The more widely a climate change model is believed, the more likely people are to take action to stop it happening, while the more widely a climate change model is not believed, the more likely it is that its predictions will 'come true'. This is the point: modeling, frameworks and game playing are all ways of thinking about possible futures and attempting to imagine better their variety and properties – in order to decide how, when and where to act with a view to helping to push the future in one direction, or to avoid another.

This focuses on the use of modeling of different kinds in order to help learning occur. As an example, let us consider a multi-agent model of a relatively simple problem (see Figure 8.2) concerning the production

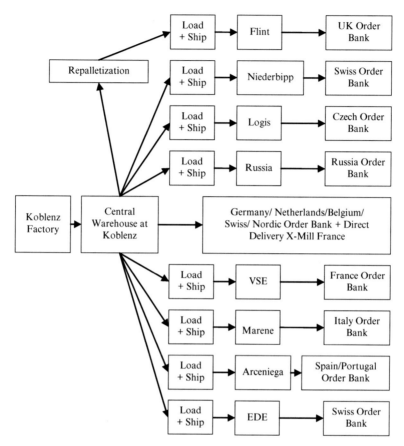

Figure 8.2   Supply network structure

of different types of paper products and their successful distribution to different retail markets (Allen et al. 2006).

The system is looked at in terms of a set of interacting agents: a factory agent running the central machine; a central warehouse agent distributing the production in response to the orders coming in from the many different local market agents running the national warehouses supplying retailers in some 25 countries. Each agent has behavior that is governed by rules which are triggered by the information coming from the agents to which it is connected. So, warehouse agents reorder stock when they consider that theirs is low, and future demand may lead to a stock-out. The factory agent considers the orders from the central warehouse agent and decides when to switch production from one product type to another, giving rise to changeover costs. The data concerning orders, decisions and flows were sufficient to allow us to find the rules and parameters to mimic current behavior responding to the fluctuating level of retail orders. This behavior was reasonable, but somehow represented a limit on what the agents in that system could learn from experience, since there were time delays in the response to orders, and also different priorities in the behaviors and choices of the other agents. In short, learning in the real world was difficult because the feedback from any behavioral experiment could not be read clearly.

The real point was that if demand were entirely predictable there are undoubtedly many ways of optimizing production and shipping for such a system. But in reality, demand is always somewhat unpredictable, and so reality inevitably deviates from forecasts, so the problem arises as to how the behavior of the agents deals with the imbalances. Often, initially small disturbances are in fact amplified by the agents, and in any case, it is difficult for anyone to know how they should behave. By building the model, we are able to explore millions of possible behavioral rules and parameter values, and also to add different information flows between agents. This enabled us to find resilient behavioral rules for the different agents that eliminated stock-outs and required lower inventory to be carried by the system, and with less time lost in changeovers for the machine.

Of course, this type of model is an 'operational' one, designed to explore the possible functioning of a chosen 'infrastructure' of production, of transport and of distribution. In Figure 8.1 this is represented by to the model corresponding to three assumptions – boundary, variables, and typical components. The fluctuating flows that result from uncertain demand can be studied and the rules of operation of the system – including information exchanges and sharing – lead to successful operations. However, for middle managers charged with running this, they could also explore models with different infrastructure – fewer or more separate warehouses, different routes, and so on – and they could examine how the different structures compared. Strategic managers could examine the bigger question of whether this 'market' is a good one to be in, and whether there is a new domain, or new technology that they need to try to get into. Their model would correspond to evolutionary models, with changing objectives, competences and skills, as a result of innovation and novelty.

This is a very simple model of part of an industrial ecosystem. It could be extended to include the supply side, the flows of wastes, and the linkages into other sectors and domains. However, what it illustrates is that we need to represent the effects of multiple agents within it, attempting to solve their own problems, and affecting others. We also see the difficulty of learning – even in such a simple situation as a paper factory making and delivering a range of products.

Without the modeling, people are really learning by doing, and as we have seen, this can only lead to relatively poor performance.

The observation we can make is: if it is difficult to understand how the behavior of each agent impacts on the overall system, and people are not using models and frameworks to reflect on the collective behavior, then clearly we are in a world of 'trial and error'. It really will be difficult for even well-intentioned agents to know how to behave for the overall good. Learning how to create more sustainable industrial ecosystems, for example, is not at all easy, and in essence requires the kind of frameworks and models that are discussed in this section.

The point is to be able to 'imagine' the different responses that can occur, and how they are connected, and what this produces overall. In addition to modeling, then, model-based gaming systems are excellent, because they can provide ideas about possible innovative responses that are not yet observable in the 'data', and also they provide some degree of experience that can rehearse possible actions or events, and make unexpected consequences less unexpected.

In summary, then, Part III of this volume opens the way to the issue of learning and evolution of industrial ecosystems, which is ultimately the most important issue. A dynamic model of a particular situation tells us about how things would continue under various 'what-if' experiments, but this assumes that the mechanisms and variables of the system do not change. However, evolutionary models can also explore how and which new variables, mechanisms and problems may emerge in the system under different policies, decisions or changes in environment or technologies, and through this provide a basis for exploring the resilience and sustainability of the region.

REFERENCES

Allen, P.M. (1994), 'Evolution, Sustainability and Industrial Metabolism', in R. Ayres and U. Simonis (eds), *Industrial Metabolism: Restructuring for Sustainable Development*, Tokyo: United Nations University Press, pp. 78–100.

Allen, P.M. and J.M. McGlade (1987), 'Evolutionary Drive: The Effect of Microscopic Diversity, Error Making and Noise', *Foundation of Physics*, 17(7): 723–8.

Allen, P., P. Datta and M. Christopher (2006), 'Improving the Resilience and Performance of Organizations using Multi-Agent Modeling of a Complex Production-Distribution Systems', *Journal of Risk Management, Special Issue: Complexity, Risk and Emergence*, 8(4): 294–309.

Allen, P.M., M. Strathern and J.S. Baldwin (2006), 'Evolutionary Drive: New Understanding of Change in Socio-economic Systems', *Emergence Complexity and Organization*, 8(2): 2–19.

9. A framework for analysis of industrial networks

Ruud Kempener, Brett Cohen, Lauren Basson and Jim Petrie

9.1 INTRODUCTION

Industrial networks play an important role in providing products and services to both meet basic human needs and fulfill wider societal aspirations. As such, their operations underpin all aspects of economic activity. At the same time, such networks impact upon the natural environment through consumption of natural resources and generation of wastes. Their social function is related to such things as their employment generation potential, their spatial interplay with residential communities, and their (often perceived) contribution to quality of life – either positive or negative. Consequently, understanding how industrial networks function is key to understanding their contribution to sustainable development.

Moving businesses towards more sustainable operation demands that systemic approaches, cognizant of all explicit and implicit dynamic interconnections, be adopted. Traditional organizational theories of business practice are unable to cope with this complexity. In 1995, Gladwin argued that 'new insights about system dynamics and predictability emerging from the study of complex systems may become critical in making these connections' (Gladwin and Kennelly 1995). Spiegelman (2003) and Ehrenfeld (2004) support the view that complex system theories will be used in developing science to advance understanding of sustainability. These theories can support the development of more rigorous methodological tools to model the dynamic, non-linear and unpredictable behavior of real networks.

Whilst industrial networks themselves may be relatively simple entities involving only a few players, they can also be complex interacting structures embracing multiple value chains. Equally, their interaction with their broader environment may be either steady state or dynamic, but is in no case passive. Industrial networks tend to become more dispersed, more dynamic and more complex due to globalization, increasing competition within industries, and the increasing speed of the innovation cycle (Castells 2000). As a result, it is important to be able to capture this full complexity in any attempt to model the behavior of existing networks, or to design new networks against a set of multiple (and often conflicting) objectives. Added to this challenge is the underlying uncertainty which pervades all aspects of network structure, function and behavior, and the need to understand how such uncertainty informs the decision-making processes which define network operation.

Most industrial networks consist of several organizations linked to each other through the exchange of resources. Some of these resources are tangible, such as the delivery of goods to the supermarket; while other resources are intangible, such as the knowledge or technical assistance provided by an engineering company to a production company (Wernerfelt 1984). Furthermore, there are many non-industrial organizations involved in industrial networks at the level of interested and affected parties (IAPs), such as governmental organizations, consumer groups, industry representatives, universities and so on. All these IAPs contribute to the functioning of the industrial network by, for example, providing information, setting rules, introducing innovations, setting standards or providing the demand for network outputs. Although all may profess to want to work together with respect to the functioning of the industrial network as a whole, the reality is different, as each has its own individual agenda. For example, industrial organizations are interested in maximizing profit; governmental organizations can be interested in increasing the contribution of the industrial network to national welfare; and environmental organizations want to reduce the negative environmental impact of the industrial network. The IAP grouping contributes to defining the external environment in which a given network will operate. The interplay between the individual decision-making processes of network players, and those of the IAPs, and how this is shaped by the transactional exchanges between network players, results in industrial networks which are typically dynamic, and which evolve continuously.

Since the early 1950s, several professional disciplines such as economics, management sciences and engineering have developed modeling approaches to improve the understanding of the performance of industrial networks (Forrester 1961; Hakansson 1987; Winston 1994; Sterman 2000). Approaches to modeling can be classified into two main groups, based on the literature – namely, those that consider the organizations in an industrial network as autonomous decision-makers, and those that do not. This is akin to distinguishing between two levels of analysis, namely 'aggregated' and 'disaggregated' approaches. The former considers the network as a whole, and focuses on aggregated flows (for example of materials, energy and capital). It can be argued that such a 'global' perspective is consistent with the level of analysis required by governments or strategic planners who may be interested in optimizing systems as a whole. Under these circumstances, some of the organizations in the network may be disadvantaged (for example financially or in terms of the constraints placed on their operations), while others may benefit. Such global models of networks may assist policy-makers and planners to design appropriate instruments (for example regulations, taxes, incentives, subsidies and so on) to promote the achievement of the global optimum.

However, the pursuit of self-interest by entities may lead to a suboptimal configuration and operation of the network – a situation which may be exacerbated by an imperfect or inappropriate policy or legislative environment. In order to understand what behavior is likely to be manifested and how this might differ from the global optimum or perceived ideal, it is necessary to analyze the network from a disaggregated perspective, that is, considering the operating environment and corresponding behavior of each node in the network. It has been argued that even for policy, an aggregated perspective of industry is inadequate and that a disaggregated approach to analysis is required to develop the necessary understanding of the 'values, knowledge and incentives faced by various actors in both the demand and supply sectors' (Axtell et al. 2002). Such disaggregated approaches to analysis are referred to as 'agent-based' (Deffuant 2001; Axtell et al. 2002; Bonabeau 2002; Bousquet and Le Page 2004; Monticino et al. 2004; Valkering et al. 2004). The level of disaggregation required for the modeling and analysis of networks is clearly dependent on the goal of the analysis.

Models that do not treat agents as autonomous decision-makers are used generally to explore the potential performance of the industrial network with regard to a single, clearly defined objective. For example, such modeling approaches have been used to study the minimum environmental impact or the maximum economic output that can be achieved in an industrial network. The level of detail within these models can range from broad sectoral considerations, to detailed technological assessments within network organizations. These models can be used to determine the potential performance of networks in relation to the specified objective, the constraints around network functioning, and may even be able to suggest how network performance can be enhanced, albeit within the imposed behavioral rules of network players. However, regardless the levels of detail, aggregated models do not address the autonomy of organizations and therefore cannot capture the full complexity of industrial networks.

Where modeling approaches do incorporate autonomous decision-making power of the organizations in an individual network, these can provide an understanding of the functioning of industrial networks in real life. However, most of the existing models are based on the premise that all organizations within the network are rational optimizers, which of course does not reflect reality (Conlisk 1996; Thaler 2000). In real decision situations, organizations are confronted by a large number of uncertainties which make it impossible to evaluate accurately the different consequences of their activities (Rao and Georgeff 1991). Therefore, despite their engagement with decision-making and its impact on network function, the ability of these models to develop an understanding of how industrial networks evolve is limited. New models of network function, supported by appropriate modeling tools, need to be developed to assist all network players and IAPs better to understand network behavior, and thus support strategic decision-making related to the evolution of the network in question. This is the aim of this chapter.

In order to address this aim, this chapter starts by exploring the characteristics of industrial networks, highlighting how these give rise to complex behavior, and showing the consequences for network modeling purposes. On the basis of this overview, a two-stage modeling approach is proposed. The first stage is the development of an integrative framework, which takes into account the complexity of industrial networks, and provides a better insight into how organizational structures affect the performance of network systems. The second stage is a modeling approach which derives from this framework, within which agent-level decisions are enabled, and through which the evolution of the network's performance can be tracked.

9.2   COMPLEXITY IN INDUSTRIAL NETWORKS

Industrial networks have often been described in terms which fit the description of complexity or, more specifically, the definition of complex adaptive systems (Holland 1995; Axelrod 1999; Choi et al. 2001). It is important to understand the underlying characteristics of such networks, how these give rise to system complexity, and what the consequences are for network modeling.

9.2.1   Resource Scarcity

The main driver for the existence of industrial networks is resource scarcity, resulting in interaction between those organizations which control particular resources, and others which require them. Here we adopt a deliberately broad definition of 'resources', to cover both exhaustible resources such as material and capital, and other tangible and intangible resources, such as brand names, and in-house knowledge around such aspects of business performance as technology, financing, contract management, production efficiencies and so on (Wernerfelt 1984). In this chapter, we refer to the attributes of the various resource exchanges within an industrial network (such as price, quality and so on), together with legislative and other policy instruments that impact on resources scarcity, as the 'functional' characteristics of an industrial network.

The notion of resource scarcity is important, because it is only those organizations perceived as having rare, valuable, non-substitutable or 'difficult to imitate' resources that can sustain their position in industrial networks and create competitive advantage over other organizations (Dyer and Singh 1998). The only way to create and maintain a competitive position is to cooperate with other organizations (Hakansson 1987), hence providing the modus vivendi for the network. Resource scarcity thus gives rise to the relationships that exist between organizations in the industrial network. Furthermore, these relationships define the internal structure of the system (Manson 2001) and thus the efficiency and effectiveness of the industrial network as a whole (Wilkinson and Young 2002).

The concept of resource scarcity suggests three distinct requirements for the modeling of industrial networks – the ability to capture: (1) the functional characteristics of the network; (2) the control by some organizations over these resources; and (3) the requirement to establish relationships within the network. How, when and why these three elements interact depends on the specifics of the resources, the nature of control and the potential relationships available.

9.2.2   Multiple Autonomous Decision-Makers

Since there is no organization that controls all resources in the industrial network (otherwise there would be no network), each organization in the network has agency: the ability to intervene meaningfully in the course of events in the system (Giddens 1984). Since all organizations within a network share the same environment, this implies that they are always to some extent dependent on each other, and that the network structure is always partial and temporary (Newton 2002). Hence, the structure, and thus the future performance of the network, especially in the long term, always differs from the current situation.

The notion that the network environment can, at any moment, be changed by the autonomous behavior of any of the organizations within the network has important implications for organizational behavior. Organizations try to create some kind of order by developing mental models or schemas, which play a role in two ways. Firstly, such models assist organizations in making sense of their surrounding environment by reducing complexity through the use of information cues, assumptions, predictions and simplifications (Schein 1996; Sterman 2000; Weick 2001; Maital 2004). Secondly, they provide a basis for the development and selection of appropriate courses of action through the use of routines, norms and values (Nelson and Winter 1982; Sterman 2000; Thaler 2000; Gigerenzer 2001). We refer to these cognitive and normative aspects as the 'implicit' characteristics of the network. These define how an organization evaluates different decision alternatives at any stage of network evolution (Simon 1957; Schein 1996; Sterman 2000; Thaler and Mullainathan 2000; Hertwig et al. 2004).

The notion that organizations in industrial networks always operate with a certain degree of autonomy, or 'dimensionality' in complexity terms (Choi et al. 2001), is the fundamental characteristic used to distinguish this class of complex adaptive systems from other complex systems (Kauffman 2000). Additional network complexity arises from the observation that the behavior of organizations cannot be described as rational decisions between different functional alternatives, but depends on a range of implicit characteristics, which we have defined above. Modeling the dynamics and evolution of industrial networks therefore requires the explicit consideration of both the autonomy of the individual organizations in the network, as well as the implicit characteristics that organizations use to interpret their environment. It also suggests that any relevant modeling approach should allow for continuous feedback between the organizational decision-making processes and the organization's environment.

9.2.3 Learning and Adaptation

In a changing environment, organizations need to respond to changes in their environment and adapt their strategies in order to continue and survive (Hannan and Freeman 1984; Kraatz 1998). Such adaptation is subject to different learning processes, which are both internal and external to the organization, and include such behavior as rule-following, problem-solving, learning, dealing with conflicts, imitation and so on (March 1981). Internally, organizational adaptation can occur by evaluating the consequences of decisions and adapting decision strategies or selection criteria accordingly (Argyris and Schon 1978). Externally, organizations can observe the performance of other organizations and adapt the strategies or norms and values that seem to be successful (Haunschild and Miner 1997). Adaptation can result in significant changes in organizational attributes, such as technology performance, organizational policies or goals, or even existing relationships with other organizations. Each of these changes will affect the functionality and resilience of that particular organization in the network. There is a knock-on effect too. Such change stimulates changes in other organizations, and results in the evolution of industrial networks through time.

However, organizational adaptability is subject to resistance. Some of the factors that generate this so called 'structural inertia' are internal factors such as sunk plant costs, equipment and personnel; while others, such as legislation, contracts and cultural values, are external (Hannan and Freeman 1984). The interplay between resistance and adaptability in industrial networks creates a situation in which the system's feedback loops attempt to maintain its current state. However, when system change does occur, it can be very rapid and even catastrophic (Kay and Regier 2000).

The learning and adaptation processes in industrial organizations are linked to the notion of path-dependency and co-evolution. However, and contrary to most biological systems, the evolution processes in industrial systems can be much quicker and more severe due to the large turnaround of organizations entering and leaving the network. This is easy to comprehend when it is realized that biological networks are the product of natural evolution, which instills in them a certain resilience or robustness. This cannot be said for industrial networks, which suggests that models of these networks need to reflect multiple and nested feedback loops between network organizations and their environment, and capture fast response times; and that such feedbacks be defined in terms of both functional as well as implicit characteristics.

9.2.4   Background Systems

No industrial network can be seen in isolation of its dynamic environment (March 1981; Limburg et al. 2002). For example, organizations are often linked to more than one industrial network, so changes in one network can percolate from one network to another. Furthermore, the environment's exogenous variables (for example consumer demand or stock market performance) change over time. Network dynamics are thus an important characteristic that affects the structure, performance and evolution of industrial networks. Therefore, analytical models of industrial networks should be able to accommodate both functional and implicit characteristics that change over time within the overall environment in which individual organizations, and their associated network(s), operate.

9.2.5 Social Embeddedness

Finally, as a consequence of the interrelations between different organizations, industrial networks become inherently social (Grabher 1993). Social embeddedness can be defined as 'the extent to which economic action is linked to, or depends on, action or institutions that are non-economic in content, goals or processes' (Granovetter 2005), such as underlying social networks' culture, politics and religion. The emergence of social institutions is attributed to the cognitive ability of organizations to evaluate the performance of other organizations in the network, and to assign social status to organizations depending on their short-term or long-term success (Jost 2005). Institutions are also formed through long-term interaction between specific organizations, through professionalism and through imitation because of uncertainty (DiMaggio and Powell 1983).

Institutionalization affects the behavior of individual organizations in several ways: on a cognitive level, it provides guidance for making sense of the environment in which an organization, and its network, function; and on a normative and regulatory level, it provides justification for decision-making and action (Schein 1990; Barley and Tolbert 1997). Social embeddedness thus has an important effect on the functioning and evolution of industrial networks and, through the impact of regulatory, normative and cognitive rules and values, on the decision-making processes of organizations within the network. The social embeddedness of industrial networks therefore requires that relevant network models accommodate those functional and implicit characteristics that play a role in this process of institutionalization. Both these characteristics, and the institutionalization process itself, need to be modeled at a network level, in which all the organizations that are active within the industrial network contribute to the establishment, or breakdown, of these institutional structures. Furthermore, individual organizations should be modeled such that social institutions are taken into consideration throughout any local decision-making process. This is no small task, particularly as institutional structures are themselves dynamic.

9.3   AN ANALYTICAL FRAMEWORK

The preceding discussion has identified a significant number of challenges for any modeling exercise which aims to capture some semblance of the complexity which defines industrial networks. Whilst these challenges are not to be understated, an even bigger one exists – and that is to define a structure within which the interplay between the salient features of such

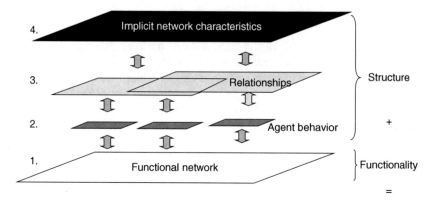

Figure 9.1   Four-level analytical framework for network analysis and design

networks is identified and can be made operational, and the associated information management protocols can be articulated. This amounts to the definition of an analytical framework. Such a framework should not only reflect the associations of functional and implicit characteristics of the network and its subentities, and map their connections, but also capture their evolution over time. A four-level framework is proposed here (Figure 9.1).

9.3.1   Level 1 – Functional Level

The first level of the framework represents the functional environment of industrial networks. It describes the different resources (capital, land, labor, and selected information relating to quantities of material required and available, price, delivery times and so on) that are under control of different organizations, or available through existing relationships. Furthermore, the functional level represents the extent to which an organization has access to information or control over resources in the network depending on its current functionality and relations, the geographical constraints, the existing infrastructure, and other functional parameters.

9.3.2   Level 2 – Organizational Decision-Making

The second level of the framework represents the decision-making processes which any organization employs to effect transformation or transaction of resources within the network. The scientific literature is well served by sources which discuss how agents make decisions, what information they use, what assumptions they make during decision-making and how they evaluate the consequences of decisions in the face of complexity (Simon 1957; Cyert and March 1963; Nelson and Winter 1982; DiMaggio and Powell 1983; Giddens 1984; Wernerfelt 1984; Schein 1990; Levy 1994; Thaler and Mullainathan 2000). These aspects can be divided into three categories: the functional characteristics of the different decision alternatives, the implicit characteristics that play a role in assisting organizations to make sense of their environment, and the implicit characteristics that form the basis of consequent decision strategies.

The functional characteristics are aspects such as price, quantity and quality of a product or service that need to be considered when choosing between alternative products or services. The relevant implicit characteristics are those cognitive aspects that define how the organization evaluates different decision alternatives – and include those modeling assumptions, estimations and predictions which help organizations and agents comprehend their place within their environment (Simon 1957; Schein 1996; Sterman 2000; Thaler and Mullainathan 2000; Hertwig et al. 2004). These implicit characteristics are supported by others which capture the decision rules that an organization uses to select a preferred course of action. Depending on the quality of information available to support network objectives, such decision rules can span classic optimization approaches to simple heuristics (Nelson and Winter 1982; Sterman 2000; Gigerenzer and Goldstein 2000).

9.3.3 Level 3 – Relationships between Organizations

Social considerations become more important in supporting decisions to establish or change business relationships in uncertain situations (Pfeffer et al. 1976). Much research has been done in the field of inter-organizational relationships to understand why and how relationships are established or terminated, and the effect of existing relationships on the behavior of the involved agents (Granovetter 1985; Eisenhardt 1989; Haunschild 1994; Podolny 1994; Ring and Van De Ven 1994; Haunschild and Miner 1997; Uzzi 1997). Many of these researchers suggest that there are several implicit characteristics of relationships that have an impact on the decision-making processes. One of the most important implicit characteristics of a relationship is the level of trust that exists between two partners (Luhmann 1984; Ring and Van De Ven 1994; Uzzi 1997). Other implicit characteristics are the level of fairness, benevolence, reliability, loyalty, past experience or status (Kumar et al. 1995; Ridgeway et al. 1998; Selnes and Gonhaug 2000; Narayandas 2005).

We contend that all these aspects of interorganizational relationships can be incorporated into the third level of the analytical framework, typically by the use of proxy measures in heuristic form. Some discussion of how this might be achieved is offered in section 9.5 below. Each organization may choose to attribute different implicit characteristics to existing and potential relationships. Furthermore, there are several characteristics of the relationship itself that inform the use of other implicit characteristics in the decision-making processes of organizations within the network. For example, if the organization operates in a market which is highly uncertain, then the probability increases that agents will favor a potential partner with which they have had positive interaction experience in the past (Podolny 1994).

9.3.4   Level 4 – Industrial Network Characteristics

The fourth level of the analytical framework represents those implicit characteristics of the network as a whole that play an important role in the decision-making processes of the individual organizations and thus in network evolution. Much work has been done in the field of sociology and economics to describe and understand the interaction between the individual decision-making processes of the organizations and the institutions on a network level (DiMaggio and Powell 1983; Giddens 1984; Granovetter 1985; Hodgson 1988; Haunschild and Miner 1997; Newton 2002). Multiple factors come into play here. Firstly, trade policies and legislation imposed by governments and industry organizations set the framework within which agents can trade legitimately. Legitimacy originates from interaction between organizations and is an emergent property on a network level, but as soon as legitimacy is formalized it can be mapped directly on the functional level of the analytical framework. Secondly, norms and values are established within the network as a whole, and players who do not conform to these are likely to be excluded. Finally, societal expectations as a whole will impact on the 'licence to operate' of any agent in the network.

It is not only important to recognize the effect of network institutions on individual decision-making processes, but also to pay attention to the process of the establishment and change of institutions. Organizations with value systems different to those of organizations within established networks will find difficulties in entering the network, since they do not fit into the existing order. Although the process of institutionalization introduces some stability in terms of entrenched structures, it also reduces the flexibility of the network as a whole by constraining its adaptability, much like any overdetermined system. As such, it simultaneously creates an environment which is vulnerable to exogenous forces. Examples of exogenous disruptions are new technologies, new regulation or laws, or major economic shifts. The potential for disrupting exogenous forces is a characteristic of a network and amplifies market uncertainty within that particular network (Barley and Tolbert 1997). It is in this process of establishment and change of institutions where non-industrial agents, such as governmental agencies, advocacy groups and customers, affect the performance and evolution of industrial networks.

These theories on organizational behavior in networks suggest that the evolution of industrial networks cannot be studied independently of the individual decision-making processes of the agents themselves, and the relational characteristics between agents and the institutions of the industrial network as a whole. Any meaningful analytical framework, and resulting modeling approach(es), needs to recognize this.

9.3.5 Interconnectivity between Different Levels of the Framework

Two key aspects of the structure of the proposed analytical framework require elaboration. Firstly, the different functional and implicit characteristics that affect network evolution and functioning will not always necessarily fit uniquely into a single level of the framework, and all factors may play a role at various levels within the framework. For example, a company's routine that is identified on the decision-making level of the organization (Level 2 of the framework) can be transposed to the network level (Level 4 of the framework) if the company is successful and it becomes a standard procedure for most companies within the network. Secondly, the interrelationship between the different characteristics on the different levels should be highlighted. As an example, the decision to invest in a new production technology can attract a large number of new customers, which subsequently has a positive effect on the status of that particular organization in the network, which in turn makes the organization more attractive to new suppliers.

9.4   APPLICATION OF THE ANALYTICAL FRAMEWORK

The analytical framework presented above is able to capture the full range of industrial network characteristics, and thus provides a more realistic basis for understanding the evolution of such networks. Of course, a framework alone is of little use without a modeling approach that supports the capture of the necessary information to populate the different levels of the analytical framework. The aim in developing the modeling approach

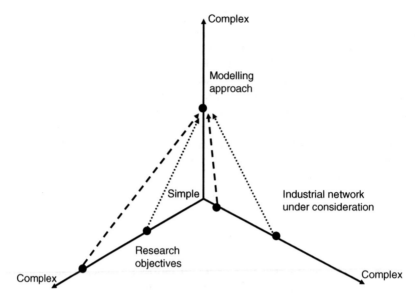

Figure 9.2   *The development of modeling approaches on the basis of the research objectives, the character of the specific industrial network under consideration, and the analytical framework*

should be to provide a comprehensive understanding of the dynamics of industrial networks, and thus assist in the development of responsive business strategies and policies by all players in the network.

The question as to which modeling approach should be developed in studying industrial networks depends on two factors: the research objectives and the particularities of the industrial network under consideration. Figure 9.2 suggests how the relative complexity of both might map onto an appropriate modeling approach. The three axes each represent a continuum from 'simple' to 'complex'. This progression captures the increase in the number of regularities, feedback loops and relationships between the different system characteristics on the different system scales, which needs to be described to represent any given system concisely (Gell-Mann 1995). The more interdependency between different scales (that is, the more interdependency between behavioral, relational and network characteristics), the more complex a system is and therefore the more complexity needs to be represented in the modeling approach (Bar-Yam 2005).

The complexity of research objectives can be characterized by the time and space dimensions of the problem, the scope of the system and the specific number of research objectives. For example, supply chain management is a discipline that has developed modeling approaches for industrial networks over many years. In this case, analysis objectives have focused mainly on the operational aspects of supply chains, covering logistics, inventory control and production times, and so on (Yee and Platts 2006). Performance measures reflect short time scales of months, days or hours, and the external environment can be treated as an equilibrium. Furthermore, these analyses typically focus on only one aspect of the system, namely economic performance, while other objectives such as contribution of the network to environmental or social welfare are disregarded. Such an analysis would be defined as 'simple', in that the regularities (the rules that describe the behavior of the system) are localized, are connected through predetermined, and restricted time-space, represent no feedback between the environment and the system, and interact only in terms of economic characteristics. In contrast, when considering for example the strategic performance of an industrial network against sustainability objectives, the regularities that are needed to describe the network increase vastly, and the analysis requirements are much more 'complex'. The interaction between local decisions and the environment can have long-term impacts (for example lock-in effects of investments). Simultaneously, uncertainty increases the importance of implicit characteristics. Incorporating environmental and social impacts increases the number of characteristics and interactions that affect the decision-making processes; and the learning processes that need to be represented increase the feedback loops between actions, the consequences and the adaptation processes within organizations.

The second axis represents the industrial network itself. Section 9.2 identified those characteristics of a network which give rise to its underlying complexity. The particular degree of complexity can be understood only by examining the specific network in more detail. With respect to resource scarcity, complexity increases if resource exchanges serve multiple purposes (for example conversion of materials to multiple products) and if resources can be used in different ways. Both characteristics increase the number of alternatives available to the organizations within the network, and therefore system complexity. The complexity also increases due to limits in the level of control that particular organizations have within the network. For example, in an environment with limited control, organizations rely on their trust in other organizations to make decisions about resource exchange (Li and Berta 2002). The modeling of trust requires the incorporation of implicit characteristics on a relational level, which in turn requires more feedback loops and interaction to be modeled. The same arguments hold for other implicit characteristics, such as those that play a role in learning and adaptation, the effects of the background system and the degree of social embeddedness of the system.

The complexity of the modeling approach should match the complexity of both research objectives and the specific industrial network in question. This complexity is determined through two modeling decisions: (1) the level of aggregation with which the organizations in the network are represented; and (2) the number of levels of the analytical framework that are captured. The level of aggregation depends on the level of control that agents have within the network, and how this affects network performance. An increase in the number of levels of the analytical framework results in an increased number of emergent properties, the inclusion of more characteristics and more feedback loops and interactions between them, and thus a more comprehensive representation of industrial network complexity. If the research objective is to understand the evolution of industrial networks, the modeling approach should consider the potential for organizations to make autonomous decisions. The choice of the level of aggregation is less important here, as the level at which decisions take place itself determines the requisite level of model detail. However, the way in which decision-making processes are modeled becomes an important consideration. From simple heuristics (of the 'if then else' variety), through classic optimization routines, to more participative decision-making processes with explicit consideration of value judgments or imitation, the decision-making process will dictate the extent to which implicit characteristics are considered.

Overall, it is our view that the more uncertainty which exists within models of network structure and performance, the greater is the need for consideration of implicit characteristics at any level of the framework. Explicit modeling of organizational decision-making processes requires, by definition, an agent-based modeling approach. However, such an approach can be augmented with system dynamics modeling approaches to represent institutional processes on a network level. The challenge is to work with (a set of) modeling approaches which allow key uncertainties to be identified, quantified where possible, and their impact explored systematically.

9.5 DEVELOPMENT OF THE MODELING APPROACH

Section 9.4 emphasized the need to consider explicitly the research objectives and the particular detail of the network under investigation as part of model development. Whilst this is perhaps obvious, it poses real challenges to modelers seeking to develop generic approaches. There is no 'one size fits all' modeling approach. That said, the structure of the analytical framework provides a useful skeleton upon which to hang various modeling tools.

As a demonstration of this approach, consider an industrial network whose contribution to sustainability is the key research question. This provides sufficient context for the following discussion about modeling approaches. The performance of such a network depends on: (1) the individual contributions of organizations to sustainability; and (2) the relationships and exchange of resources between the different organizations involved. In recent years, it has been recognized that, especially in terms of environmental performance, large gains can be achieved by introducing innovations and instruments for total supply networks instead of focusing on the performance of the single organization (Weizacker et al. 1997; Day 1998). It is therefore important to focus on how the network configuration impacts upon the overall sustainability of the network, which can only be modeled by explicit consideration of how individual organizations choose between different potential partners and how these choices affect the evolution of the network (Hodgson 1988; Grabher 1993; Gadde et al. 2003). Figure 9.3 shows the position of strategic decision-making within the analytical framework (Level 2) and how such decisions are affected by different network characteristics.

The decision structure displayed in Figure 9.3 is a simplified version of general models for strategic decision-making found in management

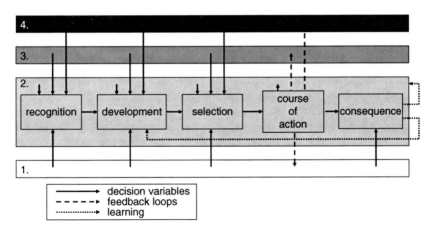

Figure 9.3   The effect of functional and implicit characteristics on the decision-making process of organizations, and the effects of feedback between organizations and their environment

sciences (Cyert et al. 1956; Cyert and March 1963; Cohen et al. 1972; Mintzberg et al. 1976; Clemen 1996). The decision process consists of three stages; recognition, development and selection. In the 'recognition' phase, the organization identifies particular stimuli that trigger the need for strategic decisions. These stimuli can be exogenous, or problems or opportunities that occur or arise within the organization, or within the network (Moss 1981); or they can be developed intentionally through periodical evaluation of the organization's position (Moncrieff 1999). The recognition of stimuli is informed by the functional characteristics of the organization and its environment. However, it is also informed by implicit characteristics, such as an organization's interests, the uncertainty associated with the stimuli or the perceived benefits of taking action (Mintzberg et al. 1976). On the basis of these stimuli, organizations develop alternative courses of action to respond to the stimuli. This stage is often referred to as strategy formation (Mintzberg et al. 1976; Mintzberg and Lampel 1999). Sometimes these responses can be straightforward, in other cases less so. For those latter situations, organizations use implicit characteristics as 'guidelines', 'rigidities' or routines (Nelson and Winter 1982; Hodgson 1988) to make sense of their environment and react upon the information they receive.

The last stage is the selection of the appropriate course of action, which often is a choice between action and no action, and which is a function of the subjective and shared values of the decision-makers (Schein 1996). Several models are available which describe how decision-makers either explicitly or implicitly deal with data, values and criteria in their final decision (Tversky and Kahneman 1981; Howard 1988; Belton and Stewart 2002).

Consequently, feedback loops exist between the course of action and the functional and implicit characteristics of the agent, or those of its relationships, or of the network as a whole. This is shown by the various connections between Level 2 of the framework, and the other levels. For example, the choice by an organization of a specific partner affects the implicit characteristics of that particular relationship, such as the length of their relationship, the loyalty between the two partners, or the level of trust between them.

The last stage is the learning process that occurs after each decision process. The agent becomes aware of the consequences of its action and can compare this with its initial intent. If the consequences are positive, the strategy formation in the development phase is reinforced (single-loop learning) or the norms and values used to recognize stimuli or develop and select actions are reinforced (double-loop learning) (Smith 2001). In the case of negative outcomes, strategy formation or norms and values can be altered in order to achieve better outcomes in the next decision process.

9.5.1 Choice of Modeling Tools

The modeling approach described above highlights the information flows and feedback loops which drive network evolution. However, it says little about the selection of tools necessary to generate this information, or to quantify the effect of the various feedback loops. What is clear is that the evolution of the network is informed principally by activity at Level 2 of the framework, that is, at a level of decision-making by the individual organizations or agents within the network. Hence it is appropriate to focus here on tools which support agent-level decision-making and, in particular, on ways of capturing those key implicit characteristics at the various levels of the analytical framework which affect agent cognition.

The constraints within which individual agents operate may either promote or inhibit the establishment and/or termination of relationships between agents. However, understanding how such relationships evolve is vital for understanding the performance of the overall performance of the network, whatever the research question. In terms of sustainability assessment, previous studies have identified that 'mutual trust' and loyalty are key factors that determine whether or not sustainability can be achieved (Sterr and Ott 2004). But how can trust and loyalty be incorporated into modeling tools? According to the German philosopher Luhmann, trust should be understood specifically in relation to risk. Trust presupposes the awareness of risk by individual agents, who develop responses in accordance with their predisposition to risk (Luhmann 1984). However, Giddens argues that another feature of trust is confidence: the 'more or a [*sic*] less taken-for-granted attitude that familiar things will remain stable' (Giddens 1990).

Trust as a response position to business risk, and trust on the basis of confidence in another's goodwill within the relationship (fairness) are two different perspectives, both of which need to be accommodated in strategic decision-making by agents (Ring and Van De Ven 1994). The risk perspective an organization takes to other organizations can be decomposed into three characteristics. Firstly, the risk perspective is related to the risk profile of an organization: the production methods used, the insurance mechanisms in place and the quality of the product and/or resource. These are functional characteristics of an organization. Secondly, risk perspective is determined by past experience. Podolny (1994) found that if uncertainty is high, organizations will prefer to engage with those organizations with whom they have transacted in the past. He also found that if market uncertainty is high, the probability increases that organizations engage in transactions with those of similar status. Status has two structural components: the size of the organization and the number of connections an organization has. The size of the organization is used as an approximation for how successful an organization is and can be measured in terms of production volume, turnover or number of employees, depending on the industrial network (Haunschild and Miner 1997). The number of connections an organization has does not only provide an indication of the scope of resource exchange between organizations, but the presence (or absence) of connections also provides information about the underlying quality of that organization (as perceived by other organizations to which it is connected) (Podolny 2001). In conclusion, the risk perspective related to trust can be decomposed into the risk profile of a potential partner, past experience and status; where status can be decomposed into the size of the organization and the number of connections an organization has.

The second characteristic of trust is a perspective of the level of 'fairness' within a relationship. The level of fairness can be seen as a determinant of relationship quality (Kumar et al. 1995) and operates as a lower-band constraint on choosing the appropriate partner. It operates as a heuristic that permits organizations to be responsive to stimuli and to speed up decision-making (Uzzi 1997). Kumar et al. (1995) suggest that reliability and benevolence are two key factors that determine the perception of fairness within a relationship. An organization is perceived as reliable when it continuously satisfies the agreed conditions about transactions of material and information. Benevolence is perceived as the willingness of the other organization to act in a way that benefits the interests of both parties. These implicit characteristics of organizations have a strong positive effect, directly and indirectly, on the degree of fairness between two organizations (Selnes and Gonhaug 2000).

Similarly, the notion of 'loyalty' can be decomposed into a set of functional and implicit characteristics on the different levels of the analytical framework. Selnes and Gonhaug (2000) found that reliability and benevolence are two attributes that not only affect the level of 'fairness' between two organizations, but also increase the loyalty between two partners through an increased mutual satisfaction. Both attributes are required to explain loyal behavior. Reliability informs the level of satisfaction associated with exchange of resources between organizations, and this gives rise to a stronger sense of loyalty. However, satisfaction alone is not sufficient to explain loyal behavior (Narayandas 2005). An organization needs also to display a level of benevolence, associated with the provision of services beyond those for which it has been contracted. The third characteristic that affects loyalty is the length of a relationship. Ring and Van de Ven (1994) found that, as the temporal duration of the relationship between two organizations increases, the likelihood decreases that the organizations will terminate their relationships when a breach of commitment (the fourth characteristic) occurs. The reason for this behavior is that past experience provides a great deal of information about the other organization, while the search for new partners will confront an organization with an uncertain situation.

The above discussion provides a basis for decomposing the rather elusive notions of trust and loyalty into implicit characteristics for which it is possible to find proxy attributes. For example, 'reliability' explicitly refers to relationship outcomes, and can thus be measured in terms of the numbers of years that a supplier delivers according to contract agreements. 'Benevolence' refers to the process of the relationship, and can be measured by the degree to which the supplier is willing to divide the benefits and burdens of the relationship. The benefits of a relationship are the parties' earnings in comparison to other potential partners, while the burdens constitute efforts and investments to establish and/or maintain the relationship.

Figure 9.4 presents a simplified example of how trust and loyalty can be modeled in terms of the functional and implicit characteristics that impact upon the decision outcome. The example in Figure 9.4 describes a situation in which a particular organization recognizes that it is being outperformed by its competitors and seeks to explore alternative supplier

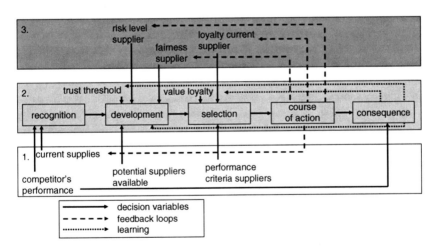

Figure 9.4   Process of modeling the effects of trust on the decision-making process of individual agents and the evolution of the network

contracts as a means of addressing this (the 'recognition' stage of Figure 9.3).

It is suggested here that the organizational decision-making can be modeled as a two-stage process. In the development phase, potential partners are screened on the basis of trust (this being a 'yes'/'no' criterion, based on the 'risk level' and 'fairness' argument made above). Without previous experience, the risk level of a potential partner is assessed against a particular threshold, which is determined by functional characteristics of the environment itself. A young, innovative network will have lower thresholds than an established industrial network. If organizations do have previous experience with a potential supplier, the proxies for reliability and benevolence can be used to assess whether or not the potential supplier is trustworthy. Only those potential partners that can be trusted will then be considered in the selection phase (Figure 9.3) on the basis of the performance criteria of the decision-maker. This selection forms the second phase of the decision-making exercise by agents. It is here that formal approaches to multi-criteria decision analysis (MCDA) can be applied, whereby decision-makers can evaluate the performance of courses of action based on a wide range of (often conflicting) criteria, and informed by value judgments relating to preference. The performance criteria may be either quantitative (as in the case of most functional characteristics), or qualitative (for example loyalty).

MCDA incorporates a range of evaluation techniques (Belton and Stewart 2002). For the agent-level decisions considered here, we propose that value function methods hold most promise, in that they allow for articulation of intra-criterion preference relationships, as well as intercriteria ones. What is attractive about such methods is their intuitive ease of application. They rely on the formulation of partial value functions for each criterion, which map performance scores onto a nominal value basis. Such partial value functions can be created for quantitative indices, or for qualitative metrics captured by constructed scales. Thereafter it is possible to develop a sense of the overall desirability of any course of action by simple additive weighting of these partial value scores. Here, weights are scaling constants which map the preference relationships of the decision-maker, and are informed explicitly by the range of performance scores in each individual decision criterion.

Our prior experience in the use of MCDA approaches for business decision-making (Petrie et al. 2004; Basson and Petrie 2007a, 2007b) has demonstrated that it is possible to overlay explicit considerations of risk and uncertainty on the MCDA approach. We contend that these methods and tools can be taken up directly for the analysis of industrial networks, and have demonstrated this for a particular energy network

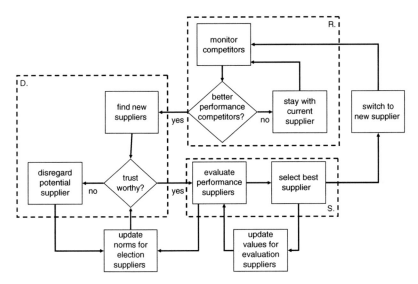

Figure 9.5   Modeling logic for agents making strategic decisions about choice of suppliers

(Kempener et al. 2006; Beck et al. 2008), though details of this case study are not given here. At this stage, and by way of example only, we show in Figure 9.5 the modeling logic which can be used by individual agents in selecting partners with whom to transact resource exchanges. The important point here is that both functional and implicit characteristics inform the decision-making practices of individual agents.

Here, the R, D and S components refer to the recognition, development and selection stages of Figure 9.3, and parallel the various stages of a rigorous decision analysis cycle. At the level of decision-making by individual agents, learning takes place through the feedback of organizational performance into the adaptation of the norms in the development stage, and the value functions and weightings in the selection stage.

The example presented above does not explicitly consider the impact of implicit characteristics at a network level on the strategic decision taken by individual agents. However, as a general rule, to engage with the social complexity of industrial networks, explicit consideration of implicit network characteristics is required. Examples of the impact of social complexity are (Basson 2004):

- the asymmetry of power and conflict both within organizations within the network, and among the IAPs which inform the social environment in which the network operates;

- differences in access to information, knowledge and extent of political and social empowerment amongst participants in the network;
- changing worldviews and their underlying political and economic realities.

These and other examples of models engaging with the effects of social complexity on the performance and evolution of industrial networks can be found in Petrie et al. (2006), Kempener et al. (2006) and Beck et al. (2008).

9.6   CONCLUSION

There is much interest in analyzing the functioning of industrial networks in order to guide improvements in their performance – no longer focusing on economic realities alone, but spurred on by a commitment to sustainability. Recognizing that such networks are complex entities, operating within an even more complex and uncertain environment, poses real challenges for analysts and designers.

In this chapter we have attempted to characterize industrial networks according to their key features, focusing largely on where and how decision-making power is exercised, and what the implications of this are for network learning and evolution. We have used this to suggest that networks are defined by a mix of functional and implicit characteristics, the articulation of which is necessary to engage with network operation (or design). Beyond this, we have proposed a hierarchical framework for network analysis, which captures the requisite information flow around network function, and points to the modeling detail required to populate the framework. The key challenge for any analysis of industrial networks is to provide the requisite information to key decision-makers in an accessible, and internally consistent, format. This is where the proposed framework has real value, as it helps track information flow in the context of a specific analytical objective.

There is no 'one size fits all' modeling approach to support this framework. Here, we advocate the use of a combination of agent-based, and systems dynamic approaches, within which use is made of the tools of multi-criteria decision analysis to inform decision-making practices by agents within the network, and soft systems 'problem-structuring' approaches to guide the formulation of analysis objectives. Such an approach provides a comprehensive platform for consideration of all the relevant agent and network characteristics.

REFERENCES

Argyris, C. and D.A. Schon (1978), *Organizational Learning: a Theory of Action*, Reading, MA, Addison-Wesley.

Axelrod, N.N. (1999), Embracing Technology: The Application of Complexity Theory to Business, *Strategy and Leadership*, **27**(6): 56–8.

Axtell, R.L., C.J. Andrews and M.J. Small (2002), 'Agent-Based Modeling and Industrial Ecology', *Journal of Industrial Ecology*, **5**(4): 10–13.

Barley, S.R. and P.S. Tolbert (1997), 'Institutionalization and Structuration: Studying the Links Between Action and Institution', *Organization Studies*, **18**(1): 93.

Bar-Yam, Y. (2005), 'About Engineering Complex Systems: Multiscale Analysis and Evolutionary Engineering', in S. Brueckner, G. Di Marzo Serugendo, A. Karageorgos and R. Nagpal (eds), *Engineering Self Organising Systems: Methodologies and Applications*, Berlin: Springer-Verlag, pp. 16–31.

Basson, L. (2004), 'Context Compensation and Uncertainty in Environmental Decision Making', Department of Chemical Engineering, University of Sydney, Sydney.

Basson, L. and J. Petrie (2007a), 'An Integrated Approach for the Management of Uncertainty in Decision Making Supported by LCA', *Environmental Modeling and Software*, **22**(2): 167–76.

Basson, L. and J. Petrie (2007b), 'A Critical Systems Approach to Decision Support for Sustainable Business', *Computers and Chemical Engineering*, **31**(8): 876–88.

Beck, J., R. Kempener, B. Cohen and J. Petrie (2008), 'A Complex Systems Approach to Planning, Optimization and Decision Making for Energy Networks', *Energy Policy*, **36**(8): 2803–13.

Belton, V. and T.J. Stewart (2002), *Multiple Criteria Decision Analysis: An Integrated Approach*, Dordrecht, The Netherlands: Kluwer Academic Publishers.

Bonabeau, E. (2002), Agent-Based Modeling: Methods and Techniques for Simulating Human Systems, *PNAS*, **99**(90003): 7280–87.

Bousquet, F. and C. Le Page (2004), 'Multi-Agent Simulations and Ecosystem Management: A Review', *Ecological Modeling*, **176**: 313–32.

Castells, M. (2000), *The Rise of the Network Society, The Information Age: Economy, Society and Culture*, Vol. 1, 2nd edition, Oxford: Blackwell Publishers.

Choi, T.Y., K.J. Dooley and M. Rungtusanatham (2001), 'Supply Networks and Complex Adaptive Systems: Control versus Emergence', *Journal of Operations Management*, **19**(3): 351–66.

Clemen, R.T. (1996), *Making Hard Decisions: An Introduction to Decision Analysis*, Pacific Grove, CA: Duxbury Press.

Cohen, M.D., J.G. March and J.P. Olsen (1972), 'A Garbage Can Model of Organizational Choice', *Administrative Science Quarterly*, **17**(1): 1–25.

Conlisk, J. (1996), 'Why bounded rationality?', *Journal of Economic Literature*, **34**(2): 669.

Cyert, R.M. and J.G. March (1963), *A Behavioral Theory of the Firm*, Cambridge, MA: Blackwell Publishers.

Cyert, R.M., H.A. Simon and D.B. Trow (1956), 'Observation of a Business Decision', *Journal of Business*, **29**(4): 237–48.

Day, R.M. (1998), *Beyond Eco-Efficiency: Sustainability as a Driver for Innovation*, Washington, DC: World Resources Institute.

Deffuant, G. (2001), 'Improving Agri-Environmental Policies: A Simulation Approach to the Cognitive Properties of Farmers and Institutions (Final Report)', Aubière Cedex, France, Cemagref; http://wwwlisc.clermont.cemagref. fr/ImagesProject/FinalReport/references_list.htm.

DiMaggio, P.J. and W.W. Powell (1983), 'The Iron Cage Revisited: Institutional Isomorphism and Collective Rationality in Organizational Fields', *American Sociological Review*, **48**(2): 147–60.

Dyer, J.H. and H. Singh (1998), 'The Relational View: Cooperative Strategy and Sources of Interorganizational Competitive Advantage', *Academy of Management Review*, **23**(4): 660.

Ehrenfeld, J. (2004), 'Can Industrial Ecology be the "Science of Sustainability"?', *Journal of Industrial Ecology*, **8**(1–2): 1–3.

Eisenhardt, K.M. (1989), 'Agency Theory: An Assessment and Review', *Academy of Management Review*, **14**(1): 57.

Forrester, J.W. (1961), *Industrial Dynamics*, Cambridge, MA: MIT Press.

Gadde, L.-E., L. Huemer and H. Hakansson (2003), 'Strategizing in Industrial Networks', *Industrial Marketing Management*, **32**(5): 357–64.

Gell-Mann, M. (1995), 'What is Complexity?', *Complexity*, **1**(1): 1–9.

Giddens, A. (1984), *The Constitution of Society*, Berkeley and Los Angeles, CA: University of California Press.

Giddens, A. (1990), *The Consequences of Modernity*, Stanford, CA: Stanford University Press.

Gigerenzer, G. (2001), 'Decision Making: Nonrational Theories', in N.J. Smelser and P.B. Baltes (eds), *International Encyclopedia of the Social and Behavioral Sciences*, Oxford: Elsevier Science, pp. 3304–9.

Gigerenzer, G. and D.G. Goldstain (2000), 'Reasoning the Fast and Frugal Way: Models of Bounded Rationality', in T. Connolly, H.R. Arkes and K.R. Hammond (eds), *Judgement and Decision Making*, Cambridge: Cambridge University Press, pp. 621–50.

Gladwin, T.N. and J.J. Kennelly (1995), 'Shifting Paradigms for Sustainable Development: Implications for Management Theory and Research', *Academy of Management Review*, **20**(4): 874.

Grabher, G. (1993), 'Rediscovering the Social in the Economics of Interfirm Relations', in G. Grahber (ed.), *The Embedded Firm, on the Socioeconomics of Industrial Networks*, London: Routledge, pp. 1–33.

Granovetter, M. (1985), 'Economic Action and Social Structure: The Problem of Embeddedness', *American Journal of Sociology*, **91**(3): 481–510.

Granovetter, M. (2005), 'The Impact of Social Structure on Economic Outcomes', *Journal of Economic Perspectives*, **19**(1): 33–50.

Hakansson, H. (1987), *Industrial Technological Development: A Network Approach*, London: Croom Helm.

Hannan, M.T. and J. Freeman (1984), 'Structural Inertia and Organizational Change', *American Sociological Review*, **49**(2): 149–64.

Haunschild, P.R. (1994), 'How Much Is That Company Worth? Interorganizational Relationships, Uncertainty, and Acquisition Premiums', *Administrative Science Quarterly*, **39**(3): 391–411.

Haunschild, P.R. and A.S. Miner (1997), 'Modes of Interorganizational Imitation: The Effects of Outcome Salience and Uncertainty', *Administrative Science Quarterly*, **42**(3): 472–500.

Hertwig, R., G. Barron, E.U. Weber and I. Erev (2004), 'Decisions from

Experience and the Effect of Rare Events in Risky Choice', *Psychological Science*, **15**(8): 534–40.

Hodgson, G.M. (1988), *Economics and Institutions*, Cambridge: Polity Press.

Holland, J.H. (1995), *Hidden Order, How Adaptation Builds Complexity*, Reading, MA, Menlo Park, CA and New York: Addison-Wesley Publishing Company.

Howard, R.A. (1988), 'Decision Analysis: Practice and Promise', *Management Science*, **34**(6): 679–95.

Jost, J. (2005), 'Formal Aspects of the Emergence of Institutions', Santa Fe Institute Working Papers, New Mexico, 13.

Kauffman, S. (2000), *Investigations*, Oxford: Oxford University Press.

Kay, J. and H.A. Regier (2000), 'Uncertainty, Complexity, and Ecological Integrity: Insights from an Ecosystem Approach', in P. Crabbe, A. Holland, L. Ryszkowski and L. Westra (eds), *Implementing Ecological Integrity: Restoring Regional and Global Environmental and Human Health*, Dordrecht, The Netherlands and Boston, MA: Kluwer, pp. 121–56.

Kempener, R., L. Basson, R. Malan, B. Cohen, J. Beck and J. Petrie (2006), 'The Use of MCDA to Model Agent Decisions in Complex Industrial Networks', 18th International Conference on Multiple Criteria Decision Making 2006, Chania, Greece.

Kraatz, M.S. (1998), 'Learning by Association? Interorganizational Networks and Adaptation to Environmental Change', *Academy of Management Journal*, **41**(6): 621–43.

Kumar, N., L.K. Scheer and J.B.E.M. Steenkamp (1995), 'The Effects of Supplier Fairness on Vulnerable Resellers', *Journal of Marketing Research*, **32**(1): 54–65.

Levy, D. (1994), 'Chaos Theory and Strategy: Theory, Application, and Managerial Implications', *Strategic Management Journal*, **15**(Summer Special Issue): 167–79.

Li, S.X. and W.B. Berta (2002), 'The Ties that Bind: Strategic Actions and Status Structure in the US Investment Banking Industry', *Organization Studies*, **23**(3): 339.

Limburg, K.E., R.V. O'Neill, R. Costanza and S. Farber (2002), 'Complex Systems and Valuation', *Ecological Economics*, **41**(3): 409–20.

Luhmann, N. (1984), *Social Systems*, Stanford, CA: Stanford University Press.

Maital, S. (2004), 'Daniel Kahneman: On Redefining Rationality', *Journal of Socio-Economics*, **33**: 1–14.

Manson, S.M. (2001), 'Simplifying Complexity: A Review of Complexity Theory', *Geoforum*, **32**(3): 405–14.

March, J.G. (1981), 'Footnotes to Organizational Change', *Administrative Science Quarterly*, **26**(4): 563.

Mintzberg, H. and J. Lampel (1999), 'Reflecting on the Strategy Process', *Sloan Management Review*, **40**(3): 21–30.

Mintzberg, H., D. Raisinghani and A. Théorêt (1976), 'The Structure of "Unstructured" Decision Processes', *Administrative Science Quarterly*, **21**(2): 246–75.

Moncrieff, J. (1999), 'Is Strategy Making a Difference?', *Long Range Planning*, **32**(2): 273–6.

Monticino, M., M. Acevedo, B. Callicott, T. Cogdill, M. Ji and C. Lindquist (2004), 'Coupled Human and Natural Systems: A Multi-Agent Based Approach', in C.

Pahl-Wostl, S. Schmidt, A.E. Rizzoli and A.J. Jakeman (eds), *Complexity and Integrated Resources Management: Transactions of the 2nd Biennial Meeting of the International Environmental Modeling and Software Society, Volume 1*, Manno, Switzerland: iEMSs, pp. 196–202.

Moss, S. (1981), *An Economic Theory of Business Strategy*, Oxford: Basil Blackwell.

Narayandas, D. (2005), 'Building Loyalty in Business Markets', *Harvard Business Review*, **83**(9): 131–9.

Nelson, R.R. and S.G. Winter (1982), *An Evolutionary Theory of Economic Change*, Boston, MA: Belknap Press.

Newton, T.J. (2002), 'Creating the new Ecological Order? Elias and Actor-Network Theory', *Academy of Management Review*, **27**(4): 523.

Petrie, J., L. Basson, P. Notten and M. Stewart (2004), 'Multi Criteria Decision Analysis: The Case of Coal to Electricity in South Africa', in A. Azapagic and R. Clift (eds), *Sustainable Development in Practice: Case Studies for Engineers and Scientists*, London: John Wiley, pp. 367–96.

Petrie, J., B. Cohen, L. Basson and R. Kempener (2006), 'Analysis and Design of Industrial Networks for Sustainability Objectives', 21st European Conference on Operational Research Reykjavik, Iceland.

Pfeffer, J., G.A. Salancik and H. Leblebici (1976), 'The Effect of Uncertainty on the Use of Social Influence in Organizational Decision Making', *Administrative Science Quarterly*, **21**(2): 227–45.

Podolny, J.M. (1994), 'Market Uncertainty and the Social Character of Economic Exchange', *Administrative Science Quarterly*, **39**(3): 458–83.

Podolny, J.M. (2001), 'Networks as the Pipes and Prisms of the Market', *American Journal of Sociology*, **107**(1): 33–60.

Rao, A.S. and M.P. Georgeff (1991), 'Modeling Rational Agents within a BDI-Architecture', in M.N. Huhns and M.P. Singh (eds), *Readings in Agents*, San Francisco, CA: Morgan Kaufmann Publishers, pp. 317–28.

Ridgeway, C.L., E.H. Boyle, K.J. Knipers and D.T. Robinson (1998), 'How do Status Beliefs Develop? The Role of Resources and Interactional Experience', *American Sociological Review*, **63**(3): 331–51.

Ring, P.S. and A.H. Van De Ven (1994), 'Developmental Processes of Cooperative Interorganizational Relationships', *Academy of Management Review*, **19**(1): 90.

Schein, E.H. (1990), 'Organizational Culture', *American Psychologist*, **45**(2): 109–19.

Schein, E.H. (1996), 'Culture: The Missing Concept in Organization Studies', *Administrative Science Quarterly*, **41**(2): 229–40.

Selnes, F. and K. Gonhaug (2000), 'Effects of Supplier Reliability and Benevolence in Business Marketing', *Journal of Business Research*, **49**(3): 259–71.

Simon, H.A. (1957), 'A Behavioral Model of Rational Choice', in H.A. Simon (ed.), *Models of Man: Social and Rational*, New York and London: John Wiley & Sons, pp. 241–60.

Smith, M.K. (2001), 'Chris Argyris: Theories of Action, Double-Loop Learning and Organizational Learning', *the encyclopedia of informal education*, available at http://www.infed.org/biblio/b-learn.htm.

Spiegelman, J. (2003), 'Beyond the Food Web: Connections to a Deeper Industrial Ecology', *Journal of Industrial Ecology*, **7**(1): 17–22.

Sterman, J.D. (2000), *Business Dynamics, Systems thinking and Modeling for a Complex World*, Boston, MA: Irwin McGraw-Hill.

Sterr, T. and T. Ott (2004), 'The Industrial Region as a Promising Unit for Eco-Industrial Development: Reflections, Practical Experience and Establishment of Innovative Instruments to Support Industrial Ecology', *Journal of Cleaner Production*, **12**(8–10): 947–65.

Thaler, R.H. (2000), 'From Homo Economicus to Homo Sapiens', *Journal of Economic Perspectives*, **14**(133–41).

Thaler, R.H. and S. Mullainathan (2000), 'Behavioral Economics', NBER Working paper series, Cambridge, MA, 13.

Tversky, A. and D. Kahneman (1981), 'The Framing of Decisions and the Psychology of Choice', *Science*, **211**(4481): 453–8.

Uzzi, B. (1997), 'Social Structure and Competition in Interfirm Networks: The Paradox of Embeddedness', *Administrative Science Quarterly*, **42**(1): 37.

Valkering, P., J. Krywkow, J. Rotmans and A. van der Veen (2004), 'Simulating Stakeholder Support for River Management', in C. Pahl-Wostl, S, Schmidt, A.E. Rizzoli and A.J. Jakeman (eds), *Complexity and Integrated Resources Management: Transactions of the 2nd Biennial Meeting of the International Environmental Modeling and Software Society, Volume 1*, Manno, Switzerland: iEMSs, pp. 184–9.

Weick, K.E. (2001), *Making Sense of the Organization*, Malden, MA: Blackwell Publishing.

Weizacker, E. von, A.B. Lovins and L.H. Lovins (1997), *Factor Four: Doubling Wealth – Halving Resource Use: A Report to the Club of Rome*, London: Earthscan.

Wernerfelt, B. (1984), 'A Resource-Based View of the Firm', *Strategic Management Journal*, **5**(2): 171–81.

Wilkinson, I. and L. Young (2002), 'On Cooperating: Firms, Relations and Networks', *Journal of Business Research*, **55**(2): 123–32.

Winston, W.L. (1994), *Operations Research: Applications and Algorithms*, Belmont, CA: International Thomson Publishing.

Yee, C.L. and K.W. Platts (2006), 'A Framework and Tool for Supply Network Strategy Operationalisation', *International Journal of Production Economics*, **104**(1): 230–48.

10. Understanding and shaping the evolution of sustainable large-scale socio-technical systems

Igor Nikolic, Gerard P.J. Dijkema and Koen H. van Dam

10.1 INTRODUCTION

The focus of this chapter is on the creation of a framework for modeling and simulating the growth, evolution and dynamics of regional industrial clusters. Why is this relevant? Currently the world is experiencing dramatic and rapid change. Regional industrial clusters dominated by process industry, such as the Rotterdam-Rijnmond area and Groningen Seaports in the Netherlands, the German Ruhr Area, the Antwerp region in Belgium, Le Havre in France and Teesside in the United Kingdom that largely evolved in the twentieth century must find a way to make timely adaptations to novel and stringent ecologic, economic and supply chain pressures and demands. These include, amongst others, the nascent reduced availability of cheap fossil feedstock, dwindling of suitable metal ore resources, dilution of metal stock, limits to or penalties on CO_2 emissions, and global competition for feedstock and commodity, specialties and pharmaceuticals markets (Verhoef 2004; Dijkema 2004).

The objective of this chapter is the creation of a framework that will support systematic and rational shaping of sustainable networked industrial systems on a regional scale. One may also understand this work as a plea to recognize and study the effects of the decentralization of decisions that determine network growth.

The work presented in this chapter represents the theoretical background of a decision support tool developed, amongst others, in the course of the CostaDue project (Dijkema and Stikkelman 2006). Due to the confidential nature of the underlying project data, all specific references to industrial activities in the actual cluster have been removed.

In the CostaDue project, Groningen Seaports, a regional development agency (RDA), together with the Groningen province authorities initiated a process to transform the Delfzijl and Eemshaven industrial areas from a chlorine-based chemical site to a bio-based energy cluster. By modeling the industrial network growth, the RDA is supported in deciding which interested clients to accept in the region and which ones not to accept, in order to achieve the best possible transition path for their region.

10.2 APPROACH

To meet the objective the central question addressed is how to understand and formalize the evolutionary mechanisms of industrial cluster evolution. To this end, we suggest viewing these systems as large-scale socio-technical systems and to model their evolution.

10.2.1 Large-Scale Socio-Technical Systems: λ-Systems

'Large-scale socio-technical systems' is a term used in Thomas Hughes's system theory (Hughes 1987; Bijker et al. 1987). To avoid the lengthy acronym, we propose the term λ-system. The term indicates a class of systems that span technical artifacts embedded in a social network, by which a large-scale, complex socio-technical artifact emerges. λ-systems include, for example, organizations, companies and institutions that develop around and sustain a particular industrial system, be it a single plant, industrial complex or set of interconnected supply chains.

   In any λ-system a physical network is intricately connected with a social network to form a complex socio-technical system. The physical network comprises manufacturing installations (nodes) and infrastructure such as pipelines, roads, power grids and so on (links). The social network consists of stakeholders: operating companies, investors, local and national governments, regional development agencies (RDAs), non-governmental organizations, customers and so on. Their interconnections consist of social information exchange, contracts, ownership relationships and so on.

10.2.2 Industrial Ecology and λ-systems

Industrial ecology (IE) research has extensively studied the materials and energy exchange, cascading and loop closure in λ-systems. These include, for example, the chemical processes and metal manufacturing industries and the utility industries for electric power and natural gas. These studies predominantly focus on technical artifacts and physical systems, and often neglect the social network. In λ-systems, however, soft but important relationships exist on top of the materials–energy links. In the operational and tactical layers of this social network, middle management takes short-term economic decisions on the exchange of feedstock, products, utilities and services in response to market dynamics. In the strategic layer private and public actors decide on and influence the structure of the network by adding, changing or removing physical assets (Dijkema et al. 2005). Operational, tactical and strategic behavior of specific agents is determined by their identity. In this layer stakeholder identity is defined, be it governmental control or entrepreneurial spirit. Thus, the social network adds non-physical yet fundamental dimensions to the system and its behavior.

While the technical subcomponents of λ-systems can be engineered, the social network and the system network structure cannot. Rather, their present state has evolved as the result of a series of discrete events and of continuous optimization, which are determined by the actions, interests and influence of the stakeholders. Their decisions and actions are driven by the pressures exerted from the λ-system's external environment: global markets; (inter)national rules and regulations; availability of and access to capital, knowledge and skilled labor.

Reversing the argument, λ-systems may be shaped in this evolutionary process. However, one of the fundamental properties of an evolving system is that their ultimate fate cannot be determined in advance. They are intractable (Dennet 1996). Thus no model or simulation can be fully predictive of the details of the development of any particular cluster in response to a series of deliberate actions.

10.2.3 Objective and Hypothesis

The dos and don'ts of industrial cluster development are the holy grail for any regional development authority, because the societal cost of waiting for industrial clusters (not) to evolve may be dramatic. An important objective of the work, therefore, is to increase our knowledge of λ-system growth patterns by simulation of physical and social network evolution, where technologies and stakeholder identities as well as external regimes vary. The ultimate goal is to provide decision support for those involved in steering the development of industrial clusters.

As stated, the development of industrial clusters, λ-systems, is intractable. We propose, however, that a managed evolution in both physical and social dimensions is required to shape λ-systems and ensure their sustainable future and feasibility. Furthermore, we propose that such evolutionary process can be steered by the design of the λ-system's external world (top-down) and the adaptation and expansion of the available set of technologies or system components (bottom-up).

Our hypothesis is that the use of adequate models of λ-systems evolution will improve decision-making on industrial cluster development. By playing out scenarios in a simulation, we may reduce uncertainty by answering 'what if?' questions and communicate the insights back to the systems stakeholders.

10.2.4 Focus and Structure

The subject of this chapter is the development of a framework to help understand and shape the evolution of λ-systems, which consists of a modeling methodology for λ-systems and a simulation environment.

First, the foundations for the framework are introduced. Subsequently, the modeling methodology is presented, with an emphasis on the development of generic agent representations. In section 10.5 the outline of the simulation environment, its implementation, use and limitations are addressed. Finally, conclusions are drawn and future work is discussed.

10.3   FOUNDATIONS

In this section a succinct introduction is given of the theoretical foundations used for understanding the required state and for shaping the evolution of λ-systems. No attempt is made at extensively reviewing the theoretical foundations from industrial ecology, complex adaptive systems theory, network evolution theory, agent-based modeling and knowledge engineering.

10.3.1   Industrial Ecology

The IE community has postulated useful paradigms on the required state of λ-systems (sustainability) and preferred structure (networked ecosystems) (Frosch and Gallopoulos 1992). While providing an image of the system's physical performance, the images from life cycle assessment, mass flow accounting, and substance flow analysis concern largely static systems, however, and suffer from lack of content on system structure and technology representation.

In the situation where the dynamics of systems are important and where, rather than analysis, system design is called for, IE approaches are largely inadequate (Verhoef 2004; Dijkema 2004). An action-oriented industrial ecology approach is needed (Nikolic et al. 2005a) to develop a body of knowledge on the evolution of λ-systems. Therein, answering the 'how come?' rather than 'how to make?' is the leading question. Answering it requires an explicit description of the external regime, decision and learning processes of agents that determine λ-system evolution.

10.3.2   Complex Adaptive Systems Theory

D.C. Mikulecky (2001) defines complexity as the property of a real-world system that is manifested in the inability of any single formalism to be adequate to capture all its properties. λ-systems are made up of a physical network and a social network. In theory, the physical network may be completely described by first principles models, because all model behavior follows from universal laws of nature. The social network however cannot, because natural laws (first principles) are not the basic elements of behavior. They are just boundary limits to what behavior is possible. It may thus be seen that the making of useful λ-system descriptions requires distinctly different formalisms for the description of each distinct system aspect. Since these formalisms are not derivable from each other, Mikulecky's criterion is met: λ-systems are complex.

A complex adaptive system (CAS) is a system consisting of many agents that interact with each other in various ways. Such a system is adaptive if these agents change their actions as a result of the events in the process of interaction (Vriend 1995). In λ-systems the physical network evolves over time because of actions in the social network. Thus, λ-systems are adaptive systems, where the system structure and content can be changed from within the system, by agents that develop new behavior (through learning and strategic behavior), accept new agents or adopt novel technologies. This is confirmed by Kay (2002), who also identified similar characteristics of λ-systems.

By adopting a CAS view and by inclusion of multiple dimensions, dynamic patterns of system behavior emerge from local interactions between system elements (Kaufmann 1992, 1995, 1996; Holland 1996; Newman 2003; Kay 2002). System structure is not prescribed in advance. Interaction occurs at multiple dimensions and across multiple levels. Thus, whilst the span and nature of interactions is defined, the total system behavior is not – it emerges.

CAS theory recognizes that, in order to understand the evolution of real, complex adaptive systems a multitude of perspectives is required to capture the richness of the dynamics of the system and the behavior of subcomponents. Key characteristics of λ-systems are: they exhibit emergent properties, have the ability to learn, their evolution is path-dependent, and they are restricted in their ability to respond to inputs.

10.3.3   Network Evolution Theory

According to Newman (2003) a network is a set of items called nodes, with connections between them called links. 'Network' is thus a conceptualization of reality, where any system component is either a node or a link; either a thing or a connection between things.

One of the main issues of interest when studying industrial networks is the relation between network structure and network function. This is especially evident in the case of petrochemical clusters and their performance on sustainability. Is it possible to maintain the industry's societal function, the production of chemicals and energy, while reorganizing its structure to deal with a resource problem and at the same time increase its sustainability performance (Dijkema 2004)?

One of the dominant approaches to studying network growth is through using NK models (Kauffman 1992, 1995). We maintain Kauffman's basic idea, nodes searching for other nodes to connect to. We could reduce the element of stochastics as used for example by Barabasi et al. (2001), however, because we can introduce realistic observed decision-making processes and technology descriptions of petrochemical clusters. Furthermore, in λ-systems nodes are capable of creating new nodes only under certain conditions.

When discussing evolution, the concept of fitness is of paramount importance. A fitness landscape is a description of the conceptual environment of an individual where every point in the landscape implies a certain fitness. The landscape has peaks, which the individual tries to reach. This search requires adaptation, and thus represents the process of evolution of an individual or a species. A species evolutionary process never happens in isolation, however, as there is always more than one species evolving. Since it is likely that the evolution of one species changes the fitness landscape of the other – and vice versa – the fitness landscapes of both species are coupled and dynamic (Hordijk and Kauffman 2005). This represents the situation of most stakeholders in the social network, which have to deal with competition.

Through the evolutionary process, λ-systems adapt to exploit or discover as much of the available design space as possible (Dennet 1996). Such self-organizing hierarchical open (SOHO) systems always expand to maximize the use of exergy available in the environment (Kay 2002). Thus, λ-systems emerge when there is enough energy, knowledge or economic potential. These principles of self-organization are the basic drivers of our agents. A petrochemical firm will try to make as much money as possible from the market and its assets, so that it can make more 'firm biomass' in the form of assets.

Once a network has evolved, its characteristics need to be defined, preferably by a set of metrics. In network theory, however, to date metrics have been developed for networks consisting of one type of node and one type of link only (Newman 2003). These may provide a starting point for suitable metrics of λ-systems that capture multiple types of nodes (industrial facilities) and links (mass, energy, money, information).

10.3.4   Agent-Based Modeling

Jennings (2000) defines an agent as 'an encapsulated computer system that is situated in some environment, and that is capable of flexible, autonomous action in that environment in order to meet its design objectives'. Agents are reactive, proactive, autonomous and social software entities.

Furthermore one should realize that agent-based models (ABMs) can be understood as state machines, which historically originate from cellular automata (CA) research (Mitchell et al. 1994). State machines are mathematical descriptions of systems which consist of a set of states and the transitions between these states. An ABM in effect is a scaled-up state machine, where instead of two states, we have several hundred states, distributed across a multidimensional parameter space. Instead of a few transition rules, we have business heuristics and game-theoretical models for state transition.

Other noteworthy uses of agent-based models in understanding different aspects of λ-systems are the land use claims model of Ligtenberg et al. (2001), the model of innovation in industrial districts by Albino et al. (2006), and models of a small firm by Andrews et al. (2005).

Garcia-Flores and Wang (2002) and Aldea et al. (2004) suggest that agents not only need a communication language and a standard interface, but, in order to interact, they also need a shared model of the world. We have used knowledge engineering principles to develop such language and interface.

10.3.5   Knowledge Engineering

In the artificial intelligence community ontologies have been developed as a useful means of knowledge representation. Ontologies are formal descriptions of entities and their properties, relationships, constraints and behavior that are not only machine-readable but also machine-understandable. When two agents are communicating about certain concepts we want to be sure that they give the same interpretation to these concepts. Therefore it is of the utmost importance to specify unambiguously each concept and its meaning. This equates to the creation of a standard interface by defining a common language.

In an ontology the meaning of each concept is stored not only in subclass relationships ('is a', for example apple is a fruit, red is a color) but also in property relationships ('has a', for example an apple has a red color).

In other words, an ontology contains explicit formal specifications of the terms in the domain and the relations among them (Gruber 1993).

The actual mechanism of the λ-system's evolution is the decision-making in the social network. Ontologies provide a representation for domain knowledge that the agents base their decisions on. This separates domain knowledge (ontology) from the operational knowledge (decision-making rules). The formal description of the domain can be used to formalize the decision-making rules, which are the intelligence of the agents. There are several ways to formally model the 'intelligence' of agents (Luger and Stubblefield 1993). We will use rule-based reasoning (Forgy 1982) which is commonly used in expert systems to model tacit knowledge. The inference engine of an expert system checks each rule against the known facts in the knowledge base, executing rules that apply. The Rete algorithm (Forgy 1982) is an efficient implementation of the rule search and matching algorithm. It consists of a dynamic network of nodes, where each node is a rule having a memory of facts which satisfy that node.

Mathematical optimization is used to complement the expert system approach. In cases where agents are optimizing we will use mathematical game theory as a model of their behavior. Concepts that can be used are Stackelberg and inverse Stackelberg games (Olsder 2005), and Nash bargaining games (Nash 1950). These games can be played to reach local optima, Pareto optima or system-level optima.

10.3.6   Conclusion

To date the industrial ecology paradigm has largely been elaborated by focusing on the required state of physical networks and their analysis. λ-systems however, are complex, adaptive systems that consist of interconnected physical and social networks. They evolve and exhibit emergent properties and behavior. Therefore, their representation and simulation must be based on network evolution concepts. Agent-based network models can be ameliorated by incorporating adequate technology and agent descriptions. Knowledge engineering principles can be used to formalize external world description, technology and agent characteristics. Rule-based reasoning and game theory provide models for agent behavior and interaction.

10.4   MODELING METHODOLOGY

λ-systems are inherently complex. With time, system structure, content and behavior evolve. In this section, a new modeling methodology is presented that respects and captures these characteristics, in order to enable the creation of meaningful simulation models to outplay λ-system evolution. Therein, instead of *ex ante*, prescriptive modeling of system structure, content and behavior, we present a model of the evolution of λ-systems that will allow *ex post* evaluation of the system structure, content and behavior.

We have labeled this methodology 'action-oriented industrial ecology' (AOIE), which has been extensively described in Nikolic et al. (2006b). In the AOIE model, only the possible ingredients of the system (technologies, agents) and their characteristics are defined; the evolution of the λ-system is governed only by the external regime and the complex, adaptive system's internal dynamics.

10.4.1 Overview

The AOIE methodology (the modeling methodology as discussed in this section) comprises a knowledge application development cycle to capture the problem and formalize an appropriate model and a simulation cycle wherein the model is combined with case-specific agents and information to visualize the AOIE results (see Figure 10.1). The methodology is an extended version of that developed by Nikolic et al. (2005b) and van Dam et al. (2006). Only the system decomposition and formalization steps are addressed here.

On completion of the inventory and structuring phases of the system decomposition, an ontology can be created. Thereby, the domain and system description are formalized and generalized. This is the foundation for the creation of an ontology. A more extensive discussion on ontology creation can be found in Noy and McGuinness (2000).

An ontology for the formal description and modeling of industrial networks as λ-systems has been developed using Protégé (Gennari et al. 2001). An excerpt of the full ontology (Nikolic et al. 2006a) is presented as Figure 10.2.

In the following sections part of the ontology is used to discuss the agents interface, their layout and their decision-making behavior.

10.4.2 Agent Interface and Decision-Making

The interface between all model components – technologies, agents and the external world – is based on the λ-system ontology. It provides a standard naming scheme for agent functions and structure for all components. A single, common interface gives the possibility to compartmentalize the model as it uniquely defines communication between any two parts of the

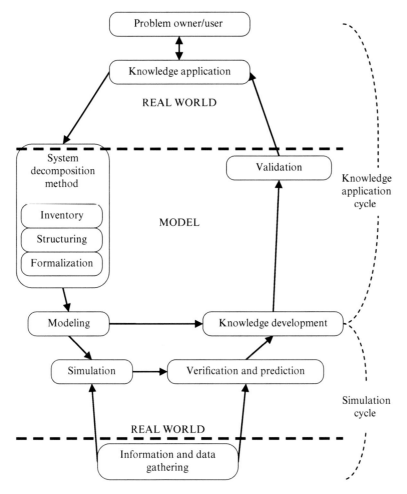

Figure 10.1   Structure of the action-oriented industrial ecology approach

model. It also opens the way to define a variety of links: physical flows, social relations in the form of contracts, financial transactions and so on.

Decision-making rules (for example strategic decision-making based on technology and economic parameters) can be written by, or defined in close cooperation with experts in the field. Once the relevant parts of the ontology are defined, it allows formalization of the design problem in the domain experts' language. By adhering to a standard ontology, these components become modular and reusable. This is crucial in developing evolutionary models because it allows for parts of the model to evolve and change.

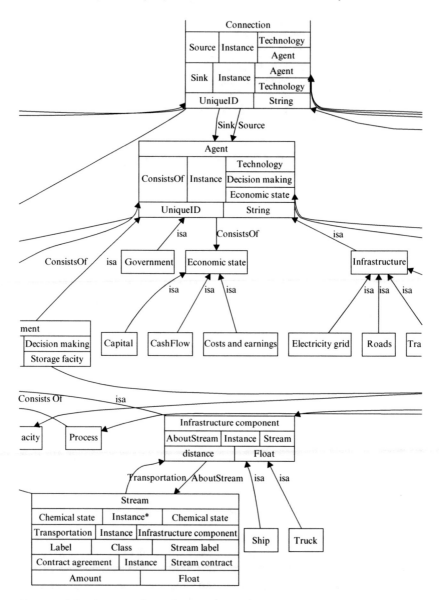

Figure 10.2   Excerpt from the AOIE ontology

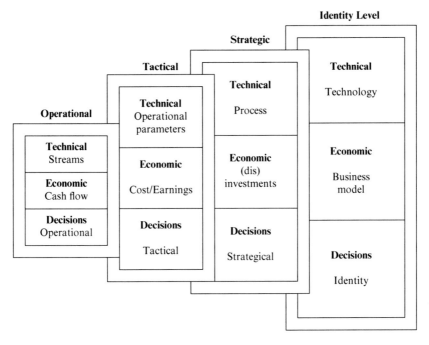

Figure 10.3   Internal layered structure of the agent

10.4.3   Multilevel Decision-Making

In our approach to model λ-systems, we consider both the physical network and the social network to consist of agents (nodes) that are linked. The general agent model structure is presented in Figure 10.3. Agent behavior can be defined at four levels: identity, strategic, tactical and operational. These represent decision-making rules and data on different temporal scales. Together with deciding on which activities to perform, the higher hierarchical levels also influence the behavior of the agent by constraining decisions on the lower level. The resulting hierarchy of behavior and meta decision-making leads to a 'behavioral selection algorithm'.

At each level an agent may have three components: technology, economics and decision-making. This set-up allows us to define any kind of agent. An industrial plant in the physical network, for example, will have a technology. Its behavior is: 'when provided with the right inputs, specified outputs will be generated'. Some of its economics will be fixed (for example invested capital); others will be determined by the market, such as product prices.

In the social network, agents can be specified that represent different roles in a production organization. There are many different ways a decision can be made. In the operational domain, for example, when selecting a contract, an agent can just choose the cheapest or consider the element of trust or familiarity with the supplier. At the tactical level the decision-making determines which of these two modes of operational behavior are to be employed. Previous experiences of an agent can influence tactical behavior by choosing different tactical subsets of behavior at the strategic level. Thus, in the simulation, the overall agent behavior is a result of the decision-making process across all levels and compartments, defined by appropriate rule sets and reasoning algorithms.

In the following sections, we will discuss this internal structure of the agents.

10.4.4   Operational Level

At the operational level, very short-term, practical decisions are made. They answer questions of the agent like: 'Do I have the resources that I need to produce my products?', 'Do I have enough cash flow to afford the resources?', and 'Am I making enough money from the sale of my products?'

At this level the technology is represented by a transformation function, expressed through the ontology, where the exact stoichiometry of the process is encoded. It states that for each x units of input, be it a resource or utility, y units of output are produced. Whether these products are considered waste or a product is indicated using a classification structure from the ontology. Furthermore, at this level, the making and breaking of short-term contracts is executed. In this trading process the availability of resources from suppliers and ability of clients to handle products is considered.

10.4.5   Tactical Level

At the tactical level the medium-term decisions and operational behavior selections are made. Questions answered can be: 'Which specific technical configuration will I employ, at which capacity level do I operate the process?', 'What are my costs and earnings?', 'When do I invest to optimize or scale the process at hand?' and 'How do I have to adapt my sourcing and sales contracts to optimize my cash flow?'

In reality and in the model most technologies are scalable, with minimum and maximum capacities. Many are able to switch between operational modes. Each transition in state has an associated cost and transition time. Other economic data at this level are prices of resources and products.

Decision-making at this level can be an optimization of costs considering the supply and demand of resources and products, the costs of switching and medium-term expectations of price developments. As already mentioned, these can be either optimizations or heuristics. The tactical level may include rules that set operational behavior.

10.4.6   Strategic Level

At the strategic level, the following types of questions are answered: 'What is the economic profile of the currently implemented type of technology?' and 'Which type of the technology should I implement, considering the long-term market developments for products and resources and the costs of the technology?'

Economic data on this level are related to bringing new technologies into being: investment, running costs and decommissioning costs; duration of development, implementation, decommissioning and so on. The agent's strategic level considers the life phase of its asset portfolio and chooses the appropriate economic models. Tactical economic decisions are set to different types during the development phase – normal operation or phase-out of a technology.

Decision-making at this level may determine which types of tactical behavior can be employed.

10.4.7   Identity Level

This level answers questions such as: 'Which type of an agent am I?', 'Which main economic model do I use?' and 'How and when do I want to change these elements?'

The identity of the agent describes whether this is a production, infrastructure, government and so on type of agent. It selects the subset of possible technical components from all possible technological components available in the model. The main type of economic model is selected at this level. These can be for-profit, not-for-profit, charity and so on. Each main type is associated with a possible subset of types, such as aggressive optimizations, passive heuristics and so on.

10.4.8   The Simulated World

Apart from agents and links, the simulated world contains three other important components: scenarios, world market and the natural environment.

A scenario contains dynamics observed in the external world that cannot be influenced by the agents. A scenario describes, for example, how the world market behaves and which set of technologies and identities are available to the agents. The scenarios represent the modelers' will in the simulation.

The world market is the aggregation of all the other agents that are not explicitly modeled. If an agent in a regional cluster needs a certain resource that is not produced within the region, it can always be sourced from the world market. Likewise, all outputs that cannot be sold locally can be exported to the world market. The world market has its own internal price and demand dynamics, which are considered to be a part of a given scenario.

The natural environment is modeled as a single agent, whose behavior is to receive all streams labeled 'waste', and to provide all the resources labeled 'ubiquities', freely available resources such as air. Depending on the scenario, agents may need to pay a certain amount for emitting wastes to the environment.

10.4.9   Conclusion

The foundations have been used to develop a generic methodology for the modeling and simulation of λ-systems. The methodology for action-oriented industrial ecology rests on a generic ontology for λ-systems. Therein, agents are the nodes in both the physical and social network. The generic model of an agent consists of four levels: identity determines strategic, tactical and operational behavior. The agent may have any subset of three compartments: technology, economy and decision-making. Scenarios, world market and (natural) environment are part of each simulated world.

10.5   SIMULATION

In this section some implementation aspects, the types of outcomes from the simulation, ways it can(not) be used, and some metrics are discussed as well as the simulation scope and limitations. Finally, validation and verification are addressed.

10.5.1   Implementation

A short overview of the tools used for implementation is given. The design goal of the implementation was to develop a generic, modular, expandable simulation environment for λ-systems.

The simulation is written in the Java 1.5 programming language. It uses the Repast (North et al. 2006) agent-based framework. The ontology is defined through the Protégé library. The ontology structure and instances is stored in a PostgreSQL database on a Linux server. Prior to a simulation run, the database is consulted, the Protégé knowledge base is constructed, and instances translated into an isomorphic Java class structure and instantiated. Repast agents are initialized and receive these objects, as prescribed in the ontology. Actual decision-making within the agents is performed using the JBoss Rules forward chaining inference engine. This allows for an unprecedented flexibility in layering decision-making code at run time, without the need to change the agent code.

10.5.2   Agent Network Evolution

Resulting from the interactions between different levels within an agent, in the process of following its decision-making and depending on its environment, agents display a particular behavior. Agents search for resources, and attempt to sell their products to other agents, or on the world market. As a result of these interactions, which were not predetermined, an interaction network structure evolves. The types of interactions are summed up in Figure 10.4.

In Figure 10.4 we see five types of connections between agents. For example, at the identity level we see ownership and social group interactions. At the strategic level we see trust relationships. At the tactical level we see joint infrastructural connections, both physical and monetary. Finally, at the operational level we see contractual and mass and energy flow relationships. Each of these connections has its own properties such as duration, distance, price, capacity and so on. Exact details are specified in the ontology.

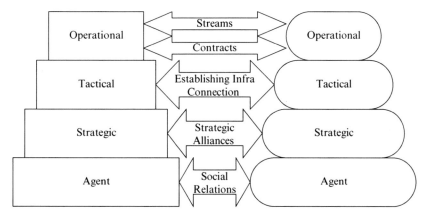

Figure 10.4   Types of connections between agents

From the interactions between the agents a complex multidimensional network emerges. As a part of the emergent structure this network also has temporal dynamics. The communication between different agents determines what actions the agent can perform. It effectively limits their behavioral space. Since agents influence and depend on each other, their interaction effectively forms a coupled fitness landscape, as described in the introduction. Each change in an agent's behavior directly affects how successful, or fit, the other agents are. By running the simulation in discrete time steps, we create generations of agent networks, allowing evolutionary processes to take place.

10.5.3   Use

The modeling methodology and the ontology help the user make very explicit assumptions about the mechanisms and objects that exist in 'world'. This in turn allows for creation of very explicit scenarios. The simulation is thus a 'what if?' scenario testing tool. It allows us to reflect on possible system structures arising from the now explicit dynamics of industrial ecosystems. The simulation's predominant advantage is that it offers greater insight in a complex problem, where many unobvious interactions exist.

Using the presented modeling methodology and simulation, one can take encoded assumptions on the world and behavior of the agents and observe the possible types of system behavior. Assuming the computer makes no mistakes, these are then the necessary consequences of the encoded assumptions. It is therefore a test for 'common sense' when trying to understand the evolutionary processes in λ-systems.

More specifically, we use the model to elucidate the dynamics of industrial ecosystems. First, we grow possible network structures from given description of firms and their decision-making in a region. The similarities and differences between evolved structure, and the structure observed in reality, give a sense of alternatives and directions for development. Furthermore, this gives an estimate of real-world deviations from the ideal situation described by the model.

Subsequently, by introducing realistic dynamics in the world market, we can observe the network's response: such as the effects of an extreme oil price on a mixed chemical and bio-based cluster. Another application we developed examines the effects of new disruptive technologies on the cluster. During simulation runs, the simulation world 'creates' new technological options randomly or in a predefined order. We can observe changes in the cluster metrics and economic indicators as a response to this system-level innovation.

Related to the world market scenarios, we can adapt the simulation world's parameters to model new policies, taxes, subsidies or laws. These can be either exogenous, or can be introduced by the government agent according to its own internal logic.

10.5.4 Metrics

In order to understand the emerging system structure we have developed a number of metrics which we will briefly present here.

When studying the network structure of the emergent cluster, we use graph metrics such as the average shortest path length (Dijkstra 1959), global network efficiency, degree of connectivity, degree of completeness and degree distribution. In addition we perform a Fruchterman–Rheingold graph layout analysis to identify cluster structure (Fruchterman and Reingold 1991).

Apart from graph metrics, we perform an economic cluster analysis by tracking the fraction of internal links/total links, the fraction of internal circulating mass/total mass, the fraction of internal circulating money/total money, the profit per invested unit of capital, the margin per invested unit of capital and the total asset value of the cluster. The simulation also tracks the average price of all goods traded within the simulated network, as well as the margins, profits and total assets of each individual agent. These are calculated using standard accounting algorithms.

In the next section, we will discuss the main limitations of the method and simulation.

10.5.5 Limitations

It is important to realize the limitations to this approach. In the first place, the simulation is not an expert system; it cannot make a decision on how to influence λ-systems. Its maximum temporal resolution is a quarter of a year. Furthermore, with the current data, the model cannot predict or describe the exact future behavior of a single specific player. It only models classes of agents and their typical behavior. The economic parameters are not suited for exact prediction of costs or profits of individual agents. To expect accurate quantitative predictions of clusters economic performance is not realistic.

The model is not suitable for highly detailed planning of infrastructures, such as exact paths of pipelines and such. Since the model focuses on the regional cluster level, it will not predict mega trends in the external world. However, if such trends are available, they can very easily be incorporated into the scenarios.

In summary, the simulation is meant only to explore the space of possible types of structure and dynamics patterns.

10.5.6   Verification and Validation

In order to validate the correct functioning of the model, several approaches can be taken. First, extreme parameter settings are applied to the simulation in order to check for logical consistency. Subsequently, parameter sweeps are performed across the entire parameter space. While this is computationally intensive, the parameter sweeps allow us to create attractor maps (Milnor 1985), which couple portions of the parameter space to model states. The number and location of the attractors offer insight into both the logical consistency and the spread of possible outcomes of the model.

Sensitivity analysis can be performed around the edges of the attractor space to identify any chaotic components. Most simulations will have a number of parameters that will cause the model to become chaotic, and they need to be identified correctly.

Validation offers very different challenges. Since λ-systems are path-dependent, exact replay of their evolutionary path requires very detailed knowledge and availability of data, and a detailed description of the mechanisms of interaction. When constructing models, it is impossible to discriminate whether a deviation from the real world is due to an inaccuracy of the input data or due to the inadequacy of description of the behavioral mechanisms. However, historical replays remain as the main validation technique.

10.5.7   Summary

An outline of the λ-system simulation framework developed is given. The main use of simulation of λ-system evolution is to underpin strategic management and policy-making. Model verification is feasible. Model validation by exact replay of historic evolution probably cannot be achieved, but from useful λ-system models evolutionary patterns emerge that resemble historic development.

10.6   CONCLUSIONS AND OUTLOOK

In this chapter a framework for modeling and simulating the growth, evolution and dynamics of regional industrial clusters has been presented.

The framework consists of a modeling methodology coupled with a simulation environment. Therefore it can be seen as a generic methodology to realize action-oriented industrial ecology. Both the methodology and the simulation model have been embedded in an umbrella knowledge application and rest on a generic AOIE ontology.

The framework is generic: it gives us the possibility to develop models of any large-scale socio-technical system or λ-system and simulate it. Thus, we can elucidate λ-system evolution and study the possibilities of 'directed growth' under conditions of decentralized decision-making on network growth. In short, the framework is our means to explore the (im)possibilities of shaping λ-systems. In retrospect, its development can also be understood at a meta-level: our objective was to develop the framework, our means is the modeling methodology and the result is a simulation environment.

The central theme of our research is to elucidate the dynamics of regional λ-systems evolution in order to help shape their transition towards sustainability. The completion of the AOIE framework suggests that it is feasible to enhance our knowledge of regional λ-systems and shape them for sustainability.

At the time of writing, we have completed a model of the Groningen Seaports industrial cluster transition to a bio-based industrial cluster (Blokker 2006; Nikolic and Dijkema 2006). In this model, we have examined the possible transition paths from a chlorine-based cluster to a bio-based cluster. The model source code is available for inspection to the interested reader.

As future work, we are starting a model of syngas industry–infrastructure co-evolution in the Rotterdam-Rijnmond region, and a prototype model of CO_2 emissions trading and electricity production portfolio development has been developed (Chappin 2006).

The framework and the results from these cases provide ample directions for future work. The first direction is the collection of more suitable data. An extensive cataloguing campaign is being set up to create a library of technology descriptions, optimization algorithms and business heuristics. The second direction is a more tight and extended integration between modeling and simulation within the framework. The ontology can be used as a knowledge management system for agent models and as a foundation of a human language interface to define the elements of the simulation.

The third area is work on the creation of an even more generic ontology that spans a very large diversity of λ-system domains and descriptions. A final area is the implementation and use of traditional IE metrics derived from mass and energy balances in the methodology, such as energy dissipation, material diffusion and exergy loss. This would allow tracking of system performance during network evolution, and tracking of the amount and energy content of resources and utilities used for system functioning.

ACKNOWLEDGMENTS

The authors acknowledge the support received from the Next Generation Infrastructures Foundation (http://www.nginfra.nl). The authors wish to thank A. Jamaković for help with the network metrics, S. Blokker and E. Chappin for help with computer code and illustrations.

REFERENCES

Albino, V., N. Carbonara and I. Giannoccaro (2006), 'Innovation in Industrial Districts: An Agent-Based Simulation Model', *International Journal of Production Economics*, **104**(1): 30–45.

Aldea, A., R. Banares-Alcantara, L. Jimenez, A. Moreno, J. Martinez and D. Riano (2004), 'The Scope of Application of Multi-Agent Systems in the Process Industry: Three Case Studies', *Expert Systems with Applications*, **26**(1): 39–47.

Andrews, A., A. Baptista and A. Patton (2005), 'A Multi-Agent Model of a Small Firm', http://radburn.rutgers.edu/andrews/projects/abm/EPAppr4-6-04.pdf.

Barabasi, A.L., H. Jeong, Z. Neda, E. Ravasz, A. Schubert and T. Vicsek (2001), 'Evolution of the Social Network of Scientific Collaborations', arXiv:cond-mat/0104162 v1, 10 Apr 2001, available at http://arxiv.org/pdf/cond-mat/0104162.

Bijker, W.E., T.P. Hughes and T.J. Pinch (1987), *The Social Construction of Technological Systems: New Directions in the Sociology and History of Technology*, Cambridge, MA: MIT Press.

Blokker, S.B. (2006), 'Co-Evolution in the Process Industry: An Agent Based Model for the Eemshaven Chemical Cluster', MSc Thesis, Delft.

Chappin, E.J.L. (2006), 'Carbon Dioxide Emission Trade Impact on Power Generation Portfolio. Agent-Based Modeling to Elucidate Influences of Emission Trading on Investments in Dutch Electricity Generation', MSc Thesis, Delft.

van Dam, K.H., I. Nikolic, Z. Lukzo and G.P.J. Dijkema (2006), 'Towards a Generic Approach for Analyzing the Efficiency of Complex Networks', in Chun-Yi Su and Jagannathan Sarangapani (eds), *Proceedings of the 2006 IEEE International Conference on Networking, Sensing and Control*, Ft Lauderdale, FL, 23–25 April, IEEE, pp. 745–50.

Dennet, D.C. (1996), *Darwin's Dangerous Idea: Evolution and the Meanings of Life*, reprint edition, New York: Simon & Schuster.

Dijkema, G.P.J. (2004), 'Process System Innovation By Design: Towards a Sustainable Petrochemical Industry', Dissertation, TU Delft.

Dijkema, G.P.J., D.J. van Zanten and J. Grievink (2005), 'Public Roles and Private Interests in Petrochemical Clusters: Model-based Decision Support of the Regional Development Board', *Chemical Engineering Research and Design*, **83**(A6): 739–51.

Dijkema, G.P.J. and R.M. Stikkelman (2006), 'Positionpaper Eemsdelta, Perspectieven en kansen voor duurzame economische ontwikkeling van de Eemsdelta; Een systematisch verkenning', TU Delft, in Dutch, available upon request.

Forgy, C.L. (1982), 'Rete: A Fast Algorithm for the Many Pattern/Many Object Pattern Match Problem', *Artificial Intelligence*, **19**: 17–37

Frosch, R.A. and N.E. Gallopoulos (1992), 'Towards an Industrial Ecology', in A.D. Bradshaw, R. Southwood and F. Warner (eds), *The Treatment and Handling of Wastes*, London: Chapman & Hall, pp. 269–92.

Fruchterman, T.M.J. and E.M. Reingold (1991), 'Graph Drawing by Force-Directed Placement', *Software, Practice and Experience*, **21**: 1129–64.

Garcia-Flores, R. and X.Z. Wang (2002), 'A Multi-Agent System for Chemical Supply Chain Simulation and Management Support', *OR Spectrum*, **24**: 343–70.

Gennari, J.H., M.A. Musen, R.W. Fergerson, W.E. Grosso, M. Crubézy, H. Eriksson, N.F. Noy and S.W. Tu (2001), 'The Evolution of Protégé: An Environment for Knowledge-Based Systems Development', *IEEE Intelligent Systems*, **16**(2): 60–71.

Gruber, T.R. (1993), 'A Translation Approach to Portable Ontology Specification', *Knowledge Acquisition*, **5**: 199–220.

Holland, J. (1996), *Hidden Order: How Adaptation Builds Complexity*, Redwood City, CA: Addison-Wesley Longman Publishing Co., Inc.

Hordijk, W. and S.A. Kauffman (2005), 'Correlation Analysis of Coupled Fitness Landscapes: Research Articles', *Complex*, **10**(6): 41–49.

Hughes, T.P. (1987), 'The Evolution of Large Technological Systems', in W.E. Bijker, T. Hughes and T.J. Pinch (eds), *The Social Construction of Technological Systems: New Directions in the Sociology and History of Technology*, Cambridge, MA: MIT Press, pp. 51–82.

Jennings, N. (2000), 'On Agent-Based Software Engineering', *Artificial Intelligence*, **117**: 277–96.

Kauffman, S. (1992), *Origins of Order: Self Organization and Selection in Evolution*, New York: Oxford University Press.

Kauffman, S. (1995), *At Home in the Universe*, New York: Oxford University Press.

Kauffman, S. (1996), 'Investigations: The Nature of Autonomous Agents and the Worlds they Mutually Create', Santa Fe Institute Working Paper 96-08-072, Santa Fe, NM.

Kay, J.J. (2002), 'On Complexity Theory, Exergy and Industrial Ecology: Some Implications for Construction Ecology', in C. Kibert, J. Sendzimir and B. Guy (eds), *Construction Ecology: Nature as the Basis for Green Buildings*, New York: Spon Press, pp. 72–107.

Ligtenberg, A., A. Bregt and R. Lammeren (2001), 'Multi-Actor Based Land Use Modeling: Spatial Planning Using Agents', *Landscape and Urban Planning*, **56**: 21–33.

Luger, G.F. and William A. Stubblefield (1993), *Artificial Intelligence: Structures and Strategies for Complex Problem Solving*, 2nd edition Redwood City, CA: Benjamin/Cummings.

Mikulecky, D. (2001), 'The Emergence of Complexity: Science Coming of Age or Science Growing Old?', *Computers and Chemistry*, **25**(4): 341–8.

Mitchell, M., J.P. Crutcheld and P.T. Hraber (1994), 'Evolving Cellular Automata to Perform Computations: Mechanisms and Impediments', *Physica D*, **75**: 361–91.

Nash, J. (1950), 'The Bargaining Problem', *Econometrica*, **18**(2): 155–62.

Newman, M.E.J. (2003), 'The Structure and Function of Complex Networks', *SIAM Review*, **45**: 167–256

Nikolic, I. and G.P.J. Dijkema (2006), 'Shaping Regional Industry–Infrastructure Networks: An Agent Based Modeling Framework', 2006 IEEE Conference on Systems, Man and Cybernetics, 8–11 October, Taipei, Taiwan.

Nikolic, I., G.P.J. Dijkema and M.A. Reuter (2005a), 'Industry–Infrastructure Co-Evolution, Complexity and Industrial Ecology', *Proceedings of the 7th World Congress of Chemical Engineering*, 10–14 July Glasgow (CD-ROM).

Nikolic, I., G.P.J. Dijkema, M.A. Reuter and A.D. Pape (2005b), 'Towards Action-Oriented Industrial Ecology: Understanding and Shaping the Sustainable Co-Evolution of Industry and Infrastructure', ISIE '05 Conference Stockholm 12–15 June 2005.

Nikolic, I., K.H. van Dam, S. Blokker, M. Houwing and E. Chappin (2006a), 'AOIE Ontology', http://www.IgorNikolic.com.

Nikolic, I., G.P.J. Dijkema, K.H. van Dam and Z. Lukzo (2006b), 'General Methodology for Action-Oriented Industrial Ecology Complex Systems Approach Applied to the Rotterdam Industrial Cluster', in Chun-Yi Su and Jagannathan Sarangapani (eds), *Proceedings of the 2006 IEEE International Conference On Networking, Sensing and Control*, Ft lauderdale, FL, 23–25 April, IEEE, pp. 831–6..

North, M.J., N.T. Collier and J.R. Vos (2006), 'Experiences Creating Three Implementations of the Repast Agent Modeling Toolkit', *ACM Transactions on Modeling and Computer Simulation*, **16**(1): 1–25.

Noy, N.F. and D.L. McGuinness (2000), 'Ontology Development 101: A Guide to Creating Your First Ontology', Technical Report KSL-01-05, Stanford University, California, http://protege.stanford.edu/publications/ontology_development/ontology101-noy-mcguinness.html.

Olsder, G.J. (2005), 'Phenomena in Inverse Stackelberg Problems: Regelungs-theorie', Report No. 11/2005, pp. 603–5.

Verhoef, E.V. (2004), 'The Ecology of Metals', Dissertation, TU Delft.

Vriend, N. (1995), 'Self Organization of Markets: An Example of a Computational Approach', *Journal of Computational Economics*, **8**(3): 205–31.

11. Futures scenarios of industrial ecosystems: a research design for transportation planning

Paul Beavis, John A. Black, James Lennox, Graham M. Turner and Stephen J. Moore

11.1 INTRODUCTION

A challenge in assessing the performance of industrial ecosystems is to consider how short-term efficiency gains reconcile with effective long-term sustainability outcomes. Each industrial ecosystem makes an imprint on the anthroposphere. This imprint may be termed its peculiar system format. We must assess whether the set of processes, characteristic of the industrial ecosystem, map to outcomes of reduced resource intensity of use and environmental impacts in the long term. In materials accounting, this is a significant imponderable, due to complex physical dynamics in interaction with other industrial ecosystems, underpinned by behavioral changes. This is demonstrated in the research of impediments to achieving sustained dematerialization (Fischer-Kowalski and Amann 2001). The transportation and land use activity also requires design techniques to address this predicament. For instance, technical gains in automobile fuel efficiency may be undermined if this induces increased travel on a network.

A tractable modeling framework would deal with uncertainty in evaluating the possible tension between efficiency and effectiveness across timescales and industry sectors of certain stocks and their flows. Consequently, in a long-term context, this uncertainty is not only about the technical and sociological solutions to current problems but also about the ignorance of what to study and what programs to enact for future corrections to biophysical relations which may otherwise lead to emerging non-sustainability. We may term this process 'sketch planning the future', which involves a framework of building interacting scenarios based on the fidelity of materials accounting.

The aim of this chapter is to define and demonstrate a scenario macro-modeling framework for futures studies of industrial ecosystems, with particular reference to the urban freight and interregional passenger transportation tasks in Australia. Transportation is an industrial ecosystem in the sense of it being a core tangible metabolic activity (Brunner and Rechberger 2004). Its function is to facilitate accessibility for goods exchange as well as human interaction. As a servicing industrial ecosystem, transportation may act as a proxy for one consideration of the relative sustainability of human settlements in the context of activity influenced by spatial arrangements and linkages of processes (for example between residences and workplaces; between places of production and consumption). The pursuit of sustainable transportation then gives insights into the cross-cutting issues across industrial ecosystems necessary for restructuring.

To demonstrate our assertions in this chapter, we utilize a dynamical vintage material accounting model called the Australian Stocks and Flows Framework (ASFF). We firstly discuss the evolving research issues in transportation and how these parallel with the understanding of the nature of industrial ecosystems. We then discuss the meaning and value of industrial ecology futures scenarios. In section 11.4, the role of scenarios is explained and illustrated by investigations into the urban freight task. In section 11.5 we discuss how the Design Approach, embodied by ASFF, facilitates transition management through envelope analysis. The interregional passenger task for Australia is investigated in section 11.6. This demonstrates more extensively the use of biophysical limits to guide the feasibility of futures scenarios. The conclusion collates key insights of futures studies for industrial ecology.

11.2   RESEARCH DESIGN IN TRANSPORTATION PLANNING

Specific research tasks to inform the appropriate response to the human condition in cities and regions through policy settings are constantly evolving. This is clearly evident in the transportation field where Black et al. (1983) have outlined the shifting research imperatives for the policy challenges that have evolved in Sydney, Australia since the 1930s. Key research themes are tracked in Figure 11.1. Whilst these research thrusts are contiguous, we might discern shifts that also parallel with the evolving research themes of industrial ecology. Early infrastructure planning was seen to support the motorized mobility necessary for economic development. Often public transit made early gains, later to suffer neglect in preference to policies that supported the automobile (Mees 2000). Congested highways motivated the need to enact end-of-pipe emission controls. Land

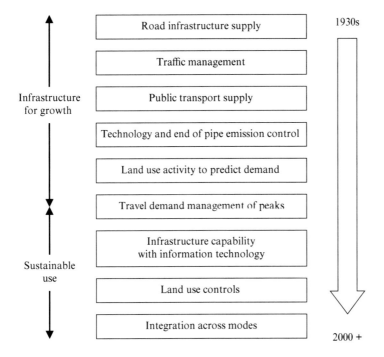

Figure 11.1   Evolving research design challenges for transportation planning

use planning was developed in order to coordinate better the generators and attractor co-locations that created traffic path 'desire lines' and to localize trips. This may be seen as an attempt to close traffic loops in the transportation task. Demand management has been investigated to price externalities (such as congestion) and follow an environmental economics thrust, or further to control behavior through frictional land use and traffic controls echoing the evolving theme of sustainable consumption. More recently, investigations into integration services across modes (passenger transit and freight hubs) may be seen as a way of controlling resource intensity. Strategic planning in transportation is also grappling with the emerging issue of rebound in industrial ecology (Hertwich 2005): new roads planned for the relief of highway congestion and to maximize travel time savings only induce more traffic demand; the infrastructure is rapidly saturated; and there can be a mode switch from public transit patronage along parallel routes.

The research task, then, in approach and technique, needs to be continuously reassessed so as to 'ensure that the research boat does not run the risk of being mis-spaced in time and space' (Black et al. 1983: 115). Research objectives and tools must be pertinent to the foreseen problem (Black and Hayashi 2005). Therefore our conception of what constitutes sustainable socio-economic organization is certainly open to further enlightenment. Westerman and Black (1983: 1312) note that research design is 'an on-going process of collective learning and selective decision making'. An objective of futures studies is to lay the foundations for research design along the transition path that is needed. How effective scenario–model frameworks are in this ambition may be discerned by their ability to identify, and by their agility to negotiate, emerging unsustainable practices projected into the future.

11.3 FUTURES PERSPECTIVES AND SUSTAINABILITY OUTLOOKS OF INDUSTRIAL ECOSYSTEMS

11.3.1 A Motivation for Futures Studies

Futures studies are an aspect of strategic thinking rather than strategic planning (see Figure 11.2). They enable strategists to become wiser and more knowledgeable about evolving physical constraints (Voros 2003). The goal of futures studies is to structure uncertainty (Herce et al. 2003). This involves tracking the propagation of unsustainable activities, and also articulating and managing the transition path to outcomes deemed sustainable. This tracking procedure is conducted along a corridor, enveloped by known and evolving physical constraints. Futures studies then provide the means to restructure an industrial ecosystem, to make the transition to more profound, and embedded, sustainable outcomes by confronting the modeler or scenario builder with necessary trade-offs, which may be counter-intuitive to their frame of reference. Unlike forecasting based on empiricism, the pursuit of futures studies represents a form of engineering design; a creative act of synthesis from extant stocks and flows to new combinations of stock and flow relationships (Mischke 1980).

A significant heritage in futures studies is the technology diffusion literature which identifies the lock-in effects of stocks with older technology of lower efficiency (Gifford and Garrison 1993; Nakićenović 1991). Technology diffusion is a central component in analyzing future paths for industrial ecosystems and the constraints to more sustainable forms of production. This has led to the necessary mechanism of vintaging in assessing macro futures (Ingham et al. 1992; Davidsdottir and Ruth

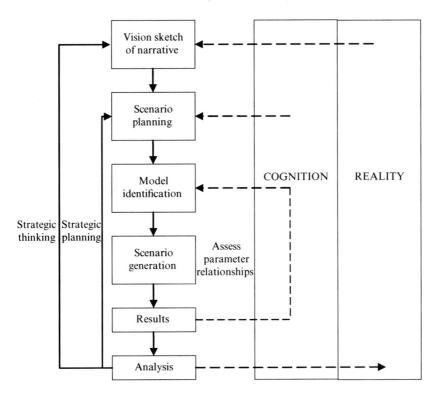

Figure 11.2   A method of system analysis

2005). Vintaging – incorporating the age structure of stocks and their relative performance parameters – permits a modeling framework to have biophysical fidelity when considering long-term futures. This measures the stock inertia, and path-dependency, known as technological lock-in.

System formats 'are like putty in these early days and turn to hardened clay as they age' (Gifford and Garrison 1993: 115). The policy implications of lock-in are profound. Repercussions of paths taken can be tracked for their lock-in effects (though often assessed only in hindsight). Inappropriate action or lack of action is also significant. Starkie (1987) recognized that the attempts of urban and transport policy-makers to backtrack over mistaken paths, or to remediate at a later date, are an example of catastrophe theory. That is, it requires many more resources later to achieve improvements at the necessary rate if wrong decisions are made. Conventional transportation systems require huge resources to maintain mobility requirements. Indeed, transportation planning seems ever fated to address a supply cycle culminating in the evolution of 'system deficiencies' (Kanafani and Sperling 1982: 67).

Model and scenario development methods for futures studies may use approaches which are normative and often better suited for the purpose of forecasting (Höjer and Mattsson 2000; Aligica 2003; Tapio and Hietanen 2002). This creates problems involving systems identification and encoding, the use of empiricism to structure uncertainty, and the role and application of the scenarios themselves. These concerns outline the propensity for mismatch between scenario design and model use which can undermine futures research.

To achieve effectiveness in futures studies of industrial ecosystems, it is essential to separate our understanding of prediction and explanation and to focus on explanatory mechanisms for decision support. Beck (1997) has recognized capturing system complexity as a major challenge for systemic studies. Excessive overt use of empiricism leads to inappropriate historical determinism. Höjer and Mattsson (2000) question the empiricism and invalid assumptions on common parameter relationships used in transportation futures research. Tying income growth with car ownership, for instance, confuses biophysical relationships with context-dependent behavior. Nowhere is this more apparent than in the highway sector where road authorities 'predict and provide' road space (Mees 2000: 51), where the supply of new infrastructure fuels more demand. Aligica (2003) observes that the core problem with this determinism is that it considers prediction as a sufficient truth and does not allow for the legitimacy of explanation. This has implications for model structure, and how we question the parameter relationships that can be validly applied in the future.

There is a danger in futures studies of overparameterizing a model. Deterministic dynamical systems have a strict basis for model identification, or how the reality of the system is encoded. If we are increasingly seeking to understand the economic–ecological interactions of the anthroposphere better, an overspecified model is likely to build in major theoretical errors. Other parameter relationships over time may come to predominance and 'new variables thus invalidate old encodings' (Haag and Kaupenjohann 2000: 125). The design approach we present through this chapter, as embodied in the Australian Stocks and Flows Framework (ASFF), attempts to address this problem by minimizing the number of system parameters to those of core biophysical relationships. The user incorporates assumptions on future parameter values separately in the scenario narrative (see section 11.5).

Integral to the technical requirements of futures studies is the approach to scenario development. The nature of the futures investigation is to develop scenarios so that we may undertake sketch planning of activities of novel combinations (Harris 2001). This entails a particular objective of generating scenarios as a means for knowledge accumulation. This concern is highly pertinent, for instance, in transportation ecosystems, where mono-modal, silo thinking dominates decision-making in the public deployment of infrastructure and private coordination of the distribution supply chain. The challenge is to generate these scenarios in a coherent and consistent fashion. This also requires that we have the means to generate these scenarios in models for appropriate reflection.

11.3.2 Sustainability and Modeling in Industrial Ecology Studies

The characterization of sustainable development in industrial ecology has significant implications for structuring model–scenario frameworks with a futures orientation. These outlooks of industrial ecology can be delineated by how they observe and formalize the interaction within the anthroposphere, and between the socio-economic and ecological realms. How a model–scenario framework evaluates and grants insights into sustainability practice will be related to its formalism of space–time causation, and its treatment of future uncertainty. Subcomponents of this formalism are the manner in which societal organization is characterized and the consideration of ecological damage on future capital maintenance. The characterization of industrial ecology and indicators to measure its sustainability have ranged from closed-loop systems to self-modifying systems (Ehrenfeld 2003). Characterizing industrial ecosystems as self-modifying systems may point to the obstacles in achieving sustained dematerialization and guide the necessary steps for a successful adaptive response (Spiegelman 2003). This leads to the research task of ecological restructuring or transition management (Picton and Daniels 1999).

This characterization of sustainable development has implications for (re)designing the anthroposphere and the particular industrial ecosystem of focus. In directing an appropriate research design, the selection of sustainability approach will influence model identification, the use of data, and the structure of a query system. We can, however, only understand the sustainability of industrial ecosystems through: (1) undertaking a deeper analysis of its interaction with ecology that assesses the resiliencies in the face of human impacts; and (2) synthesizing, with given biophysical relationships, a query system, on how best to make transitions.

From a policy perspective, assessment of the interaction with the environment has developed little since the (driving forces–pressure–state–response paradigm (OECD 1994). Haberl et al. (2002) observe two problems with this approach, namely, that it does not consider the effects of changed environmental conditions on society; and it only describes interventions of society in natural systems. The approach reduces the description of society's actions to responses only. There is, however, a need to consider the feedback relationship between socio-economic and ecological development more thoroughly.

Indicators that characterize the sustainability of industrial ecosystems can direct the formalism in scenario–model interaction necessary for industrial ecology futures studies. Haberl et al. (2002) have outlined four indicator areas: socio-economic driving forces; pressures on the environment; state of the environment; and feedback of environmental change on society. The dual concepts that encapsulate these indicator sets are socio-economic metabolism and colonization of natural processes. The second concept is often neglected in the sustainability debate. In a biophysical model of a nation, sufficient resolution of specific ecological interactions remains a problem. The land appropriations that it represents have long-term repercussions for the sustainability of the anthroposphere. In lieu of regionally specific damage functions, ASFF takes an approach of exposing dilemmas in the prevailing metabolism. A decline in land resource stock yields means that fewer commodities are exported, or more are imported, and thus shows as a reduction in the indicator of national income. This forces the recognition of a dilemma to be resolved.

With a basis in biophysical relations, ASFF attempts to incorporate the future tension associated with loss of some key biophysical stocks (land and declining agricultural yields, water, and fossil fuel stocks) as the economy grows. It therefore underpins the limits in substitution of man-made capital for natural capital. Similarly, transportation networks, as they grow, increase the carbon intensity of human habitation and have huge maintenance requirements. Functional innovation in land use and transportation networks, such as demand management or introducing transit hubs, allow greater leverage in the existing stock of physical infrastructure for improved mobility and accessibility (Gifford and Garrison 1993). The modeler is confronted with the need to develop such novel scenarios and strategies to control resource intensity of use.

The aspects to assess the scope and orientation of scenario–model interactions as effective frameworks in the formulation of industrial ecology futures studies are summarized in Table 11.1. These aspects and constituents might be considered typology which can be used as a checklist to evaluate a specific planning endeavor which combines a unique set of scenario ambition, available modeling mechanisms, and a conception of environmental sustainability. This typology is not comprehensive: frameworks may still grant significant insights into future vectors of non-sustainability without adhering to tight criteria.

Table 11.1   Aspects of the practice of industrial ecology futures studies

Aspects	Constituents	Comment
Goal-oriented approach	Whether the study is focused on the means or the end goal	This directs the practice of a model towards feasible steps or back-casting
Prediction versus explanation	The use of data in the model, to calibrate key variables or to be used more deterministically	Whether we are interested in structuring uncertainty or wish for a more predictive outcome
Paradigm of industrial ecology	Whether the study is focused on closing loops or structuring the evolution of self-modifying systems. How ecosystem carrying capacity and damage are considered	Determines our interest in anticipatory or adaptive management; whether the colonization of ecosystem functions (biophysical yields and their limits) are considered
Dimensions of the system boundary	Process-oriented or a structural approach. Impacts occur statically in space and time or dynamically	To what extent we are capturing cross cutting issues and laying the basis for multi-sectoral solutions. To what extent we can incorporate numerous trajectories into a corridor approach
Degree of human–machine interaction	To what extent and when the user can intervene in the process	To what extent can we track the trajectory (make feasible steps) or must we assume a given path
Scenario creation	Morphological technical analysis and/or qualitative description	The role of public participation and the degree of articulation of technical system formats. The depth of discussion in irreducible functional relationships
The accounting mechanism of the model	Physical, economic or hybrids	Identify the nature of feasibility measurement. The stocks and flows basis: the relationship between gradual and quick dynamics

11.4   THE ROLE OF SCENARIOS

The design approach has the potential to address concerns on the appropriateness of modeling and scenario development methods in futures studies (Gault et al. 1987). It addresses the formation of those macro models in industrial ecology that consider the interaction of infrastructure, population, affluence and technology on environmental outcomes (resource depletion and pollution), and attempts to unravel the materializing tendencies of interacting industrial ecosystems.

It is these tendencies, fueled by population growth, that may frustrate dematerialization goals (Fischer-Kowalski and Amann 2001). This section outlines the integral role of scenarios in analysis and design. We illustrate the evolution of scenario and strategies with reference to the urban freight industrial ecosystem.

At the macro strategic level, judgments 'require more dimensions of analysis than models can provide' (Harris 2001: 67). For instance, we cannot easily cover the necessary resolution to incorporate the impacts of regional ecological damage. Therefore, conceptual validity is of paramount importance (Black and Blunden 1988). Models should operate in a system of analysis (a framework) rather than be simply calculation machines. This has implications for both the approach to the formal model and the interpretation of quantified results. Human–machine interaction is another significant characteristic in the systems approach of which scenario–model frameworks are an integral part.

The understanding between perceptions of reality and the degree of acceptance of different science theories describing reality has been well established (Maruyama 1980). This profoundly affects the sustainability outlook of the modeler and thus the modeling ambition and outcome. Furthermore, there remains conflict on how new knowledge to reduce uncertainty in modeling economic–ecologic interactions is to be acquired. This is termed 'epistemic uncertainty' (Haag and Kaupenjohann 2001). Such concerns include identifying the valid frames of observation for complex systems. Scenarios, as 'the frame conditions of the system to be modeled' (Pesonen et al. 2000: 22), have major implications for knowledge accumulation. As noted in Figure 11.2, strategic thinking (or sketch planning), where scenario futures play a central role, becomes an indispensable part of systems analysis through allowing a critical reflection process.

The process of scenario narrative development, at the initial level of speculation, can be decomposed into a number of steps (Schwarz 1998). Scenario development starts with a hypothesis to be tested. The structures at play, or focal issues and parameters as driving forces, are identified. Interactions of driving forces can be insightfully depicted in a spider diagram (Nijkamp et al. 1997). Predetermined elements are then described for assessment. These include: slow-changing relationships (technology development in specific sectors); constraints (initiatives that are in the pipeline, such as new transportation corridor infrastructure); collisions (the development of land scarcities); and critical uncertainties (changing population distributions with respect to their places of work and study and their requirements with increasing affluence, for instance). Within scenarios, more technically based strategies can be developed using a morphological approach (Argiolu et al. 2004). This approach allows various technological combinations to be organized into logical and feasible strategies according to the functions that need to be serviced. This approach is more explanatory – it reflects on logical alternate futures and builds on the speculative direction.

When a number of interacting policies are required to produce transition, feasible pathways need to be assessed that capture cross-cutting issues (Rotmans et al. 2001). For instance, the activity of urban goods freight is rising due to logistics drivers, and control of operations from a systems point of view seems elusive (Rodrigue et al. 2001; Golob and Regan 2002). Light goods vehicles represent an increasing traffic load in the Australian urban transport network, representing 30 percent of the urban road traffic and 33 percent of the urban transport fuel consumption (BTRE 2003, Figures ES.1, 2.6, 3.4). The total energy intensity of freight is 43.5 megajoules/tonne-kilometer (48 MJ/ton-km) (Lenzen 1999), which is surprisingly high compared to other freight types due, primarily, to the low load factors. Applying different scenarios and strategies, we considered how to control the energy intensity of urban freight. We initially investigated the effects of introducing electric vehicles into the fleet at different diffusion rates to gauge the prospects of reducing hydrocarbon energy demands (Low Elect and High Elect) and then hydrogen-fueled vehicles (Elect & Hydro). We then considered accelerating retirement of the existing stock as well (High & Retire). A new scenario approach was considered when it was realized that the gains were delayed by stock inertia. This scenario was based on network restructuring by improving logistics hub arrangements so that pickup and put-down delivery consignments are consolidated (Reduce Intensity). Finally, a combination of these innovations was made (Combination) From an analysis in ASFF, the peak control of energy and emissions from urban goods freight requires a combination of aggressive technological improvements, network and land use restructuring around public distribution hubs, receiver–sender cooperative agreements, and renewable energy sources and suitable infrastructure refueling and recharging depots if Australia is to reduce fossil fuel consumption in this sector to 1990 levels by 2030 (see Figure 11.3).

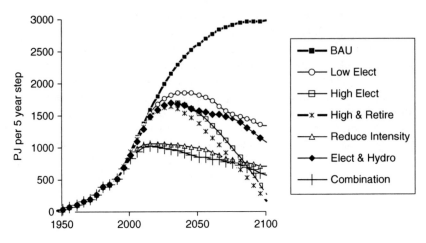

Figure 11.3   *Urban freight hydrocarbon direct energy requirement with different strategies (ASFF output)*

Applying a vintaging model to scenario narratives reveals that there is no single optimum transport technology for long-term sustainability (Mees 2000). Speculative, and then exploratory, narratives need to be applied to structure a scenario query system which facilitates this necessary interdisciplinary response. Significantly, the engagement with the framework enables the user to be educated in the interactive nature of the driving forces such as population and demand, physical network typology, and logistical service drivers affecting the urban freight task.

The linking of scenario narratives can be an even more powerful technique in futures strategic thinking. Höjer and Mattsson (2000) observe that scenarios can have an ambition additional to devising some alternate future: scenarios provide a means of searching for new paths along which development could take place. This is particularly appropriate when conventional paths do not solve a problem, or only suggest marginal improvements. In this sense, the model is used to explore how a desirable state might be reached, which is essentially the nature of a transitions approach. Transition management is a method of devising trajectories of scenarios (Rotmans et al. 2001). Such transition management requires the ability to develop complex scenarios and assess their biophysical implications. The nature of scenario generation, through model framework mechanisms, affects further scenario development. A procedure for scenario generation, and the response to it, is vital for knowledge accumulation. This procedure ought to consist of a constructive method, an improvement procedure, and a rule for stopping and selecting new scenarios when trade-offs are no longer acceptable (Harris 2001). By this means, future uncertainties can be structured and thus policy responses developed which exhibit traits of adaptive flexibility for the system format devised (Rammel and Van den Bergh 2003).

11.5 ENVELOPE ASSESSMENT IN THE DESIGN APPROACH

Effective futures studies require a scenario generation process which is exploratory, mediated by controlled simulation with explanatory outcomes. In addition to using design information to construct models for simulation, the Design Approach constructs alternative futures through repeated simulation. The Design Approach was developed conceptually by Gault et al. (1987). The scope and mechanisms of the Australian Stocks and Flows Framework (ASFF) have been described by Turner and Poldy (2001) and Foran and Poldy (2002, 2004). Key tenets of the Design Approach, and how these are applied in our case study using ASFF, include:

- The formation of futures based on physically feasible relations, according to known constraints of existing stock and flow relationships and levels. In the ASFF platform there was a calibration of 50 years of core parameter relationships.
- The separation of decisions from actions, thus separating the human–machine space so that behavioral assumptions are made transparent. ASFF runs a sophisticated scenario management system whereby variable settings can be separately recorded as instances and applied to scenarios. This allows scenarios from past experience to be composed. The user can then be actively engaged in system learning (Gault et al. 1987).
- An open-loop system without behavioral feedbacks, where disequilibria are exposed. That is, there are no explicit feedbacks where economic behavior and physical relations are jumbled together. Endogenous dynamics are based on demonstrated physical relations.

In the Design Approach it is the nature of the human–machine interaction that distinguishes the significant features of this approach from conventional system dynamics and leads to its assessment as an appropriate tool for futures studies to decipher feasible transitions. To gain guidance on desirable frameworks for human–machine interaction that track transitions, real-time control theory should be considered, although it is impossible to condense the future and manage it in real time. A possible proxy is the use of scenario management that maps a feasible transition pathway into this future and notes the limits on deviations from certain paths. Rarely are paths and their disturbances known. Therefore, a transitional management approach is most necessary for futures studies. The user should be able to intervene at different points in time according to the system response (De la Barra 1989). In this way, the user in ASFF sets control variables which are enacted for intermediate assessment and alteration. This process was conducted in the urban freight illustration. Parameter interventions were made to increase the rate of uptake of electric vehicles, retire hydrocarbon stocks, and change the rates of land use restructuring to increase terminal hubs and load factor opportunities in order to reduce fossil fuel energy use. The effect of these initiatives induced further strategies to be packaged and generated so that we could gain a crucial understanding of how we might best overcome the retardation effects of stock inertia. It is this stock inertia that projects the evolving envelope of constraints.

An envelope approach, which fosters the resolution of futures dilemmas, revealed by biophysical constraints, allows a corridor path to be tracked. This corridor can be seen as negotiating the interplay of multiple parameter trajectories. This is a vital capability for simulating futures studies. Beck (1997), when discussing economic–ecological interactions, observes that up until now our 'strategic' engineering response has been to control a single point on an entire curve, whereas with a true response we need to accommodate the distortions of a continuum of other frequencies on that curve section. Incorporating multiple-order effects in the anthroposphere is one way to accommodate this systems approach requirement. ASFF provides a measurement across the time spectrum according to the interplay of the different vintages of stocks with their associated material needs, energy requirements for operations, emissions and need for recycling processes.

11.6   MODEL–SCENARIO INTERACTION

An example of the interregional passenger transportation ecosystem is now provided to demonstrate the nature of scenario–model interaction using Design Approach principles which expose fundamental biophysical dilemmas. This scenario considers the mobility effects of shifting the population to regional centers in Australia over time. The scenario–model mechanism employed is based on a transitional path investigated by a combination of feasible steps and some backcasting.

Table 11.2   Parameter setting for layered scenarios (town clusters)

Scenario	Strategies	Population growth	Intercity per capita travel yield [km/yr]	Auto share	Mode share (after auto share)		
					Air	Bus	Rail
BAU		Medium	7 500	50%	55%	40%	5%
Town clusters	Hi mobility	Medium	10 000	50%	10%	40%	50%
	Low mobility	Medium	5 000	30%	10%	40%	50%
	Hi pop/ low mobility	High	5 000	30%	10%	40%	50%
	Hi pop/ med mobility	High	7 500	30%	10%	40%	50%

The intensification of networking activities and cooperation at a regional level is a necessary prerequisite for sustainable development (Wallner 1999). Satellite communities that live closer to their environment, sourcing their needs locally, might be considered as organizing units capable of achieving more sustainability. This form of settlement has been termed 'qualified density' (Hahn 1991). Poor transportation infrastructure and communications technology, insufficient water resources and low employment prospects act as barriers for the growth of Australian towns (Beer et al. 2003). In a futures context, the distribution settlement pattern of Australia's future population is a critical challenge: Australia would need 90 new cities the size of Canberra (population 300 000) if it were to avoid state capital city populations of 8–10 million by the year 2100 (Foran and Poldy 2002).

For the whole of Australia, we consider a 'business as usual' (BAU) scenario and also a regional towns scenario with cluster strategies of high and medium population growth with location of future households such that the current capital city populations are stabilized (backcasting initiative). The main control parameter settings defining the scenario and strategies are detailed in Table 11.2 The intercity travel requirements of a network of town clusters throughout Australia are explicitly analyzed. These requirements were anticipated to the significant. Foran and Poldy (2002) noted that the interregional and intercity non-auto passenger task will be between 120–160 billion pkm/yr by 2050. This compares with an urban public transit requirement of 30–40 billion pkm/yr – about a quarter the size. All modes of transport are included to calculate the full interregional and intercity task. As well

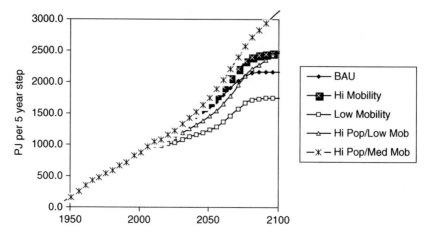

Figure 11.4   Trajectory hydrocarbon direct energy requirement of town cluster strategies for interregional and intercity travel (ASFF output)

as changing population levels, we consider the mobility demands of dispersed populations, their use of cars and the modal share of public transit.

From the fuel consumption results presented in Figure 11.4, it seems essential to control mobility demand growth with the development of a regional network of cities. Controlling the growth of regional air transportation is also significant. Creating populations of a critical mass where employment, entertainment and other facilities are located in the one regional city may engender a reduced requirement for interregional travel. A high population growth setting can frustrate any reasonable reduction in per capita mobility. There are other, severe biophysical constraints in realizing a regional qualified density future with the above parameter settings. Train operations grow from a very low biophysical base. The material needs of these new vehicles for each scenario becomes considerable compared to the baseline scenario (see Figure 11.5). The need for new track and rolling stock may be beyond the available productive capacity and financial resources of Australia to provide (see Figure 11.6).

The framework calculates, in a hierarchical, linear fashion what are the domestic production and import impacts of these additional vehicles and rolling stock with changes in mobility. A growth in imports greater than exports will lead to an increase in international foreign debt. The enhanced requirement for domestic production will necessitate growth in mining for materials and energy resources. The growth rate in mining is limited by the rate of deposit discoveries. The biophysical summary is represented in the

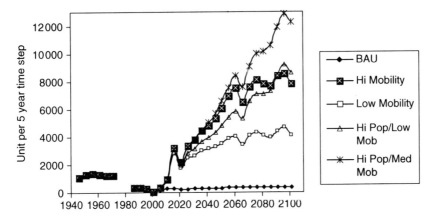

Figure 11.5   Rail vehicle requirements for interregional and intercity travel (ASFF output)

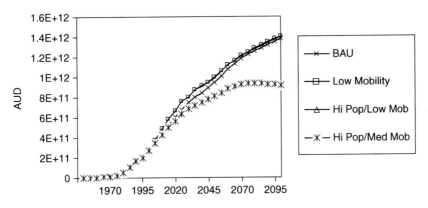

Figure 11.6   Current Account Tensions (ASFF output)

aggregate net Current Account in the International Trade Calculator (see Figure 11.6). Interacting conditions potentially represent the biophysical limits and dilemmas of composite scenarios. Higher mobility requirements lead to a larger deterioration in the net Current Account (hi pop/med mob trajectory). It requires high reductions in interregional mobility to achieve a Current Account comparable to the 'business as usual' result. This set of results should spur research efforts in how to decouple mobility from economic growth.

This economic indicator represents a proxy to the economic, social and environmental welfare of futures scenarios and thus acts as a trigger for user investigation of the dilemma. From this final indicator, the framework can be interrogated backwards to identify how the Current Account can be maintained. This procedure provides the ceiling of the corridor to guide transition management.

We may consider how this illustration responds to the aspects flagged in Table 11.1 for model–scenario frameworks to achieve effective futures studies. Our goal orientation is structuring uncertainty through the use of a feasible steps approach to track and develop composite strategies, such as, what should be the rates of transition to other transport modes given existing stock limitations. The system boundary necessarily extends beyond the industrial ecosystem to investigate the cascading relationships that prevent change due to inertia of interlocking industrial ecosystems: we find increased motorized mobility is not a sustainable solution to maintaining accessibility (Knoflacher 1996). The need for motorized mobility is likely to be heightened with dispersed clusters of population centers. An 'environmental' solution from available system formats (trains shuttling between cities) has major investment requirements, which are not financially sustainable with the current stock and structure of the Australian economy, unless Australia is to expand its commodity export base. Low intercity travel yields the best prospects for neutral sustainability outcomes. The scenario creation process involves the high-level speculative scoping and then a number of morphological strategies where parameter changes are made. New scenarios need to be scoped when assumptions underpinning the last set of strategies raise non-negotiable biophysical dilemmas, that is, the system formats, seemingly nimble, have become hardened clay.

11.7   CONCLUSIONS

Appropriate futures studies in transportation industrial ecosystems remain ill-defined. Consequently, there is confusion regarding the necessary minimum content, structure and output of studies to assess the complementary nature of strategy and sustainability. This chapter has raised awareness for the need to formulate practice in modeling industrial ecology futures scenarios. This is a vital research agenda given the problem of demonstrating sustained dematerialization across interlocking industrial ecosystems.

In this chapter, we have described the components required for industrial ecology futures studies and have demonstrated how the scenario–model procedure works. We have deciphered some of the biophysical dilemmas associated with two transportation industrial ecosystems in Australia: the urban freight and interregional passenger tasks. Through engaging the model framework, we practiced transitional management to discern the rate of structural and technical change necessary to achieve sustainability goals (reducing hydrocarbon fuel use).

The design approach, as currently embodied in the ASFF platform, can address issues in industrial ecology futures studies on the basis that it represents a calibrated framework of biophysical relations of the economy. Separating choices from the consequences of choices means that scenarios can be generated, and their physical feasibility gauged. The scenario development framework allows a learning-by-doing approach where knowledge is created. The evolution of dilemmas allows new scenarios to be created 'midstream' of the trajectory, and evokes the continuous engagement of the human–machine interaction process. We then become involved in the negotiation of a transition to a more sustainable future with more flexible system formats.

ACKNOWLEDGMENTS

The authors thank Petrie Tapio of Finland Futures Institute for insights into transportation futures planning and for his generous comments on an earlier draft. We are grateful to *whatIf?*™ (formerly Robberts Associates) for ongoing support with the ASFF platform. Barney Foran and Franzi Poldy of National Futures, Sustainable Ecosystems Division of the Commonwealth Scientific and Industrial Research Organisation (CSIRO) are also gratefully acknowledged for the construction of ASFF and their groundbreaking study *Future Dilemmas*, the insights of which have been added to this chapter.

REFERENCES

Aligica, P. (2003), 'Prediction, Explanation and the Epistemology of Future Studies', *Futures*, **35**: 1027–40.

Argiolu, R., R. van der Heijden and V. Marcher (2004), 'ITS Policy Strategies for Urban Regions: A Creative Exploration', Proceedings from the 10th World Conference on Transportation Research, 4–8 July, Istanbul, Turkey.

Beck, M.B. (1997), 'Applying Systems Analysis in Managing the Water Environment: Towards a New Agenda', *Water Science Technology*, **36**(5): 1–17.

Beer, A., A. Maude and B. Pritchard (2003), *Developing Australia's Regions: Theory and Practice*, Sydney: UNSW Press.

Black, J.A. and W.R. Blunden (1988), 'On the Economic Evaluation of Private–Public Sector Transport Projects', Proceedings from the 13th Australasian Transport Research Forum, Christchurch, New Zealand.

Black, J.A. and Y. Hayashi (2005), 'Trans-Disciplinary Framework: The Challenges of Modeling the Sustainable City', Proceedings from the 9th Computers in Urban Planning and Management (CUPUM) Conference, 29 June – 1 July, University College London.

Black, J.A., C. Kuranami and P. Rimmer (1983), 'Transport–Land Use Issues, Problems and Policy Implications: Sydney Since the Thirties', Proceedings from the 8th Australian Transport Research Forum, 18–20 May, Canberra, Australia.

Brunner, P.H. and H. Rechberger (2004), *Practical Handbook of Material Flow Analysis*, Advanced Methods in Resource and Waste Management, Boca Raton, FL and London: Lewis Publishers.

BTRE (2003), Urban Pollutant Emissions from Motor Vehicles: Australian Trends to 2020. Report for Environment Australia. Canberra: Australian Government Department of Transport and Regional Services. Bureau of Transport and Regional Economics.

Davidsdottir, B. and M. Ruth (2005), 'Pulp Non-Fiction: Regionalized Dynamic Model of the US Pulp and Paper Industry', *Journal of Industrial Ecology*, **9**(3): 191–211.

De la Barra, Tomas (1989), *Integrated Land Use and Transport Modeling: Decision Chains and Hierarchies*, New York: Cambridge University Press.

Ehrenfeld, J. (2003), 'Putting a Spotlight on Metaphors and Analogies in Industrial Ecology', *Journal of Industrial Ecology*, **7**(1): 1–4.

Fischer-Kowalski, M. and C. Amann (2001), 'Beyond IPAT and Kurznet Curves: Globalisation as a Vital Factor in Analyzing the Environmental Impact of Socio-Economic Metabolism', *Population and Environment*, **23**(1): 7–41.

Foran, B. and F. Poldy (2002), *Future Dilemmas: Options to 2050 for Australia's Population, Technology, Resources, and Environment. Report for the Australian Commonwealth Department of Immigration and Multicultural and Indigenous Affairs*, Canberra: CSIRO Sustainable Ecosystems.

Foran, B. and F. Poldy (2004), 'Modeling Physical Realities at the Whole Economy Scale', in J.C.J.M. van den Bergh and Marco A. Jansen (eds), *Economics of Industrial Ecology: Materials, Structural Change, and Spatial Scales*, Cambridge, MA: MIT Press.

Gault, F.D., K.E. Hamilton, R.B. Hoffman and B.C. McInnis (1987), 'The Design Approach to Socio-Economic Modeling', *Futures*, **19**(1): 3–25.

Gifford, J. and W.A. Garrison (1993), 'Airports and the Air Transportation System: Functional Refinements and Functional Discovery', *Technological Forecasting and Social Change*, **43**: 103–23.

Golob, T.F. and A.C. Regan (2002), 'Trucking Industry Adoption of Information Technology: A Multivariate Discrete Choice Model', *Transportation Research C*, **10**: 205–28.

Haag, D. and M. Kaupenjohann (2000), 'Biogeochemical Models in the Environmental Sciences: The Dynamical System Paradigm and the Role of Simulation Modeling', *International Journal for Philosophy of Chemistry*, **6**(2): 117–42.

Haag, D. and M. Kaupenjohann (2001), 'Parameters, Prediction, Post-normal Science and the Precautionary Principle: A Roadmap for Modeling for Decision-Making', *Ecological Modeling*, **144**: 45–60.

Haberl, H., M. Fischer-Kowalaski, F. Krausemann, H. Schandl, H. Weisz and V. Winiwarter (2002), 'Theoretische Grundlagen für die Gesellschaftliche

Beobachtung Nachhaltiger Entwicklung' ('Theoretical Foundations of Societal Observation of Sustainable Development'), *Die Bodenkultur*, **53**: 55–63.

Hahn, E. (1991), 'Ecological Urban Restructuring: Theoretical Foundation and Concept for Action', Working paper FS II 91-402, Wissenschaftszentrum Berlin für Sozialforschung, Berlin.

Harris, B. (2001), 'Sketch Planning: Systematic Methods in Planning and its Support', in R.K. Brail and R.E. Klosterman (eds), *Planning Support Systems*, Redlands, CA: ESRI, pp. 59–80.

Herce, J.A., F. Duchin, F. Fontela and T. Lindh (2003), 'To Sum Up: Avoiding Unsustainable Futures', *Futures*, **85**: 89–97.

Hertwich, E.G. (2005), 'Consumption and the Rebound Effect: An Industrial Ecology Perspective', *Journal of Industrial Ecology*, **9**(1–2): 85–98.

Höjer, M. and L.-G. Mattsson (2000), 'Determinism and Backcasting in Future Studies', *Futures*, **32**: 613–34.

Ingham, A., J. Maw and A. Ulph (1992), 'Testing the Barriers to Energy Conservation: An Application of a Vintage Model', *Energy Journal*, **12**(4): 41–64.

Kanafani, A. and D. Sperling (1982), *National Transportation Planning*, The Hague: Martinus Nijhoff.

Knoflacher, H. (1996), *Zur Harmonie von Stadt und Verkehr*, Wien: Böhlau.

Lenzen, M. (1999), 'Total Requirements of Energy and Greenhouse Gases for Australian Transport', *Transportation Research D*, **4**: 265–90.

Maruyama, M. (1980), 'Mindscapes and Science Theories', *Current Anthropology*, **21**(5): 589–608.

Mees, P. (2000), *A Very Public Solution. Transport in the Dispersed City*, Melbourne University Press: Melbourne.

Mischke, C. (1980), *Mathematical Model Building: An Introduction to Engineering*, Iowa State University Press

Nakićenović, N. (1991), 'Diffusion of Pervasive Systems: A Case of Transport Infrastructures', *Technological Forecasting and Social Change*, **39**: 181–200.

Nijkamp, P., H. Ouwersloot and S.A. Rienstra (1997), 'Sustainable Urban Transport Systems: An Expert-based Strategic Scenario Approach', *Urban Studies*, **34**(4): 693–712.

OECD (1994), *Environmental Indicators – OECD Core Set*, Paris: OECD.

Pesonen, H.-L., T. Ekvall, G. Fleischer, G. Huppes, C. Jahn , Z.S. Klos, G. Rebitzer, G.W. Sonnemann, A. Tintinelli, B.P. Weidema and H. Wenzel (2000), 'Framework for Scenario Development in LCA', *International Journal of LCA*, **5**(1): 21–30.

Picton, T. and P.L. Daniels (1999), 'Ecological Restructuring for Sustainable Development: Evidence from the Australian Economy', *Ecological Economics*, **29**: 405–25.

Rammel, C. and J.C.J.M. van den Bergh (2003), 'Evolutionary Policies for Sustainable Development: Adaptive Flexibility and Risk Minimizing', *Ecological Economics*, **47**: 121–33.

Rodrigue, J-P., B. Slack and C. Comtois (2001), 'Green logistics', in A.M. Brewer, K.J. Button and D.A. Hensher (eds), *Handbook of Logistics and Supply Chain Management*, Amsterdam: Pergamon Press, pp. 339–50.

Rotmans, J., R. Kemp, M. van Asselt, F. Geels, G. Verbong, K. Molendijk and P. van Notten (2001), 'Transitions and Transition Management: The Case for a

Low Emission Energy Supply', Working Paper IO1-E001, International Centre for Integrative Studies (ICIS), Maastricht.

Schwarz, P. (1998), *The Art of the Long View: Planning for the Future in an Uncertain World*, Chichester: Wiley.

Spiegelman, J. (2003), 'Beyond the Food Web: Connections to a Deeper Industrial Ecology', *Journal of Industrial Ecology*, 7(1): 17–23.

Starkie, D. (1987), 'Configuring Change: Reflections on Transport Policy Processes', in P. Nijkamp and S. Reichman (eds), *Transportation Planning in a Changing World*, Aldershot: Gower in association with European Science Foundation.

Tapio, P. and O. Hietanen (2002), 'Epistimology and Public Policy: Using a New Typology to Analyze the Paradigm Shift in Finnish Transportation Futures Studies', *Futures*, **34**(7): 597–620.

Turner, G.M. and F. Poldy (2001), 'Let's Get Physical: Creating a Stocks and Flows View of the Australian Economy', in F. Ghassemi, D.H. White, S. Cuddy and T. Nakanishi (eds), *Integrating Models for Natural Resource Management Across Disciplines, Issues and Scales. Proceedings from the International Congress on Modeling and Simulation, The Australian National University, Canberra, Australia, 10–13 December*, Perth: Modeling and Simulation Society of Australia and New Zealand, pp. 1637–42.

Voros, J. (2003), 'A Generic Foresight Process Framework', *Foresight*, **5**(3): 10–21.

Wallner, H.P. (1999), 'Towards Sustainable Development of Industry: Networking, Complexity and Eco-clusters', *Journal of Cleaner Production*, 7: 49–58.

Westerman, H.L. and J.A. Black (1983), 'Energy Efficient Land Use and Transport: A Research Design and Decision-Making Framework', in P. Baron and H. Nuppnau (eds), *Research for Transport Policies in a Changing World. Proceedings from the World Conference on Transport Research, 26–29 April*, Hamburg: SNV Studiengesellschaft Nahverkehr.

12. PowerPlay: developing strategies to promote energy efficiency

Matthias Ruth, Clark Bernier, Alan Meier and John 'Skip' Laitner

12.1 INTRODUCTION

Engineers have long sought technologies that deliver goods and services more effectively and efficiently. Economists and lawyers have explored mechanisms to provide incentives for the adoption of those technologies, and for the reduction of undesired side-effects. Increasingly, industrial ecologists have situated themselves at the interface of technology and society to provide a systems perspective that encompasses the environmental, technological, economic and social dimensions of resource use, provision of goods and services, and environmental impact (Graedel and Allenby 1995; Soccolow et al. 1996). As the number of 'actors' (firms, households, government agencies), that need to be considered in a systems-based analysis is larger than typically considered in more traditional approaches, as time frames are extended to capture the long-term effects of investment and policy decisions in a changing environment, and as feedbacks among various subsystems (for example different firms, different consumer groups, different resource endowments and ecosystems) are explicitly introduced in the analysis, the complexity and need for information increase. At the same time, the limits to anticipate outcomes perfectly become painfully apparent to anyone interested in planning and management (Funtowicz and Ravetz 1993; Ruth 1998).

In complex decision environments, games are a popular tools to explore with decision-makers the consequences of their decisions in situations where information flow among 'players' is limited and environmental conditions cannot be known with certainty. There is a wide range of such games. At one extreme are game-theoretic models that attempt to identify optimal strategies for two or more players in often static or comparative static settings (Osborne and Rubinstein 1994; Owen 2001). At the other end of the range are computer-based simulation games, such as SimCity (EAI 2005), that concentrate on the evolution of systems in which typically a single player interferes in a system's dynamics through various choice variables. In between the two lie studies in experimental economics (for example Smith 1992; Kagel and Roth 1995), which attempt to substantiate, in game-like settings, the postulates on which economic models are built.

Game-theoretic models assume a small number of actors and choice variables are frequently highly context-specific and require advanced mathematical skills for their solution. In contrast, computer-based simulations often lack strong theoretical ties, require considerable time to be played, and are rarely transparent enough that players can (*ex post*) clearly evaluate the success of alternative strategies within the context of myriad variables. Studies in experimental economics typically create decision environments within which researchers can explore the validity of behavioral economic assumptions. The experiments are often highly stylized in order to reduce the influence of confounding factors on behavior and to focus on key drivers behind decisions that can be easily isolated in the experiment. Few of the experimental economics approaches use sophisticated computing technology that would allow tracing the impacts of a multitude of interacting factors in a near real-world experiment.

All three types of approaches, and various combinations of them, have been used to explain the persistence of energy efficiency gaps – the presence of discrepancies between actual energy efficiency choices by households and firms, and choices that would be considered economically optimal for them (Jaffe and Stavins 1994). Optimality is typically understood in the context of rational economic decision-making. Theoretical, econometric, simulation and gaming-based investigations continue to explore the roles of market failures and the characteristics of energy users that may contribute to the emergence and maintenance of efficiency gaps (Hausman 1979; Gately 1980; Howarth and Andersson 1993; Hassett and Metcalf 1995; Goett et al. 2000; Laitner et al. 2000; Dyner and Franco 2004). Insights from this research will be relevant in determining the roles of government regulation, information dissemination and other interventions designed to promote higher energy efficiencies.

PowerPlay has been developed at the confluence of several recent approaches – theoretical, econometric, simulation-based and gaming-oriented – to understand better the evolution and dynamics of energy efficiency choices in the combined context of household, firm and regulatory decision-making. PowerPlay incorporates theoretically and empirically founded economic and engineering concepts to frame choice options for players, utilizes a dynamic computer model to facilitate the game, draws into the game experts and decision-makers, and reports back to those players and the scientific and decision-making communities the insights generated by the game.

PowerPlay is not a computer game, although its execution is facilitated by computers. The computer's role is to simulate the rest of the economy, allow for chance events to occur which influence basic economic variables, receive the choices of players as inputs into the model, compute the ramification of players' choices in the context of all other decisions and a changing economic and technological context, and report on the extent to which players were successful in meeting their objectives. The dynamic model is thus an equivalent to the game board and chance cards of many traditional family games – the means to interact with other players through the rules of the game.

In the following sections of this chapter we offer an introduction into PowerPlay, including both its development and game rules. We summarize the findings from the initial game which was played by a diverse set of actors from government agencies, think-tanks, research institutions and non-governmental organizations in the energy field. We describe the data generated by that game and present insights into opportunities for, and constraints on the development and implementation of strategies to promote energy efficiency. We also describe how PowerPlay might be used to generate elasticities and other behavioral and economic variables that can help initialize more conventional energy or economic models in the absence of actual market data.

12.2   GAME AND MODEL DESCRIPTION

12.2.1   Overview

PowerPlay explores the evolution of US electricity generation and use in an uncertain, multiplayer world. Players represent households, appliance manufacturers, electric utilities and generation technology providers. The game's facilitators serve as surrogates for the role of politician or regulator. Each group of players has its own objectives and means of influencing the system ('levers'), as summarized in Table 12.1 and detailed in the following sections.

Coordinating the decisions of the player groups is an underlying model run in the graphical programming language STELLA (Hannon and Ruth 2001; ISEE Systems 2004). The STELLA model is divided into 12 modules – one for each player group and one that models the various policy levers available. These modules are connected to one another in three markets: the households and the utility modules interact in the market for electricity;

Table 12.1   Basic elements of the PowerPlay game

Player Group (number of groups)	Objectives	Levers
Households (6)	Minimize energy-related spending, maximize style & service, minimize environmental impact	● Product line selection and timing of purchases
Consumer technology firms (3)	Maximize firm profits	● Product line attributes ● Energy efficiency R&D
Electric utility (1)	Maximize firm profits	● Choice of technology to replace generating capacity that is retired ● Amount of capacity to purchase
Generation technology firm (1)	Maximize firm profits	● R&D investments ● Generation technology prices
Politician/regulator/ facilitator (1)	Maintain flow of game and test the results of policy levers	● Performance standards ● Electricity price ceilings ● Demand side management ● Subsidies for technology adoption ● Other policies, as desired

the utility and generation technology modules interact in the market for generation infrastructure; and the household and consumer technology modules interact in the market for electricity-consuming goods.

12.2.2   Households (Consumers)

There are six household groups. Each group plays as a single household in one of six market segments, as defined by their income and personal priorities. These segments are classified along two axes – their relative economic position (determined by quintiles of income before taxes) and the group's top priority in PowerPlay (minimizing electricity-related spending, minimizing household emissions, or maximizing the style and service provided by goods), as shown in Table 12.2.[1]

Although each group plays at the scale of a single household, their decisions are treated as indicative of the decisions of all similar households in the economy. Thus, as Table 12.3 shows, group 1's decisions represent the decisions of 53 million households whereas group 5 represents only 4

Table 12.2   Group number by income and priority

Highest priority	Income Group	
	Lowest 80%	Highest 20%
Low spending	1	4
Environment	2	5
High style/service	3	6

million households. In the aggregate, the six groups represent the approximately 110 million households in the US. The groups' 'buying power' and objectives are summarized in Table 12.3.

Each group begins the game with a home well stocked with electrical goods. These have varying life expectancies (ranging from 7 to 13 years) and vintages; thus, some will soon need replacing, others will last for some years still. Each turn, 90 percent of household income is committed to non-electricity-related purchases. Some of the remaining 10 percent is spent on electric appliances and some on the electricity to operate appliances; the remainder is put towards other household purchases. These other household purchases (representing, perhaps, vacation spending or other service consumption) are assumed to be worth more to the household than are the services provided by electrical goods. Thus, the households have an incentive to maximize the share of game income going towards non-electrical purchases. How much their score depends on this share, however, is a function of the group's priorities.

Each turn, households must make choices about those electric appliances that break. Instead of replacing individual appliances, households select the product lines from which to purchase the replacements. They must distribute their purchases among the product lines currently available from the consumer technology firms. Each product line contains all of the appliances needed, with attributes – efficiency, style and service, and durability – determined by the firm offering the line. Alternatively, households may elect to repair or delay replacement of some of their broken appliances by apportioning less than 100 percent among the available product lines.

Each household group aims to have the highest score possible on a scale from 0 to 5 at the end of the game. The performance of each household group is measured along the three dimensions listed below. Each turn, a subscore is calculated for each dimension, and these subscores are combined according to the weightings given in Table 12.3 to obtain a composite score for each of the groups. The subscores are calculated as follows:

Table 12.3 Household groups

Group	Total Similar Households (millions)	Annual Disposable Income ($000)	Income at play each year ($000)	Primary Objective (weight in score)	Secondary Objective (weight in score)	Tertiary Objective (weight in score)
1	53	30	3	Minimize energy-related spending (60%)	Maximize style & service (30%)	Minimize environmental impact (10%)
2	9	30	3	Minimize environmental impact (50%)	Minimize energy-related spending (40%)	Maximize style & service (10%)
3	26	30	3	Maximize style & service (50%)	Minimize energy-related spending (40%)	Minimize environmental impact (10%)
4	11	80	8	Minimize energy-related spending (60%)	Maximize style & service (30%)	Minimize environmental impact (10%)
5	4	80	8	Minimize environmental impact (50%)	Minimize energy-related spending (40%)	Maximize style & service (10%)
6	7	80	8	Maximize style & service (50%)	Minimize energy-related spending (40%)	Minimize environmental impact (10%)

- Spending – based 50 percent on spending during the current turn and 50 percent on average annual discounted (at 10 percent annually) spending over the last ten years.
- Style and Service – based on the level of style and service the household obtains from its stock of electric appliances as compared to the minimum requirement of that household.
- Environment – based on the amount of CO_2 emissions attributable to household electricity use.

To succeed in PowerPlay, household groups must align their purchasing decisions with their objectives as given in Table 12.3.

The STELLA household modules use a vintage model to track the current inventory of electrical goods. This means that the characteristics (style/service and efficiency levels) of a given turn's purchase (a vintage) stay attached to that vintage until it is retired.

The household modules also calculate the total electricity demand by the household sector. The efficiency of each vintage in each group's module is multiplied by the number of units and by the number of households that group represents. This total energy demand is sent to the utility module to calculate generation requirements, the CO_2 emissions per kWh of electricity, and the price of electricity. These are then fed back to the household modules to calculate total spending per group on electricity and total emissions per household. Similarly, the posted prices for consumer goods are drawn from the consumer technology firms and multiplied by the number of units purchased to calculate the total spending per household on replacement appliances. The score for each household is then calculated according to the formulae described above.

12.2.3   Consumer Technology Firms (Appliance Manufacturers)

There are three consumer technology groups, each representing a manufacturer of consumer appliances. Together they (annually) supply household electrical goods worth roughly $130 billion.[2] They each begin the game with different strengths and different product lines. Each of these lines includes every type of electrical good needed by households: lighting, air conditioners (including associated insulation), space heaters, refrigerators, clothes washers and dryers, hair dryers, computers, printers, televisions, VCRs, radios, cordless telephones and other appliances. The three firms invest their resources in maintaining existing product lines, retooling existing product lines, introducing new product lines and developing more energy-efficient products.

Each turn, a firm may invest in retooling a product line for the coming

Table 12.4   Product attributes

Attribute	1 = worst, 5 = best
Efficiency	1, 2, 3, 4, 5
Style and Service	1, 2, 3, 4
Durability	1, 2, 3

period by adjusting any or all of three product attributes. The attributes are listed along with their possible values in Table 12.4. A firm may opt to close a product line that is not selling well to avoid incurring annual maintenance charges on this line. A firm may also introduce a new product line, though this is substantially more expensive than retooling an existing line. Lastly, a firm must choose a markup (or per-unit profit margin) for each of its active product lines.

Each turn, firms are free to retool existing lines or create new lines to respond to their perceptions of current consumer demand. For each line, they choose among different levels of durability, with each higher level of durability increasing the price to produce the product line. They also choose from four levels of style and service. Each household has a minimum level at which they must keep their style/service level, and also their score is partially dependent on the average style/service level of their product inventory. Thus, there will be some households that want to purchase products that give them higher levels of service or are superior stylistically and, consequently, the producers must weigh this demand against the steep increases in production price caused by high-service, high-style product lines.

Finally, the firms must decide what technology will form the base of their product lines. In PowerPlay, there are five generic technology types ranging from type 1, which just meets efficiency standards and can be mass produced at very low cost, to type 5, which is highly experimental, very efficient (in the prototype it used half the energy of the type 1, or baseline, technology), and quite expensive to produce when the game begins. Unlike the other two product attributes, the firms in PowerPlay are able to reduce the costs of producing these five technologies. Drawing on the model of production learning curves developed by Grübler et al. (1999), firms are able to bring down their production costs though learning by doing or by choosing to spend research and development (R&D) dollars directly on a given technology type.

For each active product line, PowerPlay calculates a production cost by adding together the production costs of each of the three components of the line. Thus, any line that sees active sales will have its price go down in the subsequent turn due to the decrease in the cost of the underlying efficiency technology. A product line's cost to the consumer households is determined by applying the firm's chosen markup to its cost of production. The model aggregates the information from the three firms and displays the available product lines and their prices to the entire game room over one of the projector displays. To reflect the delays experienced in setting up new product lines and marketing product and price changes, firms must make any changes during the turn prior to the turn that those changes will become available to consumers.

Each of the three consumer goods firms starts with a different product line portfolio, as well as different strengths relative to the other two firms:

- MayPool excels at bringing to market large volumes at affordable prices. It begins the game with four active product lines, all of which cater to broad market segments.
- SharperStone emphasizes image over other product attributes and historically has been most successful in marketing to style-conscious consumers. It begins the game with three active product lines.
- HomeStar is known for its energy-efficient products and begins the game with only two active product lines.

To succeed in PowerPlay, the firms must maximize their profits. PowerPlay calculates each year's profits by subtracting line costs, production costs, and R&D spending from sales revenues. Sales revenue is determined by the purchasing decisions of the six household groups and the price of available product lines. Line costs reflect not only the costs of setting up and operating physical production equipment, but also the marketing and research that goes into selling a product line.

12.3   ELECTRIC UTILITY

The utility group represents a large, regulated utility that generates the electricity used by households in the PowerPlay world. They must determine the composition of generation by choosing between five generation technologies: coal, natural gas combined cycle (NGCC), coal integrated gasification combined cycle (IGCC), wind and solar. The utility group faces the very challenging task of anticipating future changes in demand when planning new generation capacity. To mitigate this challenge, a number of simplifying assumptions are built into PowerPlay. First, the utility is only concerned with base-load generation capacity. In PowerPlay, there is no difference between peak demand and base-load electricity demand.

This relieves the utility players of the responsibility of planning for the intra-annual cycles of power consumption in addition to the inter-annual changes. Second, as explained in section 12.2.7, the absence of growth in PowerPlay means that the utility can focus on changes in end-use efficiency and not have to worry about future growth. Third, the utility group is only concerned with generation; distribution, transmission and retail functions are handled external to PowerPlay by a flat assessment fee on each kWh of electricity. Finally, the Utility is a regulated monopoly.[3]

The utility group begins the game with a stock of generating capacity comprised of units ranging in age from 1 to 80 years as described in Table 12.5. The utility must decide how much new capacity of each technology type to purchase during the coming year to replace these losses. It is also responsible for communicating with household groups to try to identify trends in home purchases that will reduce or increase electricity demand.

The utility's decisions will influence the market price of electricity. Each year, electricity demand is calculated from the aggregated stock of appliances owned by consumers. The generation mix is then determined based on existing capacity. The cost of operating this capacity (fuel costs and operation and maintenance (O&M) costs) combined with the return on invested capital is used to calculate the total revenues from electricity sales.[4]

Table 12.5   Initial generation capacity

Generation Technology	Optimal Capacity Factor (when new)	Initial Share of Generation (GWh)[1]	Initial Age Distribution (MW)[2]
Coal	80%	85%	21% 0–20 yrs 60% 20–40 yrs 18% 40–60 yrs 2% >60 yrs
Natural Gas Combined Cycle	80%	13%	50% 0–15 yrs 50% 15–30 yrs
Coal Integrated Gasification Combined Cycle	80%	1%	100% <15 yrs
Wind	35%	1%	100% <15 yrs
Solar	20%	0%	–

Notes:
[1] Generation shares from EIA (2004).
[2] EIA (2003).

When new purchases are made, the new units are assumed to operate optimally at the capacities given in the second column of Table 12.5. Wind and solar units always operate at peak capacity and the fossil-fueled generators fill in the balance of demand, divided among existing units according to available capacities. Demand above optimal capacity results in third-party electricity purchases (assumed to be from privately owned peaking units).

To succeed in PowerPlay, the utility must maximize its profits. Each year's profits are calculated by subtracting spending on new capacity and production costs (fuel and O&M) from sales revenue. Aside from making prudent investment decisions, the utility group must work closely with the regulators to keep their allowable profits high.

12.4   GENERATION TECHNOLOGY FIRMS

The generation technology group (GenTech) represents all those firms that supply generation equipment to the utility. Their 'products' are power plants that make use of the following technologies: coal, natural gas combined cycle (NGCC), coal integrated gasification combined cycle (IGCC), wind and solar. GenTech is responsible not only for building and manufacturing the facilities and equipment, but also for the research and development necessary to reduce generation costs. In addition, GenTech may make internal purchases to stimulate the development of wind and solar technologies by reducing these technologies' production costs.

GenTech also must decide how much to spend on research and development (R&D) for each of the technologies during the coming year. R&D spending on a given technology reduces the per-MW cost of producing a power plant that uses that technology. Costs of production also go down as the company gains experience in production of a given technology through sales. It must encourage the utility to invest in some borderline technologies (IGCC and wind in PowerPlay) in order to bring its costs of production down to a competitive level.[5]

GenTech can boost production of some technologies (wind or solar), and thus accelerate learning, by purchasing the technology for its own use. GenTech can then sell the electricity generated by its own units to the utility at the utility's avoided cost. The utility, in turn, will sell the electricity at retail to consumers. If the utility is not buying much of an advanced technology, such internal purchases can supplement R&D in bringing down production costs.

To succeed in PowerPlay, GenTech must maximize its profits. Each year's profits are calculated by subtracting production costs and R&D spending from revenues.

12.5   REGULATIONS AND POLICIES

In addition to the player groups, the game facilitators have at their disposal a number of policy levers. One of the purposes of PowerPlay is to see how different types of policies affect purchasing and investment decisions. Thus, we built into the game the ability to implement different policies. The policies available in PowerPlay are:

- Minimum efficiency standards. This stipulates that no products may be sold in PowerPlay below a certain minimum level of efficiency. In game terms, this amounts to outlawing production of consumer products technology with attributes 1 as listed in Table 12.4.
- Subsidies on consumer goods. This allows the government to offer subsidies on the purchase of either a given product line or on all products built with a given technology type. These subsidies, like all other subsidies in PowerPlay, are paid for by a 'tax' that is levied on each group in proportion to the amount of income they have relative to other groups.
- Demand-side management. The utility group subsidizes the purchase of certain product lines (or products with a specific technology type) by consumers. In exchange, the utility is allowed to increase the sale price of electricity by an amount that allows it to recoup the electricity it does not sell due to increased efficiency. Thus, from the utility's perspective, the PowerPlay DSM program is revenue neutral.
- Mandatory labeling program. At the beginning of PowerPlay, consumers see only vague descriptions of the efficiency of the product lines. A mandatory labeling program, if instituted, forces the companies to report the actual energy consumption figures of their products. At any time, any of the companies can choose voluntarily to institute product labeling of their own.
- Change the return to capital of the utility. The regulators can change what rate of the return on capital the utility group is allowed to factor into the pricing equation. This can be used to force the utility to share a greater burden of the effect of an increase in the cost of electricity, punish the utility for poor decisions, or reward it for a stable, low price of electricity.
- Change the maximum electricity price increase allowed. The maximum increase is meant to keep prices relatively stable and force

the utility to assume some of the risk for poor decisions. However, in the face of rapidly increasing fuel prices or a need for more capacity, the regulators might deem it prudent to allow for more rapid increases in price.

- Generation production tax credit. To encourage lower electricity-related emissions (and thus make environmentally conscious households happier), production of wind and solar electricity can be subsidized with anywhere from fractions of a cent to a couple of cents for every kWh of electricity produced by either the utility or GenTech groups. Like the product subsidies, the cost of this subsidy is paid for by a 'tax' that is spread across the groups proportional to income.
- Renewable portfolio standard. Finally, the government can require that the utility's mix of power includes a minimum percentage of renewable (solar or wind) power.

12.6 THE REST OF THE ECONOMY

These five sets of player groups interact in three markets: the market for electricity, the market for generation equipment and the market for electrical goods. Lending institutions are not explicitly included. Instead, the game treats these and other entities as external 'black boxes'. Each turn, households are provided with the portion (10 percent) of their income not saved or spent on goods and services external to the game while the remainder never enters consideration. The profits of the producing groups also leave the game. They may be distributed as dividends to investors, paid back to lenders, or deposited into the bank, but in game terms all are treated simply as 'accrued profits'. We found that if we added financial decisions (loans, savings, investment in companies) to the already complicated purchasing and production decisions then the game became unreasonably complex for players. As the player groups must make several decisions in the course of a ten-minute turn, we had to be sensitive to how much information they were faced with, and had to handle, at a time.

Finally, to simplify decision-making, we assumed that no growth occurs in the world of PowerPlay. Income for households is the same each turn, as are household size, total number of households, and thus total goods demand. This, in turn, means that new goods purchases are limited to replacement and new generation demand depends only on retirement of old units and change in the average level of residential electrical efficiency.

12.7 PLAYING THE GAME

12.7.1 Overview

The game begins with each group receiving a basic description of its current condition: disposable income, profit, revenues, energy prices, generation capacity, active product lines, and so on. Groups interact with one another directly and indirectly through their use of the levers adumbrated in Table 12.1. Direct interaction between electricity consumers and producers occurs, for example, when households or firms purchase electricity from the utility. Indirect interactions among players occur, for example, when government subsidizes the implementation of new technology and as a result electricity prices drop for consumers. A computer model captures actions and displays their impacts on individual player groups and the system as a whole.

The game is divided into multiple periods (years). At the beginning of each year, players receive basic information about the economy and their (and others') performance during the past year. They then must make all of their purchasing, investment and other decisions for the coming year. These decisions are input into the model and the model is run at the end of the round, simulating the passage of the year. The STELLA model solves a set of thousands of difference equations, capturing the interrelationships among the various model components – from vintage structures of the capital stock to budget constraints for players, to choices by players. The next year begins with the players learning how the world changed over the course of the year as a result of players' choices and exogenous developments. With this new information they must make a new set of decisions.

By chance, unforeseen events may happen, such as a technological breakthrough in power generation or end-use equipment, a major shortfall in petroleum or gas supplies that raises the cost of electricity generation, a severe weather event that brings down power lines, a decline in employment, a decrease in consumer confidence, or the introduction of a new environmental regulation or energy policy. In any given period, multiple chance events may occur. A 'news feed', posted on a projection screen in the main game room, is used to inform players of such events.

The game is either run until some major bottleneck is encountered (for example the economy collapses because of bad decisions) or stopped at some random point. It is important that the game end at a random rather than predetermined time in order to avoid strategic behavior that would be prompted by the knowledge of the terminal period. For example, telling players that the game would last for 20 periods may lead them to halt all investments from period 16 on in order to maximize profits.

12.7.2 PowerPlay Version 1.0

Following extensive beta testing, PowerPlay was officially rolled out on 26 August 2004 in Pacific Grove, California as part of the American Council for an Energy Efficient Economy's Summer Study on Energy Efficiency in Buildings. More than 100 of the attending energy efficiency professionals participated in the game during the course of an evening. Each of the 11 groups had its own workstation supplied with a laptop PC as well as player information cards and nametags to help players get into their roles. Care was taken to locate the workstations close to one another to encourage interaction between the groups. Several types of information were projected onto three large screens at the front of the room. One screen displayed the currently available product lines' prices and other attributes as well as fuel and electricity prices. Another screen displayed current and historical group scores. A third screen indicated the current round and amount of time remaining in the round. It also displayed a 'live news feed' to keep players apprised of current events and new policies that could affect energy markets. All of the PCs were networked together to allow for the exchange of information between the model, the players' computer interfaces and the projected displays.

Play was very lively: household groups negotiated with appliance manufacturers for product lines with desirable attributes. Early in the game, the utility group overshot demand with two huge investments in generation capacity. The GenTech group enjoyed record profits from those sales, but their business floundered thereafter. The household groups with a vested interest in lowering net emissions formed a coalition to lobby the politician/regulator unsuccessfully for a renewable portfolio standard. A year later, HomeStar began labeling its product lines with Energy Star-like labels. SharperStone and MayPool followed suit just two years later in attempts to recapture energy-conscious consumers. Toward the end of the game, low-income consumers and the HomeStar group successfully negotiated with the politician/regulator to introduce a 20 percent government subsidy on purchases of the most efficient consumer goods. These subsidies, funded through a tax distributed across the groups according to income, reduced the effective price of appliances using the two highest energy-efficient technologies (see Figure 12.1).

12.8 FINDINGS AND INSIGHTS

Players' decisions shaped technology investments and energy purchases on both the demand and the supply side. After 13 'years' of hectic interactions

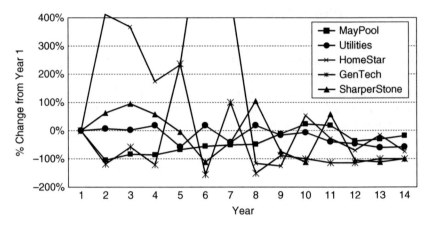

Figure 12.1   Annual firm profits

and decisions, the following characteristics of the PowerPlay world had become clear.

12.8.1   Efficiency Advocates Behave like Efficiency Advocates

With any group experience, participants bring a certain bias to the table. The participants of the 2004 Association for an Energy Efficient Economy summer study who played PowerPlay betrayed their bias through an over-whelming drive to increase efficiency regardless of their supposed group interests. It certainly was not surprising that a group of people with careers in advancing energy efficiency would act in a game setting according to the same ideals that motivate their work. What was surprising, though, was the effect that these biases had on the outcome of the game.

The utility group invested in low-emission wind and natural gas combined cycle energy to a much greater degree than American power generators are expected to over the next two decades. However, even after absorbing the impact on profits of that decision, the utility group continued to invest in the more expensive and lower-emission technologies in lieu of the two coal options. This contributed to the cost of electricity and thus ended up hurting the household groups that placed less emphasis on the environment. Indeed, the two environmentally motivated households outperformed the other four (Figure 12.2) by wide margins for this reason. The environmentally minded groups, on the other hand, were boosted as the emissions per kWh dropped over the course of the game, lowering the total emissions attributable to their energy use.

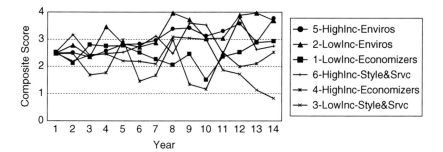

Figure 12.2   Household group scores

The utilities were not the only group behaving 'out of character' during the game. The economizing households and the style-conscious houses both invested in more efficient technologies than their starting profiles would have indicated. In the end, this hurt all four groups as the lag effect of high purchase costs early on pulled down their score through the remainder of the game.

12.8.2   Efficiency Can Lead to Higher Prices

In this run of PowerPlay, in the absence of any utility-sponsored program, household groups made their efficiency investment decisions independent of any action by the utility. However, in planning their investment in generation infrastructure, the utility failed to take these purchases into account. Coupled with the accidental overpurchase of capacity early in the game, this left the utility group underutilizing their generation stock for most of the game. As the public utility pricing system allowed them to recoup capital gains on these investments, the result was a steady increase in the price of electricity mirroring the downward movement of electricity demand (Figure 12.3).

This is reflective of the nature of power generation, where the long-term nature of generator investments leaves supply relatively inelastic. Thus, massive investments in efficiency by consumers hurt generator profits by lowering demand for the given supply. Even if the utility group had planned properly for the amount of efficiency investment that occurred, they still would have faced a loss of sales volume and thus of total profits. Only by taking part in a revenue-neutral demand-side management (DSM) program (one of the policy options available in PowerPlay) could the utility group have maintained their profits in the face of the observed consumer decisions. However, our utility group

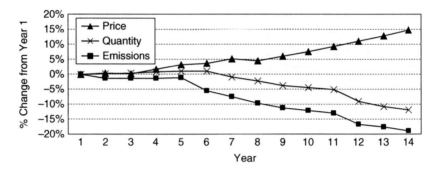

Figure 12.3   Electricity price, quantity and CO_2 emissions

expressed no desire to 'further lower demand' for electricity, and thus opted not to push for a DSM program. In reality, given the observed effect of direct subsidies (discussed below), it is likely that the utility would not have encouraged much additional efficiency through a DSM program, but would have been able to share some of the benefits of the efficiency purchases made.

12.8.3   Subsidy Programs Hurt Lower-Income Households

The subsidy (20 percent of the price of goods using tech types 4 and 5) on energy efficiency technologies, though advocated by the poorer households (who wanted to afford purchases) only ended up helping those households already making efficiency decisions. The two environmentally minded households and the high-income economizers continued to purchase roughly the same mix of efficiency goods despite the reduced price of the highest efficiencies. The low-income economizers, already burdened by the costs of their earlier purchases, were still not in a position to afford the subsidized higher efficiency goods. However, they ended up paying the bulk of the subsidies' costs. First, insomuch as the low-income economizers represented 50 percent of the households and control 30 percent of the US household income, they pay the largest share of the tax burden among the six household groups (since the tax is divided by income). Thus, they subsidized the purchase of efficiency goods by the richer households through the very policy they were convinced to lobby for.

Secondly, any efficiency purchases made due to the subsidies would raise the electricity price under a regulated utility system like PowerPlay's utility group. When the richer households bought more efficient goods, the drop-off in energy demand, with no corresponding (and pre-empted) drop-off in either generation investment or returns on capital, raises the per-unit cost of electricity. Since the subsidy was not enough to encourage efficiency investment by the lower-income households, they maintained roughly the same energy consumption profile. Thus, while the total energy spending of the other households declined or stayed even, the low-income economizers and the low-income style-conscious groups faced rising electricity spending. If the utility group had been deregulated into several separate generation companies competing in a market, then the reduction in demand would have lowered the purchase price of electricity. Under the regulated utility regime, subsidies (as opposed to the DSM system discussed above) hurt the groups they were most meant to help.

12.8.4 Separation of Markets Undermines Efficiency Gains

Over the course of each turn, the household groups had to divide their time among calculating their purchasing decisions, lobbying producer groups, lobbying the utility, and lobbying the facilitators/politicians. Inevitably, some activities took precedence over others. Interestingly, for all six households, more than half of their person-minutes were put into making the product purchase decisions. The rest of the time was split roughly evenly between asking the politicians for favors and brokering deals with the consumer goods producers. We observed no communication whatsoever between the households and the utility group, despite the fact that, unlike the real world, they had direct open access to each other. The same was true of the consumer goods groups – although they had open access to the utility group, they attempted no strategic planning with them. The utility group did attempt, a few times, to ascertain what purchase decisions consumers were likely to make. However, most of their time was spent negotiating with the generation technology groups.

The two markets modeled in the game – the market for electricity and the market for electrical goods – intersect at the level of the household. The past outcome of the electrical goods markets is the primary determinant of demand in the current electricity market. The supplier in the electricity market thus has an incentive, at least, to know what is going on in the goods market and at the most influence it. Under a regulated utility regime, the households have an economic motivation to facilitate that knowledge insomuch as better utility planning means lower electricity prices. However, in the game, as in real life, the time lag between helping the utility out and the return of lower prices makes it hard for households to justify investing their scarce time in such activities. Furthermore, the connection between telling the utility what you plan to purchase and lower prices is not apparent at first glance. This is exacerbated by the utility's clear profit motive, which makes any claims to lower price seem disingenuous at best. The result of this disconnect between the two markets in our game was that the utility group failed to adapt their planning to a rapidly changing consumer goods market, resulting in overinvestment that cancelled out much of the economic benefits of efficiency. Investment in efficiency was not enough by itself – greater gains could have been realized if these investments had been coordinated with the utility through more open information flows, through a DSM-style program, or both.

12.8.5   Generation of Experimental Data for Use by Other Models

Although not examined extensively with the set of games completed to this point, our preliminary review suggests that PowerPlay may also provide a rich source of experimental data that might be used to initialize other more conventional economic models. For example, Figure 12.3 illustrates several interesting points that may be typically overlooked in a number of traditional economic models. First, there may be a serious lag between price changes and significant changes in either energy use or emissions. In fact, the more immediate and deeper reduction of carbon dioxide emissions compared to energy use suggests that utilities may take more immediate actions to respond to price changes compared to consumers. Moreover, the long-run price elasticities may be larger than many models might otherwise suggest. The literature typically suggests own price elasticities in the range of -0.30 to -0.50. The test results shown here indicate possibilities approaching -0.75 to -1.0. This may be the result of a shift in consumer preferences not otherwise explored by traditional models. Finally Figure 12.2 indicates that while overall welfare may be largely unchanged, there may be clearly winners and losses among different household categories. To explore or confirm any of these insights will require more runs with a deeper set of data sets. But mining even these preliminary results suggest that existing models may benefit from a greater range of behavioral sensitivities than usually shown.

12.9   SUMMARY AND CONCLUSIONS

While providing participants in PowerPlay the real-life experience of making decisions about energy efficiency, the game also offered insights on how firm and household decisions are made under changing technological and market conditions. The game provided an opportunity to grasp the underlying reasons for unanticipated market dynamics and their ripple effects in energy efficiency markets. It also provided a means of testing the impact of a subsidy policy on the actors in such a market.

Most significantly, we found that rapid investment by consumers in energy efficiency in a regulated utility environment can result in a run-up of electricity prices. In today's increasingly deregulated environment, such an outcome is less likely as producers are not guaranteed a return on investment for existing capital. A decrease in demand (or, if we factor growth back into the analysis, a decrease in the rate of demand growth) should, in a competitive generation environment, result in lower electricity prices. However, inaccurate forecasts of future demand and supply changes can still swing the market the other way, with undersupply causing black- and brown-outs throughout the system.

PowerPlay also raised questions of equity with regards to efficiency investments and efficiency subsidies. Insomuch as wealthier consumers are more likely to purchase subsidized efficiency goods than are low-income consumers, such a subsidy had a regressive economic impact, effectively transferring income from low-income to high-income households. Further, if such efficiency investments have adverse effects on the dynamics of the energy market, as they did in this run of PowerPlay, then all households suffer the consequences while only the wealthier ones collect any benefit.[6]

It should be kept in mind that the insights discussed in this chapter are the results of a single run of the PowerPlay game. The observations made of future PowerPlay games could further enhance our understanding of energy-efficiency market dynamics. By changing the utility to multiple groups of deregulated generators, introducing different policy systems, or ramping up energy prices during multiple runs of the game we could collect new insights into how structure, policy and exogenous variables affect the dynamics of electricity and electrical goods markets and the decision-making of their associated actors.

ACKNOWLEDGMENT

PowerPlay was made possible in part by support from the US Environmental Protection Agency and the International Energy Agency, Organisation for Economic Co-operation and Development (OECD), Paris, France. We wish to thank the numerous participants in the alpha test, hosted at the Alliance to Save Energy, Washington DC, and the beta test, hosted at the US Environmental Protection Agency (EPA). Special thanks go to the American Council for an Energy Efficient Economy for featuring the roll-out of PowerPlay at its 2004 annual meeting in Pacific

Grove, California. We are indebted to Ari Reeves for valuable research and design support. The usual disclaimers apply.

NOTES

1. All household characteristics discussed in this section are from BLS (2003) unless otherwise noted.
2. Based on aggregate figures from BLS (2003).
3. Plans for future versions of PowerPlay involve allowing deregulation of the utility and breaking it into a number of competing generation companies.
4. O&M costs are from Narula et al. (2002). Fuel costs are based on the Energy Information Administration's (EIA's) *Annual Energy Outlook* 2003 (http://www.eia.doe.gov/emeu/aer/contents.html).
5. For an explanation of how the model treats learning curves, R&D and technology production, see the description of the same in the consumer goods group, Section 12.2 of this chapter.
6. In the case of a deregulated market (or a regulated market that properly plans for increases in efficiency), the corresponding decrease in price will still have a greater benefit for wealthy households (who consume more electricity on average) than it will for lower-income households.

REFERENCES

BLS (2003), 'Table 55. Quintiles of Income Before Taxes: Shares of Annual Aggregate Expenditures', Bureau of Labor Statistics, Washington, DC, http://stats.bls.gov/cex/2003/Aggregate/quintile.pdf.
Dyner, I. and C.J. Franco (2004), 'Consumers' Bounded Rationality: The Case of Competitive Energy Markets', *Systems Research and Behavioral Science*, **21**: 373–89.
EAI (2005), 'SimCity', Electronic Arts Inc., http://simcity.ea.com/
EIA (2003), *Annual Energy Outlook*, Energy Information Administration, US Department of Energy, Washington, DC: Government Printing Office.
EIA (2004), 'Electric Power Monthly – Table 5.1', Energy Information Administration, Washington, DC, 15 November, http://www.eia.doe.gov/cneaf/electricity/epm/table5_1.html.
Funtowicz, S.O. and J.R. Ravetz (1993), 'Science for the Post-Normal Age', *Futures*, **25**(7): 739–55.
Gately, D. (1980), 'Individual Discount Rates and the Purchase and Utilization of Energy-Using Durables: Comment', *Bell Journal of Economics*, **11**(1): 373–4.
Goett, A.A., K. Hudson and K.E. Train (2000), 'Customers' Choice Among Retail Energy Suppliers: The Willingness-to-Pay for Service Attributes', *Energy Journal*, **21**(4): 1–28.
Graedel, T.E. and B.R. Allenby (1995), *Industrial Ecology*, Englewood Cliffs, NJ: Prentice Hall.
Grübler, A., N. Nakicenovic and D.G. Victor (1999), 'Dynamics of Energy Technologies and Global Change', *Energy Policy*, **27**: 247–80.

Hannon, B. and M. Ruth (2001), *Dynamic Modeling*, 2nd edition, New York: Springer-Verlag.

Hassett, K.A. and G.E. Metcalf (1995), 'Energy Tax Credits and Residential Conservation Investment: Evidence from Panel Data', *Journal of Public Economics*, **57**: 201–17.

Hausman, J. (1979), 'Individual Discount Rates and the Purchase and Utilization of Energy-Using Durables', *Bell Journal of Economics*, **10**: 33–54.

Howarth, R.B. and B. Andersson (1993), 'Marker Barriers to Energy Efficiency', *Energy Economics*, **15**(4): 262–72.

ISEE Systems (2004), 'STELLA', http://www.iseesystems.com, accessed 22 September 2004.

Jaffe, A.B. and R.N. Stavins (1994), 'The Energy–Efficiency Gap, What Does it Mean?', *Energy Policy*, **22**(10): 804–10.

Kagel, J.H. and A.E. Roth (1995), *The Handbook of Experimental Economics*, Princeton, NJ: Princeton University Press.

Laitner, J.A.S., S.J. DeCanio and I. Peters (2000), 'Incorporating Behavioral, Social, and Organizational Phenomena in the Assessment of Climate Change Mitigation Options', in E. Jochem, J. Sathaye and D. Bouille (eds), *Society, Behavior, and Climate Change Mitigation*, Dordrecht, The Netherlands: Kluwer Academic Press, pp. 1–64.

Narula, R.G., H. Wen and K. Himes (2002), 'Incremental Cost of CO_2 Reduction in Power Plants', ASME Turbo Expo 2002, 3 June.

Osborne, M.J. and A. Rubinstein (1994), *A Course in Game Theory*, Cambridge, MA: MIT Press.

Owen, G. (2001), *Game Theory*, San Diego, CA: Academic Press.

Ruth, M. (1998), 'Mensch and Mesh: Perspectives on Industrial Ecology', *Journal of Industrial Ecology*, **2**: 13–22.

Smith, V.L. (1992), *Papers in Experimental Economics*, Cambridge: Cambridge University Press.

Soccolow, R., C. Andrews, F. Berhout and V. Thomas (eds) (1996), *Industrial Ecology and Global Change*, Cambridge: Cambridge University Press.

13. The dynamics of regions and networks in industrial ecosystems: retrospect and prospect

Brynhildur Davidsdottir and Matthias Ruth

13.1 RETROSPECT

Industrial ecosystems are complex adaptive systems, built of both man-made and physical and natural components, which closely interact with, influence and are influenced by their economic, social and environmental surroundings. As fundamental cornerstones of human economies, the development of industrial ecosystems shapes regional and national economies and influences regional and national development. System change implies a change in the structure and functioning of industrial systems in addition to the extent and quality of the interactions with their surroundings as well. Such changes ripple through the entire system through dynamic, often non-linear, lagged and feedback-driven processes and thereby generate complex behaviors that may be difficult to foresee.

Agents, such as producers and consumers, influence the behavior of industrial ecosystems through complex interaction networks. Such interactions take different forms such as cooperation, competition, symbiosis or predation with a self-interested objective in mind. At larger scales those interactions generally display more complexity due to heterogeneity of system components, agents and interactions, yet at smaller scales interaction between the system and the external natural and physical environment add increased complexity.

Given the importance of industrial ecosystems to human and natural systems, an understanding of the complex network dynamics exhibited by industrial ecosystems is pertinent to successful industrial, economic and environmental management and for successful planning of sustainable futures. The scholarship of the dynamics of industrial ecosystems is still in its infancy and thus scattered in small bits and pieces throughout the literature. This volume has brought together the various fragments that are slowly building a comprehensive paradigm, ranging from the more important concepts and analogies to the various modeling approaches that are used to analyze the dynamics of industrial ecosystems.

This volume is composed of three parts. The first focuses on basic concepts and methods, and pays particular attention to the use of analogies from biology and how they apply in industrial ecology. The second part focuses on regional dynamics, and the third focuses on industrial ecosystems as complex systems. Each part and the individual chapters within each part provide a specific perspective and illustrations. Here, we briefly review the individual contributions to each part and summarize the main conclusions. The chapter concludes with some thoughts on further developments in the field.

13.1.1 Concepts and Methods

The use of nature as a model for the emergence and development of industrial ecosystems is often a basic and coordinating precept in the study of industrial ecosystems. Marian Chertow, in her chapter 'Dynamics of geographically based industrial ecosystems', briefly identifies the various analogies on which this precept is based and then explores the commonalities between geographically based industrial ecosystems and natural ecosystems. Geographically based industrial ecosystems are comprised of those business entities that persist in geographic proximity and share resources such as water, energy, by-products and waste. Chertow's contribution expands the knowledge of such industrial ecosystems with recent findings from ecosystem studies, emphasizing the roles of diversity and stability, system openness, non-equilibrium thermodynamics and food web dynamics to illustrate the increased attention in the ecology literature on complexity and adaptation. She argues that modern ecology, with its emphasis on ecosystems as complex adaptive systems, better portrays relevant features and dynamics of industrial ecosystems. Chertow's claim is illustrated with an analysis of 50 industrial ecosystems for which she distinguishes two stylized models for geographically based industrial ecosystems: the planned eco-industrial park model and the self-organizing symbiosis model. Chertow's analysis reveals the self-organizing model to be similar to a natural ecosystem model, as it is adaptive, resilient and thus more sustainable than the planned eco-industrial park model. Her findings illustrate three emerging properties of geographically based industrial ecosystems: (1) linkages beget linkages and trades beget trades; (2) similar to change in interactions as ecosystems approximate a climax state, linkages increase in complexity as industrial ecosystems mature; and (3) adaptability sustains industrial ecosystems. As a corollary, as industries enter into a mutually beneficial relationship and as industrial systems mature, linkages and trades occur that most likely would not have occurred otherwise. Adaptability in the face of ever-changing relationships becomes an essential trait to the survival of industrial ecosystems.

13.1.2   Regional Dynamics

Industrial ecosystems, just as natural ecosystems, can be defined and modeled at various scales, such as local, regional or national. A regional perspective in many cases can be useful as it corresponds with the economic and policy framework in which the industrial ecosystem operates. Yet the environmental impact of regional dynamics is often felt at distances that fall far outside of the system boundaries that are deemed appropriate for modeling regional dynamics. As a result, the modeler must be conscious of the possibility that system boundaries may dictate model outcome, and flows across system boundaries may dictate changes within the system.

In their chapter 'Spatial and temporal life cycle assessment: ozone formation potential from natural gas use in a typical residential building in Pittsburgh, USA', authors Lloyd and Ries present a framework that incorporates geographic and meteorological information into life cycle inventory and impact assessment to enable the explicit differentiation between environmental impacts at different locations and points in time. The proof-of-concept life cycle assessment (LCA) framework is then applied to evaluate the ozone formation potential of discontinuous methane emissions that results from producing and using natural gas for residential hot water heating in Pittsburgh, Pennsylvania. The results illustrate that a simultaneous temporal and spatial understanding of a product's life cycle will more accurately capture the environmental impact of a product. The authors conclude that while one of the goals of industrial ecology is to structure industrial ecosystems as closed-loop systems, it is important to understand where and when resources are consumed and from where they originate. Such information, according to the authors, helps identify opportunities for closed-loop systems that heretofore would go unnoticed.

In regional science, the analysis of resource and commodity flows across defined regional boundaries has been prominent for a long time. Such flows are for example captured as interregional trade and are likely to become a defining feature of industrial ecosystems. In their chapter 'Estimating generalized regional input–output systems: a case study of Australia', authors Gallego and Lenzen address this issue. Various theories and models are used when incorporating trade flows into regional models, such as commodity balance, supply–demand pools, location quotients, cross-industry quotients and gravity models. The authors draw on information from those various theories and models to build an innovative input–output model and arrive at a preliminary estimate of an interregional interindustry trade flow matrix for Australia. They then use their results to describe which of the traditional theoretical assumptions of interregional trade flows best reflect Australian interindustry, interregional trade flows. The results of this work also yield insight on the impact that transport distances, relative industry sizes and other parameters have on the dynamics of interregional trade.

The chapter by Cicas, Hendrickson and Matthews called 'The economic and environmental consequences of reduced air transport services in Pennsylvania: a regional input–output life cycle assessment case study', continues the discussion of interindustry and interregional trade flows. They use an input–output model, akin to the one employed by Gallego and Lenzen combined with a life cycle model, such as that applied by Lloyd and Ries, to analyze the regional economic and environmental consequences of a decrease in air transportation services provided by US Airways. The approach enables the ability to capture both the direct and indirect sectoral impacts of a major economic event, where direct impacts are on the air transport sector itself and immediate suppliers, and indirect impacts are on the supply chain for the air transport sector.

So far in Part II, individual contributions have dealt with combining spatial and temporal dimensions of regional industrial systems using an LCA model, combining interregional trade flows using input–output (I–O) models and LCA and using I–O models to explore the structure of interregional interindustry dynamics.

In the last chapter in Part II of this volume, 'Design approach frameworks, regional metabolism and scenarios for sustainability', Baynes, West and Turner show the usefulness of the design approach when exploring the dynamics and interconnections between various components of a regional industrial ecosystem. The design approach captures separately the dynamics of the physical economy of a region and then combines that with the decision-making of socio-economic actors, by incorporating the user – a human being – as part of the modeling process. The authors illustrate how the design approach is able to represent in rigorous and rich detail the nuances of the physical economy, and at the same time be sufficiently transparent and accessible to enable stakeholder involvement. This is an important feature since long lifetime of capital and capital inertia ensures that the ramifications of investment and infrastructure decisions will last for years. Thus it becomes pertinent that stakeholders, for example involved in investment decisions, are able to participate in the modeling process as such participation yields information for the various stakeholders how they can influence different industrial futures. This may reduce myopic behavior, which is valuable, as sustainable futures need to be planned with considerable foresight. The authors illustrate that the design approach is one method to do just that, as it enables participation by decision-makers and various stakeholders to investigate various scenarios for sustainability.

13.1.3   Learning and Evolution in Industrial Ecosystems

Part III concludes this volume with five chapters that all address learning and evolution in industrial systems. The evolution of industrial ecosystems, and thus industrial futures, are influenced by the decisions and relationships between various agents or players who operate within the industrial network. Each player or agent has his own motives and aspirations that change over time as a result of learning and adaptation – which then in turn affect alternative futures. Kempener, Cohen, Basson and Petrie in their chapter 'A framework for analysis of industrial networks', address this issue. They illustrate how a linear and static analysis of industrial networks simplifies the complexity of those interrelationships, and the complexity of the industrial system. This simplification then translates into a failure of the approach to capture agent or player behavior, the impact of the external environment on agent behavior and the impact of adaptation and learning, and ultimately the failure to capture alternative industrial futures. The authors present a hierarchical analytical framework for network analysis that captures some of the complexity of industrial networks and in particular the complex interactions between the various stakeholders (or interested and affected parties, IAPs) that influence the evolution of industrial systems. The interactions are dynamic, and as a result the authors advocate using a combination of dynamic systems modeling and agent-based analysis.

In their chapter 'Understanding and shaping the evolution of sustainable large-scale socio-technical systems', Nikolic, Dijkema and van Dam continue this line of reasoning and illustrate a framework that captures the growth, evolution and adaptation of regional industrial clusters and large-scale socio-technical systems. Industrial clusters all over the world are examples of industrial ecosystems that are going to have to adapt, and as the authors argue, to become decentralized. The authors propose viewing such systems as large-scale adaptive and complex socio-technical systems, and that a managed evolution in both physical and social dimensions is required to shape those systems for sustainable futures. Such managed evolution relies on an appropriate modeling and simulation approach, which the authors call 'action-oriented industrial ecology' (AOIE). The generic model contains agents that are represented as nodes in both physical and social networks. Each agent model consists of four interconnected behavioral levels – identity, strategic, tactical and operational – and operates in three compartments – technology, economy and decision-making. The authors suggest use of the proposed framework to influence and shape the evolution of industrial systems.

While the chapters by both Nikolic et al. and Kempener et al. focus on large-scale socio-technical complexities, the complexities at smaller scales or for specific systems of technologies are no less important. Beavis, Black, Lennox, Turner and Moore, in their chapter on 'Futures scenarios of industrial ecosystems: a research design for transportation planning', illustrate the use of the design approach when planning for alternative futures of industrial systems such as transportation systems. More generally, the authors illustrate how the design approach combined with envelope analysis can effectively be used to study and plan for sustainable futures of industrial ecosystems. They present and implement a framework, model and scenario analysis for the Australian vehicle fleet with a specific focus on factors that may control and affect fuel efficiency and vehicle emissions. The results confirm the existence of multiple optimal transport technologies to enhance fuel efficiency and reduce emissions for long-term sustainability. Despite the lack of single technology optima, the authors illustrate by using envelope analysis that technology development can be expected to follow a broad technology trajectory or 'corridors', which often are defined by bio-physical constraints and structure of the already existing capital stock.

In the last chapter in this section, 'PowerPlay: developing strategies to promote energy efficiency', Ruth, Bernier, Meier and Laitner continue the discussion of the complexity of technological development in industrial systems. In this chapter the authors illustrate through the use of an innovative computer-facilitated game how the complex interactions between various agents and their simultaneous decisions affect the future development of industrial systems. Unlike many other models presented in this volume, PowerPlay was designed to be played interactively by stakeholders dealing with energy efficiency issues, ranging from members in utilities and regulatory agencies to firms engaged in innovation, development and implementation of new technology, to households making purchase decisions to maintain and enhance lifestyles. In this 'industrial ecosystem' of energy generators, suppliers and end users, two kinds of dynamics are important. First, those related to the change in structure and function of technology, economy and society represented in the model. Second, those related to information exchange and learning among stakeholders in the real communities making and living with the policy, investment and purchase decisions they made. The model, as well as results from a game that used it, points towards a new form of science-based learning environment that can help improve understanding of the dynamics of industrial ecosystems while at the same time generating data that are useful against which to compare and assess assumptions and specifications of the more traditional models used, for example in energy planning at regional and national levels.

13.2 PROSPECT

Although there lies tremendous strength in carrying out static analysis of industrial ecosystems for comparative purposes, the very nature of sustainability issues requires an understanding of both the time-varying behavior of industrial, socio-economic and environmental systems in their interrelationship as well as the spatial-varying behavior. This volume presents both the theoretical framework for assessing time-varying and spatial linkages between system components, as well as different yet complementary modeling tools that are able to capture regional complexities, socio-technical complexities and network complexities of industrial systems. The work presented in this volume suggests at least the following three avenues for further developments:

First, as valuable as analogies are to enhance understanding of industrial systems as part of larger social and ecological systems, to date the choice of analogies has largely been limited to those from mid-twentieth-century biology and ecology. In addition, interactions among components mostly have focused on the concept of symbiosis, even if other forms of interactions are no less important in nature. Significantly less attention has been paid to recent advancements in ecosystem theory, especially where it concerns complexity theory, non-equilibrium thermodynamics and related bodies of knowledge. A move beyond a focus on symbiosis is important for development in the field. But even more important for the development of industrial ecology, though, may be a move beyond analogies to actual applications of concepts and tools from those areas of research. A few first steps in that direction are presented in this volume; more are likely to come as the community of researchers grows, proliferation of methods and tools across disciplinary boundaries is encouraged and supported, and as the first insights from those first steps bear fruit in industry, economy and society.

Second, as the field of industrial ecology matures, methods are finetuned and their usefulness for analysis, as well as investment and policy support, are demonstrated through a growing number of case studies. One trend already apparent in this volume, and likely increasing over the next few years, is the confluence of methods and tools. For example, life cycle analysis makes it into dynamic simulation models or input–output models, agent-based models become increasingly used in conjunction with organizational theory and system dynamics, economics and econometrics make it into dynamic models of mass and energy flow within and across industry boundaries, and dynamic computer simulations of large industrial systems are opened up to allow for, and facilitate, dialog with stakeholders, learning, experimental data generation, and direct investment and policy support.

Third, it is increasingly recognized that sustainable solutions to engineering challenges require that economic, environmental and social constraints are not just acknowledged but are explicitly dealt with as part of the industrial ecologist's repertoire. Integrating engineering insights with models and tools from the environmental and social sciences, in itself, is an intellectual challenge for theory-building and modeling. Using those models in investment and policy-making requires attention to the combined limitations of each constituent part, error propagation when they are assembled, and effective communication of remaining uncertainties as they are communicated to decision-makers. Several of the studies presented in this volume are not only cognizant of the need for integration and sensitive to its challenges, but make efforts to move the field forward by attempting to do what has been called for elsewhere.

There clearly is no panacea for the social, economic and environmental challenges associated with industrial activities at the large scales required to meet globally growing human needs and wants. But there are smart and creative approaches to understand and manage individual aspects of these challenges better, and to clear avenues to pursue the reduction of pressures at all levels of system organization – from local and regional to global. The diversity of studies assembled in this volume should give us hope that development of flourishing industrial ecosystems is possible over the long haul, and that much can be done between now and then.

Index

accumulation 185, 188, 190
agency/agencies 3, 4, 14, 35, 44, 45, 47,
    127, 132, 139, 156, 157, 201, 203,
    221, 229
agent-based analysis 228
agent-based model 100, 162, 231
agent-based modeling 142, 159, 162
air transport 33, 83, 84, 85, 86, 87, 88,
    89, 90, 91, 92, 93, 94, 194, 227
analogy/analogies 4, 6, 7, 8, 9, 225,
    230
anthroposphere 179, 184, 185, 186,
    192
appliance 203, 205, 207, 210, 215
application 4, 5, 13, 22, 39, 65, 73, 85,
    94, 98, 139, 148, 164, 165, 172,
    175, 184, 230
Australia 14, 16, 18, 20, 35, 55, 56, 61,
    65, 66, 71, 73, 74, 98, 113, 114,
    115, 180, 189, 192, 193, 194, 196,
    226, 227
Australian 56, 57, 65, 66, 68, 73, 74, 75,
    76, 113, 114, 115, 180, 184, 189,
    191, 193, 196
Australian Stocks and Flows
    Framework 114, 115, 180, 184,
    191

backcasting 192, 193
balance 9, 56, 59, 61, 69, 106, 115, 126,
    175, 211, 226
biological analogy 6, 7
building 5, 15, 38, 40, 43, 44, 51, 52,
    55, 101, 113, 126, 179, 211, 215,
    224, 226
by-products 6, 8, 12, 17, 18, 21, 34, 40,
    67, 225

capacity 12, 32, 88, 93, 103, 104, 168,
    171, 187, 194, 204, 209, 210, 211,
    213, 214, 215, 217

capital 18, 34, 58, 64, 65, 70, 71, 72,
    73, 74, 75, 103, 104, 115, 130, 132,
    136, 158, 166, 167, 173, 185, 186,
    193, 210, 212, 214, 217, 219, 221,
    227, 229
capital inertia 227
capital stock 103, 104, 115, 214, 229
capital vintage 104
cellular automata 162
closed loop 7, 10, 15, 21, 22, 52, 185,
    226
coal 89, 209, 210, 211, 216
community 4, 10, 11, 20, 128, 159, 162,
    193, 203, 229, 230
complex 6, 7, 9, 10, 13, 15, 19, 20, 21,
    22, 31, 33, 98, 121, 122, 124, 128,
    129, 131, 133, 140, 141, 150, 157,
    159, 160, 163, 164, 172, 179, 188,
    190, 201, 213, 224, 225, 228, 229
complex adaptive systems 6, 7, 13, 15,
    19, 22, 131, 133, 159, 160, 163,
    164, 224, 225
complexity 3, 4, 6, 20, 22, 32, 103,
    123, 124, 128, 129, 130, 131, 133,
    135, 137, 140, 141, 142, 149, 150,
    160, 184, 201, 224, 225, 228, 229,
    230
computer 4, 5, 10, 97, 99, 100, 103,
    114, 162, 172, 176, 201, 202, 203,
    207, 214, 215, 229, 231
computer modeling 97, 103, 202
constraint 4, 32, 35, 56, 61, 63, 66, 67,
    68, 69, 104, 113, 123, 130, 136,
    145, 146, 162, 182, 189, 191, 192,
    194, 203, 214, 229, 231
construction 39, 52, 67, 89, 99, 101,
    197
consumer 3, 7, 8, 12, 31, 40, 44, 56, 72,
    89, 90, 129, 134, 201, 204, 205,
    207, 208, 209, 210, 211, 212, 214,
    215, 217, 219, 220, 221, 224

consumer technology 204, 205, 207
consumption 6, 40, 41, 42, 45, 46, 52,
    58, 65, 89, 90, 93, 100, 111, 114,
    128, 180, 181, 189, 194, 205, 210,
    212, 219
context 4, 59, 68, 100, 101, 103, 113,
    114, 143, 150, 179, 180, 184, 193,
    202, 203

decision makers 86, 97, 102, 110, 113,
    114, 130, 132, 144, 148, 150, 201,
    228, 231
decision making 35, 65, 100, 122, 129,
    131, 133, 135, 136, 137, 138, 139,
    141, 142, 143, 145, 146, 147, 148,
    149, 150, 159, 163, 164, 165, 166,
    167, 168, 169, 170, 171, 172, 175,
    182, 185, 202, 203, 213, 227, 229
demand 17, 31, 51, 52, 57, 58, 59, 62,
    63, 64, 65, 66, 67, 69, 71, 72, 73,
    85, 87, 93, 102, 107, 109, 125, 126,
    128, 129, 130, 134, 156, 169, 170,
    181, 184, 186, 189, 190, 194, 204,
    207, 208, 209, 210, 211, 212, 213,
    215, 217, 218, 219, 221, 226
demand side management 204, 212,
    217
dematerialization 179, 185, 188, 196
density 10, 44, 105, 109, 112, 113, 193,
    194
design approach 35, 97, 98, 99, 100,
    102, 110, 112, 113, 114, 115, 180,
    184, 188, 191, 192, 197, 227, 228,
    229
diversity 5, 9, 10, 15, 17, 20, 35, 105,
    121, 124, 175, 225, 231
durability 205, 208
dynamics 3, 4, 5, 6, 7, 8, 9, 12, 13, 15,
    16, 17, 18, 19, 22, 29, 31, 32, 34,
    35, 39, 40, 56, 71, 73, 75, 76, 83,
    84, 93, 94, 97, 99, 100, 102, 104,
    106, 113, 121, 122, 123, 124, 127,
    128, 129, 133, 134, 135, 140, 142,
    150, 156, 158, 159, 160, 161, 163,
    164, 169, 170, 172, 174, 175, 179,
    187, 191, 202, 203, 220, 221, 224,
    225, 226, 227, 228, 229, 230, 231

eco-industrial parks 13, 14, 15, 18, 21,
    72, 225

economics 4, 8, 9, 15, 31, 32, 33, 34, 35,
    55, 56, 65, 66, 73, 75, 76, 83, 84,
    85, 86, 87, 88, 89, 94, 99, 112,
    113, 115, 128, 129, 130, 135, 138,
    139, 141, 150, 156, 158, 161, 165,
    166, 167, 168, 169, 172, 173, 180,
    181, 182, 184, 185, 186, 187, 188,
    191, 192, 195, 201, 202, 203, 204,
    219, 220, 221, 224, 226, 227, 230,
    231
economy 31, 32, 33, 35, 56, 59, 72, 73,
    75, 83, 84, 86, 87, 92, 93, 94, 97,
    99, 100, 103, 104, 114, 115, 170,
    186, 196, 197, 203, 204, 213, 214,
    215, 216, 221, 227, 229, 230
ecosystems 3, 4, 5, 6, 7, 8, 9, 10, 11, 12,
    13, 14, 16, 17, 18, 19, 20, 21, 22,
    23, 31, 32, 33, 34, 35, 38, 52, 56,
    66, 76, 83, 93, 97, 98, 99, 100, 101,
    102, 104, 106, 108, 114, 115, 121,
    122, 124, 126, 127, 159, 172, 179,
    180, 182, 184, 185, 186, 187, 188,
    192, 196, 197, 201, 224, 225, 226,
    227, 228, 229, 230, 231
embedded 15, 42, 56, 157, 175, 182
embeddedness 7, 135, 142
emissions 3, 16, 38, 39, 41, 42, 44, 45,
    46, 47, 49, 50, 51, 55, 56, 84, 85,
    86, 88, 90, 91, 92, 93, 100, 101,
    102, 156, 175, 180, 181, 189, 192,
    204, 207, 213, 215, 216, 218, 220,
    226, 229
energy 3, 4, 5, 6, 7, 8, 11, 12, 13, 14, 15,
    18, 19, 20, 21, 31, 32, 33, 34, 38,
    40, 41, 42, 43, 44, 45, 46, 52, 55,
    65, 66, 67, 88, 89, 90, 93, 94, 99,
    101, 103, 104, 105, 106, 108, 111,
    113, 114, 130, 148, 157, 161, 162,
    171, 175, 176, 189, 190, 192, 194,
    201, 202, 203, 204, 206, 207, 208,
    209, 212, 214, 215, 216, 218, 219,
    220, 221, 225, 229, 230, 231
environment 3, 4, 10, 11, 16, 32, 35,
    38, 75, 83, 86, 87, 88, 92, 114, 115,
    122, 128, 129, 130, 132, 133, 134,
    135, 136, 137, 138, 141, 143, 144,
    148, 149, 150, 158, 159, 161, 162,
    169, 170, 171, 174, 175, 185, 186,
    193, 201, 202, 205, 207, 216, 221,
    224, 228, 229

environmental impact 38, 39, 47, 52, 56, 66, 129, 130, 179, 201, 204, 206, 226

feedback 4, 8, 72, 73, 74, 75, 100, 102, 103, 106, 110, 112, 113, 126, 133, 134, 140, 141, 142, 143, 144, 145, 147, 149, 186, 191, 201, 224
feedstock 8, 156, 158
firm 207, 211
flow(s) 67, 97, 99, 100, 101, 114, 115, 166, 167, 180, 184, 191
food web(s) 7, 9, 11, 12, 13, 225
fuel 8, 15, 86, 88, 89, 90, 93, 100, 179, 184, 186, 188, 189, 192, 194, 197, 210, 211, 213, 215, 229
futures studies 179, 180, 182, 184, 186, 187, 188, 191, 192, 196, 197

game 124, 162, 163, 201, 202, 203, 204, 205, 207, 208, 209, 210, 212, 213, 214, 215, 216, 217, 219, 220, 221, 229
game-theoretic models 201, 202
generation 57, 86, 90, 91, 92, 93, 104, 128, 172, 176, 183, 190, 191, 203, 204, 207, 209, 210, 211, 213, 214, 215, 217, 219, 220, 221, 231
generation infrastructure 204, 217
gravity model 61, 64, 65, 66, 69, 70, 71, 73, 226
greenhouse gases 3, 39, 55, 56, 84, 86, 88, 90, 92, 93

health 3, 4, 39, 102, 109, 115
history 13, 57, 103, 109
    historic 174
    historical xv, 75, 97, 100, 104, 108, 115, 174, 184, 215
    historically 35, 162, 209
household 33, 42, 47, 65, 101, 107, 108, 109, 110, 112, 113, 193, 201, 202, 203, 204, 205, 206, 207, 208, 209, 210, 213, 214, 215, 216, 217, 218, 219, 220, 221, 229
housing 108, 109, 110, 111, 112, 113
human–machine interaction 187, 188, 191, 197

industrial ecology 4, 5, 6, 7, 13, 22, 32, 35, 38, 157, 159, 163, 164, 165, 170, 175, 180, 181, 185, 186, 187, 188, 196, 197, 225, 226, 228, 230
industrial ecosystems 3, 4, 5, 6, 7, 8, 9, 10, 11, 12, 13, 14, 16, 17, 18, 19, 20, 21, 22, 29, 31, 32, 33, 34, 35, 52, 56, 66, 83, 93, 97, 98, 99, 100, 101, 102, 104, 106, 108, 114, 115, 121, 122, 124, 127, 172, 179, 180, 182, 184, 185, 186, 188, 196, 224, 225, 226, 227, 228, 229, 230, 231
industrial symbiosis 6, 7, 8, 12, 13, 14, 16, 17, 18, 22, 23, 32
industry 4, 10, 14, 17, 18, 21, 31, 32, 33, 34, 44, 57, 58, 59, 60, 61, 62, 63, 64, 65, 66, 67, 69, 70, 73, 75, 84, 85, 86, 93, 98, 102, 129, 130, 138, 156, 157, 161, 175, 179, 225, 226, 227, 230, 231
infrastructure 21, 39, 52, 66, 101, 103, 104, 107, 109, 115, 126, 136, 157, 166, 169, 173, 175, 176, 180, 181, 184, 185, 186, 188, 189, 193, 204, 217, 227
innovation 72, 100, 121, 124, 126, 129, 143, 162, 172, 186, 189, 229
input–output 5, 32, 33, 55, 56, 57, 58, 61, 64, 65, 66, 68, 71, 72, 75, 76, 83, 84, 85, 87, 90, 94, 101, 226, 227, 230
institution 3, 31, 32, 34, 115, 135, 138, 139, 157, 203, 213
international trade 101, 195
inventory 12, 41, 42, 51, 58, 126, 141, 164, 165, 207, 208, 226

labeled 164, 170
labeling 212, 215
land use 14, 98, 105, 106, 107, 108, 109, 110, 113, 114, 162, 179, 181, 186, 189, 192
learning by doing 127, 197, 208
life cycle analysis 230
life cycle assessment 33, 38, 41, 51, 52, 83, 84, 86, 87, 89, 159, 226, 227

market failure 202
material flow analysis 33, 52

materials 3, 4, 5, 6, 7, 8, 10, 11, 12, 13,
    15, 17, 18, 21, 31, 32, 33, 34, 38,
    52, 67, 94, 99, 101, 104, 105, 108,
    114, 121, 130, 132, 136, 141, 146,
    157, 175, 179, 180, 192, 194
markup 208, 209
metaphor 7
methane emissions 39, 44, 45, 46, 47,
    49, 50, 51, 226
model 5, 6, 9, 14, 15, 16, 17, 18, 19, 20,
    21, 22, 35, 39, 40, 41, 42, 43, 44,
    45, 46, 47, 51, 52, 56, 57, 59, 60,
    61, 64, 65, 66, 69, 70, 71, 72, 73,
    75, 76, 83, 84, 85, 86, 87, 88, 89,
    94, 97, 99, 100, 103, 115, 122, 123,
    124, 126, 127, 128, 129, 130, 131,
    133, 134, 135, 142, 143, 144, 148,
    150, 157, 158, 160, 161, 162, 163,
    164, 165, 167, 168, 169, 170, 172,
    173, 174, 175, 180, 182, 183, 184,
    185, 186, 187, 188, 190, 191, 192,
    196, 197, 201, 202, 203, 207, 208,
    209, 214, 215, 219, 220, 225, 226,
    227, 228, 229, 230, 231
    modeler xvi, 143, 170, 182, 186, 188,
        226
    modeling 4, 5, 52, 73, 75, 84, 85, 94,
        99, 100, 102, 110, 114, 115, 124,
        127, 129, 130, 131, 132, 133,
        135, 137, 139, 140, 141, 142,
        143, 145, 147, 149, 150, 156,
        157, 159, 162, 163, 164, 165,
        170, 172, 174, 175, 179, 183,
        185, 186, 188, 196, 225, 226,
        227, 228, 230, 231
    submodel 100, 101, 106, 107, 109,
        110, 113, 114
model–scenario framework 185, 196

natural gas 38, 39, 40, 41, 42, 44, 45,
    46, 47, 50, 51, 89, 90, 92, 157, 209,
    210, 211, 216, 226
nature 8, 9, 10, 11, 13, 18, 19, 31, 94,
    101, 104, 124, 132, 156, 160, 180,
    184, 187, 190, 191, 192, 196, 217,
    225, 230
network 3, 5, 6, 8, 15, 17, 18, 31, 56,
    125, 128, 129, 130, 131, 132, 133,
    134, 135, 136, 137, 138, 139, 140,
    141, 142, 143, 144, 145, 146, 147,
148, 149, 150, 156, 157, 158, 159,
    160, 161, 163, 164, 167, 168, 170,
    171, 172, 173, 175, 176, 179, 186,
    189, 190, 193, 194, 215, 224, 228,
    230
network dynamics 134, 224
network structure 17, 125, 129, 132,
    142, 158, 161, 171, 172, 173

oil 8, 15, 40, 92, 172
optimality 202
order 12, 33, 50, 51, 55, 59, 60, 66, 67,
    68, 76, 86, 87, 90, 124, 125, 126,
    130, 131, 133, 138, 145, 150, 157,
    160, 162, 164, 172, 173, 174, 175,
    181, 192, 202, 211, 214
organizational behavior 133, 139
ozone 38, 39, 47, 48, 50, 226

paradigm 22, 159, 163, 185, 187, 224
path dependency 22, 134, 183
photochemical smog 38, 39, 47
player 19, 56, 124, 128, 129, 130, 131,
    138, 140, 173, 201, 202, 203, 204,
    210, 212, 213, 214, 215, 228
policy 5, 22, 32, 83, 94, 97, 99, 100,
    102, 103, 107, 110, 112, 113, 114,
    124, 130, 132, 134, 138, 140, 173,
    174, 180, 183, 185, 189, 191, 201,
    203, 204, 212, 214, 215, 217, 218,
    221, 226, 229, 230, 231
politician 83, 203, 204, 215, 219
population 10, 35, 56, 75, 97, 98, 101,
    102, 103, 106, 107, 108, 109, 110,
    111, 114, 115, 188, 189, 190, 192,
    193, 194, 196
PowerPlay 201, 202, 203, 204, 207, 208,
    209, 210, 211, 212, 213, 215, 216,
    217, 218, 220, 221, 229
producers 3, 7, 11, 12, 31, 32, 33, 34,
    208, 214, 219, 221, 224
production cost 208, 209, 211, 212

RAS matrix balancing 57
regional 5, 19, 29, 31, 32, 33, 34, 35, 39,
    47, 51, 55, 56, 57, 58, 59, 60, 61,
    62, 63, 64, 65, 66, 67, 68, 69, 70,
    71, 72, 73, 74, 75, 76, 83, 84, 85,
    86, 87, 88, 92, 94, 97, 98, 100, 101,
    103, 105, 106, 107, 109, 110, 111,

112, 113, 114, 115, 156, 157, 158,
   170, 173, 174, 175, 180, 186, 188,
   192, 193, 194, 195, 196, 224, 225,
   226, 227, 228, 230, 231
regional metabolism 97, 100, 227
regulation(s) 130, 139, 158, 202, 212, 214
regulator 202, 203, 204, 211, 212, 213,
   215, 229
regulatory 3, 135
replacement 104, 205, 207, 213
research design 179, 180, 181, 182, 185,
   229
resource(s) 3, 6, 8, 10, 14, 16, 17, 18,
   21, 22, 31, 32, 52, 75, 84, 101, 103,
   105, 128, 129, 131, 132, 136, 141,
   143, 145, 146, 149, 156, 161, 168,
   169, 170, 171, 176, 179, 181, 183,
   186, 188, 193, 194, 201, 207, 225,
   226

scale 4, 5, 7, 17, 18, 19, 20, 31, 32, 33,
   34, 39, 40, 47, 55, 56, 75, 97, 98,
   103, 114, 140, 141, 148, 156, 157,
   162, 167, 168, 175, 179, 204, 205,
   224, 226, 228, 229, 231
scenario design 184
science 6, 22, 55, 94, 128, 129, 144, 188,
   226, 229, 231
service 33, 63, 83, 84, 85, 86, 87, 88, 90,
   91, 92, 93, 94, 101, 108, 128, 137,
   146, 158, 181, 189, 190, 201, 204,
   205, 206, 207, 208, 213, 227
simulation 5, 35, 40, 84, 97, 98, 99, 100,
   101, 102, 103, 104, 107, 110, 113,
   124, 158, 159, 163, 164, 165, 168,
   170, 171, 172, 173, 174, 175, 191,
   201, 202, 228, 230, 231
societal 128, 138, 158, 161, 185
society 4, 9, 100, 115, 186, 201, 229,
   230
spatial 17, 18, 19, 20, 31, 32, 34, 38, 39,
   45, 51, 52, 59, 60, 61, 65, 66, 73,
   97, 103, 105, 128, 180, 226, 227,
   230
spatially 21
stock(s) 97, 98, 100, 101, 102, 103, 104,
   107, 108, 114, 115, 121, 125, 126,
   134, 156, 179, 180, 182, 183, 184,
   186, 187, 189, 191, 192, 194, 196,
   207, 210, 214, 217, 229

strategic planning 97, 98, 130, 181, 182,
   183, 219
strategic thinking 182, 183, 188, 190
structure 4, 6, 7, 8, 11, 12, 13, 15, 17,
   19, 20, 21, 22, 34, 40, 57, 72, 75,
   76, 100, 101, 103, 104, 107, 108,
   109, 121, 122, 123, 124, 125, 126,
   128, 129, 131, 132, 134, 135, 136,
   138, 139, 142, 143, 158, 159, 160,
   161, 163, 164, 165, 167, 168, 171,
   172, 173, 174, 182, 183, 184, 185,
   188, 190, 191, 196, 214, 221, 224,
   226, 227, 229
subsidies 130, 173, 204, 212, 213, 215,
   218, 219, 221
subsidy 213, 215, 218, 219, 221
supplier 19, 83, 87, 168, 219, 227, 229
supply 16, 17, 31, 33, 46, 56, 57, 58, 59,
   60, 62, 63, 64, 69, 71, 73, 83, 84,
   86, 87, 88, 89, 90, 91, 92, 93, 94,
   103, 125, 126, 130, 141, 143, 156,
   157, 169, 181, 184, 185, 207, 211,
   214, 215, 217, 221, 226, 227
sustainability 35, 52, 56, 97, 98, 100,
   101, 102, 103, 104, 106, 113, 114,
   115, 128, 141, 143, 145, 150, 159,
   161, 175, 179, 180, 182, 185, 186,
   188, 190, 193, 196, 197, 227, 228,
   229, 230
system(s) 3, 4, 5, 6, 7, 8, 9, 10, 11, 12,
   13, 14, 15, 17, 19, 20, 21, 22, 31,
   32, 33, 34, 35, 38, 39, 40, 52, 55,
   56, 57, 61, 65, 66, 68, 73, 75, 76,
   85, 92, 93, 98, 99, 100, 102, 103,
   104, 113, 115, 121, 122, 123, 124,
   125, 126, 127, 128, 130, 131, 132,
   133, 134, 138, 140, 141, 142, 150,
   156, 157, 158, 159, 160, 161, 162,
   163, 164, 165, 167, 170, 172, 173,
   174, 175, 176, 179, 183, 184, 185,
   186, 187, 188, 189, 190, 191, 192,
   196, 197, 201, 202, 203, 214, 217,
   218, 219, 221, 224, 225, 226, 227,
   228, 229, 230, 231

technical change 4, 197
technological change 10, 75
temporal 18, 19, 20, 21, 33, 34, 38, 39,
   51, 52, 75, 76, 97, 147, 167, 172,
   173, 226, 227

theory 6, 11, 13, 19, 22, 35, 75, 128,
    139, 157, 159, 160, 161, 163, 183,
    188, 191, 226, 227, 230, 231
tool(s) 5, 13, 21, 34, 35, 39, 47, 52, 103,
    106, 114, 128, 131, 143, 145, 148,
    150, 156, 170, 172, 182, 191, 201,
    230, 231
transition management 180, 185, 190,
    196
transmission 40, 45, 46, 47, 50, 51, 210
transport 45, 46, 59, 62, 64, 65, 66, 126
transportation 12, 33, 61, 63, 69, 73,
    86, 87, 88, 89, 90, 91, 92, 93, 166,
    179, 180, 181, 183, 184, 185, 186,
    189, 192, 193, 194, 196, 197, 227,
    229

uncertainty 34, 40, 55, 75, 86, 87, 129,
    135, 139, 141, 142, 144, 145, 146,
    148, 159, 179, 182, 184, 185, 187,
    188, 196
urban development 109

value(s) 8, 10, 13, 35, 47, 49, 59, 60, 61,
    63, 65, 66, 67, 68, 69, 84, 85, 99,
    106, 108, 112, 113, 114, 121, 126,
    128, 130, 133, 134, 135, 138, 142,
    144, 147, 148, 149, 150, 173, 180,
    184, 208
Victoria (Australian state) 73, 74,
    97, 98, 100, 108, 109, 114, 115
Victorian Region Stock and
    Flows Framework (VRSFF) 97,
    100
vintage model 207

waste(s) 6, 11, 12, 14, 17, 31, 32, 33,
    38, 86, 91, 92, 100, 126, 128, 168,
    170, 225
water 6, 8, 11, 14, 16, 18, 39, 40, 41, 42,
    43, 44, 47, 50, 51, 56, 67, 76, 90,
    101, 103, 105, 113, 114, 115, 186,
    193, 225, 226
weight 62, 66, 68, 69, 148, 149, 205,
    206